MARY OF NAZARETH

The Mother of Jesus in the Memory of the Earliest Christians

CHRISTOPHER BRYAN

Seabury Books
19 East 34th Street
New York, NY
10016
Seabury Books is an imprint of Church Publishing Incorporated

Cover image by Giovanni Domenico Tiepolo, Madonna with Sleeping Child, 1780s

Cover design by Newgen
Typeset by Nord Compo

ISBN 978-1-64065-746-5 (paperback)
ISBN 978-1-64065-747-2 (eBook)
Library of Congress Control Number: 2024938957

For the Dean and Chapter

of the Cathedral Church of Saint Peter

in Exeter,

with gratitude and affection

The Nativity

Figure 1. The Nativity

Gherardo delle Notti,[1]

in Exeter Cathedral

CONTENTS

ACKNOWLEDGMENTS

My last major experience in theatre was when I played the Narrator in Theatre Sewanee's 2016 production of Neil Simon's *The Good Doctor*. In the wonderfully gentle, funny opening soliloquy that Simon gives to the Narrator (who is based on the person of Anton Chekhov) he says, "I ask myself a question... what force is it that compels me to write so incessantly, day after day, page after page, story after story? ... And the answer is quite simple.... I have no choice.... I am a writer.... Sometimes I think I may be mad..."

It is a basic rule of acting that we should always try to find something in the role we are playing with which we can connect. In this case, I had no difficulty at all. Those lines describe me. I enjoy writing because I enjoy telling stories. That is why I have written a number of novels, and it also lies behind my academic writings, including the present narrative, for academic writings are, after all, only stories of another kind.

But of course it is not much fun telling stories to oneself. So it occurs to me, as I sit at my desk to write this note of acknowledgment, that when it comes to gratitude, above all I must speak of those who have been kind enough over the years to indulge me by attending to my stories, which means that I am indebted to you, whoever you are, as you read this. Thank you.

Certainly there are also more specific debts of gratitude that I owe to many who have helped me. Among them, Cynthia Read, who, to my great pleasure as well as my immense benefit, has continued to work with me following her retirement from the Oxford University Press; Justin Hoffmann, Katherine Lim, Mark Powers and Airié Stuart at Church Publishing, who have been a joy to work with; the Dean and Chapter of Exeter Cathedral for the Daily Office and Eucharist that frame my working week, as well as for their permission to reproduce the Delle Notti *Mother and Child* and the East Window of the Cathdral's Lady Chapel; Romulus Stefanut for his unfailingly efficient and gracious library assistance; John Allan for his invaluable help with some of the images; and Sister Hannah, Prioress of the Community of St Mary in Sewanee, and her sisters for their prayers. Then there are a host of you—some whom "I have loved long since, and lost awhile,"—to whom I am indebted for so many conversations, suggestions, acts of encouragement, thoughtful criticisms and disagreements, recommendations for reading and exchanges of ideas over so many years that I cannot count them. Among you I must name Richard Burridge, John Crisp†, Paul Davies, Stephen and Jennifer Davis, Anne Eyre, Anne Foreman, John Gatta, Julia Gatta, Julian Gray, Jonathan Greener, David Gunn-Johnson, Morwenna Ludlow, Robert MacSwain, Susanna Metz†, Ian Morter, James Mustard, Christopher Palmer, Deborah Parsons, William S. Stafford, Leslie Stemp†, Sheila Swarbrick and Calhoun Walpole. Last but hardly least, for her love and support, her faithful companionship through life's ups and downs, I owe to Wendy my wife a debt that I can never repay.

Christopher Bryan
Julian of Norwich, 2024

ABBREVIATIONS

BDAG	Walter Bauer, rev. Frederick William Danker, W. F. Arndt, F. W. Gingrich. *A Greek-English Lexicon of the New Testament and Other Early Christian Literature*. 3rd ed. Chicago: University of Chicago Press, 2000.
BDF	F. Blass, A. Debrunner, and Robert W. Funk. *A Greek Grammar of the New Testament and Other Early Christian Literature.* Chicago: University of Chicago Press, 1961.
BG	Maximilian Zerwick, S.J. *Biblical Greek.* Ed. Joseph Smith, S.J. Rome: Editrice Pontificio Instituto Biblico, 1990.
BHGNT	Baylor Handbook on the Greek New Testament. Baylor University.
CBQ	*Catholic Biblical Quarterly*
CTD	Karl Rahner and Herbert Vorgrimler, *Concise Theological Dictionary.* Cornelius Ernst, O.P., ed. Richard Strachen, trans. Freiburg: Herder / London: Burns & Oates, 1965.
D-R	Douay-Rheims Bible
GAGNT	Maximilian Zerwick, S.J. *A Grammatical Analysis of the New Testament.* Ed. and trans. Mary Grosvenor. Rome: Editrice Ponitificio Instituto Biblico, 1993.
GELS	T. Muraoka. *A Greek-English Lexicon of the Septuagint.* Louvain: Peeters, 2009.
HG	Albert Huck and Heinrich Greeven. *Synopsis of the First Three Gospels.* Tübingen: J.C.B. Mohr (Paul Sieback), 1981.

HJPAJC	Emil Schürer, revised by Geza Vermes, Fergus Millar, and Martin Goodman. *The History of the Jewish People in the Age of Jesus Christ.* 3 vols. Edinburgh: T. & T. Clark, 1973-87.
ICC	International Critical Commentary
JB	*Jerusalem Bible*
JBL	*Journal of Biblical Literature*
KJV	King James Version of the Bible (1611): also commonly referred to as the Authorized Version
LCL	Loeb Classical Library
LHGT	Martin M. Culy, Mikael C. Parsons, Joshua J. Stigall. *Luke: A Handbook on the Greek Text.* Waco, Texas: Baylor University, 2010.
LRB	*London Review of Books*
LSJ	H. G. Liddell, R. Scott, and H. S. Jones. *A Greek English Lexicon.* 9th ed. With Supplement 1968. Oxford: Oxford University Press, 1989.
LXX	Septuagint
NAB	New American Bible (1970)
NB	*New Blackfriars*
NEB	New English Bible (1961–70)
NETS	*A New English Translation of the Septuagint.* Ed. Albert Pietesma and Benjamin C. Wright. New York: Oxford University Press, 2007.
NovT	*Novum Testamentum*
NRSV	New Revised Standard Version (1989)
NTA	Edgar Hennecke and Wilhelm Schneemelcher. *New Testament Apocrypha.* R. McL. Wilson, transl. 2 volumes. Cambridge: James Clarke, 1991.
NTS	*New Testament Studies.* Cambridge University: Studiorum Novi Testamenti Societas.
OED	*Oxford English Dictionary*

ODB	*Oxford Dictionary of the Bible.* Second edition. Ed. W. R. F. Browning. Oxford: University, 2009.
OLD	*Oxford Latin Dictionary.* Oxford: Clarendon Press, 1982.
OTP	*Old Testament Pseudepigrapha.* Ed. James H. Charlesworth. 2 vols. Garden City, N.Y.: Doubleday, 1983–85.
RB	*Revue Biblique*
RCL	*Revised Common Lectionary* (1994)
REB	*The Revised English Bible.* Oxford University Press and Cambridge University Press, 1989.
Re-Va	*Sacra Pagina Biblia.* Reina-Valera 1995. Bogotá: D.C. Sociedades Bíblicas Unidas, 1995.
RSV	Revised Standard Version (1946–57)
RV	Revised Version (1881–94)
SBLDS	Society of Biblical Literature Dissertation Series
SC	Sources chrétiennes
Smyth	Herbert Weir Smyth. *Greek Grammar.* Revised Gordon M. Messing. Cambridge, Mass.: Harvard University Press, 1984.
SP	Sacra Pagina
Spicq, *Lexicon*	Ceslas Spicq, O.P., *Theological Lexicon of the New Testament.* 3 vols. Translated and edited by James D. Ernest. Peabody, Mass.: Hendrickson, 1994.
STR	*Sewanee Theological Review*
TCGNT	Bruce M. Metzger. *A Textual Commentary on the Greek New Testament: A Companion Volume to the United Bible Societies Greek New Testament (third edition).* Corrected edition. New York: United Bible Societies, 1975.
TDNT	*Theological Dictionary of the New Testament.* Ed. Gerhard Kittel (vols. 1–5) and Gerhard

	Friedrich (vols. 6–9), trans. Geoffrey Bromiley. Grand Rapids, Mich.: Eerdmans 1964 [1933]–1974 [1973].
ThTo	*Theology Today*
TILC	*La Bibbia*. Traduzione Interconfessionale in Lingua Corrente. Rome: Alleanza Biblica Universale, 1985.
TLNT	Ceslas Spicq, O.P. *Theological Lexicon of the New Testament*. Trans. James D. Ernest. 3 vols. Peabody, Mass.: Hendrickson, 1994.
TOB	*La Bible*. Traduction Oecuménique de la Bible. Paris: Société Biblique Française & Editions du Cerf, 1988.
TSAJ	Texts and Studies in Ancient Judaism

PROLOGUE

How was Mary remembered by the earliest Christians? What kind of person did they think she was? What did they see as her role in the story of her son? To reflect on such questions, where else shall we turn if not to the records they left us? Which means, in effect, to the collection of documents that we call "the New Testament" and, in particular, to the four canonical gospels. It is true, as Beverley Roberts Gaventa has said, that glimpses of Mary given us in those documents are "fleeting."[2] That truth, however, must be weighed in light of another to which Elizabeth Schüssler Fiorenza drew our attention some years ago: that in patriarchal narrative—and of course the New Testament narratives are all examples of that—the presence of women is usually only mentioned "when women's behavior presents a problem or when women are exceptional individuals."[3]

Mary is referred to in passing, but significantly, by Paul and Mark; at somewhat greater length by Matthew; and at considerably greater length by Luke and John, each of whom give her a prominent place in entire sections of their narrative.[4] In addition to that, there is at the center of Revelation an extraordinary passage (even in that book of extraordinary passages) where we are shown a woman, crowned with stars and clothed with the sun, who brings forth "a son who is to shepherd the nations with a rod of iron"[5] -- a symbol of the people of God, as the earliest patristic exegesis saw, but a symbol that in its own terms cannot be divorced from its evident association with Mary of Nazareth, as exegesis from at least the fourth century onward also recognized. As M. Eugene Boring in his commentary on *Revelation* points out, "No Christian acquainted with the gospels can read this story of the woman who labors to bring forth the child who shall rule the nations without thinking of Mary, the mother of the Messiah, whose divine child is saved from wicked Herod by divine intervention."[6] Precisely. And, we might add, mother of the Messiah who is finally exalted from death to take his place at the right hand of the Father.

No other woman in the New Testament—or, for that matter, in the Scriptures of Israel—has anything like such coverage as this. The proper question may then be not "Why is there so little about Mary in the New Testament?" but "Why is there so much?" If Fiorenza is right, then evidently Mary was perceived and remembered, even within the lifetime of some who might have been eyewitnesses or heard about her from eyewitnesses, either as "a problem" or else as "exceptional." Why? Which? Maybe both? And in what ways?

By way of reflecting on those questions, as well as the broader questions to which I referred at the beginning of this prologue, in what follows I examine in six chapters the testimonies of each of the six witnesses to whom I have alluded, following the likely order in which they were written, and asking how they at least, among the earliest followers of Jesus, seem to have perceived and understood Mary of Nazareth. In an overview chapter I then try to bring together what we may have discerned of Mary as she was remembered by the early church, particularly bearing in mind Fiorenza's *dictum*. Throughout these parts of my study, so far as I can, I use the normal tools of literary and historical criticism, confining my enquiry to the limits imposed by those disciplines.

In this connection, I make no apology for favoring as witnesses over all other written sources of information the four canonical gospels and other documents of the canonical New Testament. As I claimed some years ago in my *Resurrection of the Messiah* (Oxford, 2012), with particular reference to the passion and resurrection narratives and, as Simon Gathercole has shown recently in his magisterial *The Gospel and the Gospels*

(Eerdmans, 2022),[7] with reference to the gospels as a whole, what the canonical gospels (including John) have in common against the non-canonical gospels is a profound commitment to the preached gospel of the church (the "kerygma"), to which Paul witnesses at 1 Corinthians 15.1-11. That kerygma was evidently early (Paul himself "received" it), and it appeared to Paul (who was surely in a position to know) to be universal ("whether it was I or they, so we preach and so you believed")—a view that is amply borne out by the evidence (see Gathercole, *Gospel and the Gospels* passim, and especially 54-77).

The kerygma itself, moreover, especially in its estimate of Jesus, is most plausibly understood as in its origins tied directly into the memory of those who had known Jesus personally, experienced him personally, and listened to his words (see my *Son of God* 126-29). It would follow, then, that they had also personally experienced those who were about him during his ministry, including naturally his mother. While it is true that the church of the first Christian centuries did not have the Scriptures or the ecumenical creeds as we have them, every source of information that we have makes clear that it was never without the apostolic gospel to which the Scriptures and creeds point, aptly summarized by Gathercole: "that Jesus is the messiah who, in fulfilment of Israel's Scripture, died a vicarious death and rose again on the third day."[8]

Of course, one need not therefore simply dismiss other early Christian writings as possible sources of information about the first Christians. It is always possible that genuine tradition from the earliest days may be preserved even in documents which appear in general to be distanced from them. That, however, does not justify an attitude which became fashionable in some scholarly circles towards the end of the twentieth century, an attitude which set the non-canonical or "apocryphal" gospels and the canonical gospels side by side as if they were more or less equal resources for information about Jesus and his earliest followers.[9] That, they most certainly are not. On the contrary, as John P. Meier put it, "most of this material, while having historical interest for a study of the picture of Jesus through the centuries, probably has nothing to do with the quest for the historical Jesus."[10] I concur with that judgment entirely, save that I would probably have deleted "probably."

The result of all this in the present work is a series of chapters that are of very uneven lengths, and that, of course, is because the materials with which I am dealing in the six witnesses are of uneven lengths. I have considered breaking the material up in some other way so as to avoid this. But the fact is the authors with whom I am dealing, although all looking to the same Lord and making essentially the same proclamation about him, are all also very much themselves, with their own styles and their own immediate concerns. Studying them each in their own plainly individual chapters is, I think, the best way of acknowledging and indeed benefitting from this. It may well be, however, that any who use this volume as a basis for study will find it helpful to consider at least the chapter on Luke in two sessions: in one considering the narratives of annunciation and nativity, in a second the narratives of Jesus' circumcision, presentation in the temple, youthful visit to Jerusalem, and Mary's appearance in Acts.

Following all this, and again in accord with my usual practice, in a postscript I reflect on the relationship between our six New Testament witnesses and subsequent Christian understanding of Mary and of the church's continuing relationship to her, beginning from the identification of her as *theotokos*—"Godbearer" or "Mother of God."[11] Lutheran theologian Robert Jenson in his *Systematic Theology* said that, "if one takes John 1 as what it is... and inserts Mary explicitly into her place in the story, the Marian doctrines immediately result"[12]—a statement marked by Jenson's usual clarity and precision, but which, given the history of Christian debate in these matters, certainly also requires explanation and perhaps defense. My postscript attempts some steps in that direction.

As is my usual practice, I have tried to keep my narrative and conclusions in the main text reasonably clear and straightforward, reserving to two appendices and to the Endnotes full references to biblical and other sources, as well as detailed discussion of particular textual, linguistic or historical problems.

1

PAUL

But when the fullness of time had come, God sent forth his Son, made of a woman, made under the law, in order to redeem those who were under the law, so that we might receive adoption as children. (Galatians 4.4-5)

I still recall, when I was very young, our parish priest, Father Crisp, describing these words as "the earliest known reference to Our Lord's Nativity—the first Christmas!" He was entirely correct. The evangelists would later portray Jesus himself declaring, "the time is fulfilled." Paul's **"when the fullness of time had come"** is of a piece with that. Behind both lies an understanding of Israel's Scriptures as enshrining promise: a promise that the present state of things, in which the world and God's people alike are in bondage to sin and death, will not last forever. The coming of Jesus is a decisive step toward fulfilment of that promise.

God **"sent forth his Son."** Although not explicit, lurking in the background here is the notion of the Son existing eternally in the bosom of the Father, like Lady Wisdom in Proverbs.[1] In Paul's thought, however, this is in preparation for an event of which Proverbs knows nothing—that same divine Son, **"made of a woman."**

Paul does not name Jesus' mother. This is by no means the only time in Scripture where a woman who is prominent in some action is not named. In Israel's Scriptures, we never hear the name of Manoah's wife, mother of the hero Samson, although the storyteller does not hesitate to speak of her in ways that make her rather more interesting and certainly a good deal quicker on the uptake than her husband.[2] In his gospel, Mark tells of a Syrophoenician woman, a gentile, who seems to get the better of Jesus in an argument involving a profoundly significant theological issue: Israel's relationship to the nations.[3] Later, he tells us of another woman who anoints Jesus with precious anointment on the eve of his passion and records for us Jesus' own word that what she had done would never be forgotten, for so long as the gospel was preached.[4] In neither case does Mark tell us the woman's name. In both cases, I daresay the tradition he received had already lost the names. In any case, it is hard not to suspect that at some point in the handing on of all these traditions, the kinds of patriarchal assumptions to which Fiorenza drew our attention have played their part.[5]

What, then, of Paul and **"made of a woman"**? First: personally, I think it extremely unlikely that Paul did *not* know the name of Jesus' mother—a name that was evidently known to the synoptic evangelists three or four decades later and needed little introduction or explanation when introduced into their narratives. Second, I believe we should dismiss as irrelevant the "anti-women" bias sometimes (and quite unjustly) attributed to Paul. Paul was anything but anti-women and was certainly willing—even eager—to name women as his fellow workers.[6] The tributes paid by him to women in the last section of his Letter to the Romans are alone sufficient to indicate this. In Romans 16, were it not that the Greek text itself indicates the gender of those to whom he refers, it would be in many cases impossible to know their gender, since the terms in which he speaks of women and of men are equally generous.[7] Nor in this respect, save in its length and the numbers involved, is Romans exceptional. Philippians 4.2-4 and 1 Corinthians 1.11 show Paul equally ready to name women as his valued colleagues and fellow workers.[8]

Why then does Paul omit Mary's name at Galatians 4.4? Because at this point what he wishes to emphasize is not the identity of Jesus' mother, but what was involved in the coming among us of the son of God. **"Made of a woman"** makes the essential point, which is *that Jesus shared the human condition.*[9] The expression is virtually proverbial:

For a mortal, born of woman,[10]
few of days and full of trouble,
comes up like a flower and withers,
flees like a shadow and does not last. (Job 14.1-2)

I have heard the idiom described as "semitic," and no doubt it is, but it can hardly be described as *merely* semitic. It is also universal. Shakespeare, fifteen hundred or so years later, is using a similar expression in exactly the same sense when he has the weird sisters tell Macbeth,

none of woman born
Shall harm Macbeth (*Macbeth* 4.1. 91–92)

leading Macbeth to infer that no human being can possibly defeat him. The weird sisters are, of course, cheating—but, then, that is what weird sisters do.[11]

We should note, moreover, that at this point in Galatians not only does Paul not name Mary, *he does not even name Jesus.* What is being asserted is the union of God and humankind: essentially the same assertion as will later be made by the fourth evangelist's "the Word became flesh" (John 1.14). Paul's expressions, **"his [God's] son"** and **"made of a woman,"** make that point. The personal names of either Jesus or Mary would arguably distract from it.

Although Paul does not tell us Mary's name, he does tell us—or rather, he implies—one very important fact about her.

Alongside Jesus being **"made of a woman"** Paul tells us that Jesus was **"born under the Law."** The "Law" here referred to is evidently *Torah*, the Law of Israel. Paul is saying that Jesus was a Jew, offspring of Abraham and so heir to the covenant.[12] In other words, not only was the son of God identified in his birth with humankind, he was identified in particular with Israel, **"in order to redeem[13] those who were under the Law so that we might receive adoption as children"** (4.4-5).

The matrilinear principle as a means of identifying Jewishness was almost certainly not yet a rabbinic norm at the time of Jesus' birth.[14] Nonetheless, Paul is here clearly implying that Jesus was born into a Jewish household: the concomitant assumption is therefore that those who composed that household, including of course his mother, were Jewish. As the legal tag has it, *res ipsa loquitur*: the thing speaks for itself. Mary of Nazareth was a daughter of Israel. She was Jewish.[15]

The proverbial nature of expressions such as "made of woman" is certainly enough to explain Paul's omission here of any mention of a father—an omission that in the past led some commentators to see reference to Jesus' virginal conception.[16] More recently, by contrast, there seems to be something of a scholarly consensus in the opposite direction. So Ernest de Witt Burton: "of such knowledge or acceptance the writings of the apostle give no hint."[17] The conclusion therefore that Paul *knew* nothing of the virginal conception is, however, an argument from silence, and arguments from silence have their dangers. We would not know that Paul was familiar with traditions of the Last Supper were it not that the Corinthians provoked him into reminding them of what he had originally taught them, as a result of which we see that clearly he *did* know such traditions, and in much the same form that we find them in the synoptic gospels.[18]

It is certainly true that Jesus' virginal conception was not an element in the very earliest public Christian proclamation, at least so far as we can reconstruct it.[19] The heart and center of that proclamation was from the beginning the life, death and resurrection of Jesus Christ the Son of God. Virtually every strand of New Testament witness indicates this, including the strand represented by Paul himself, who could hardly be clearer on the matter than he is when reminding the Corinthians what he had originally taught them:

> For I handed on to you as of first importance what I in turn had received: that Christ died for our sins in accordance with the scriptures, and that he was buried, and that he was raised on the third day in accordance with the scriptures, and that he appeared to Cephas, then to the twelve. Then he appeared to more than five hundred brothers and sisters at one time, most of whom are still alive, though some have died. Then he appeared to James, then to all the apostles. Last of all, as to someone untimely born, he appeared also to me. For I am the least of the apostles, unfit to be called an apostle, because I persecuted the church of God. (1 Cor. 15.3-9)

Strikingly, and most informatively for us, Paul goes on to say of this summary,

> Whether then it was I or they, so we proclaim and so you have come to believe. (1 Cor. 15.11)

That there were at times disagreements as to what should or should not be taught in the early church is evident (see Galatians 1 and Acts 15). But, Paul says, there was never any disagreement about this.

What then of Jesus' virginal conception? As Ambrose of Milan would later put it, *talis decet partus Deo*[20]—such a birth was *fitting* for God, but by implication not therefore necessary. Granted this and given its nature as a claim deeply personal to Jesus' family and, in particular, to his mother, that Jesus' virginal conception should not have formed part of the initial proclamation to outsiders and gentiles—some of them with pagan conceptions of virgin goddesses!—is surely as we would expect. What then if Paul's silence on this subject is *wrongly* assumed to mean that he had no knowledge of it? Is there more to say? Fr Thomas Crean OP, commenting recently on Galatians 4.4-5,[21] suggests that there might be, and even, perhaps, that there is to be, discerned in Paul's writings the very "hint" that de Witt Burton denied.

Attentive readers may have noticed that in my translation of Paul's words at Galatians 4.4, I replaced NRSV's "born of a woman, born under the law" with "**made of a woman, made under the law.**" In so doing, I reverted essentially to the KJV of 1611 (and, incidentally, the DR of 1582). Why did I do that? First, because theirs is a more accurate rendering of what Paul wrote. The word he uses is *genomenos*, the aorist participle[22] of *ginomai*, which means "come into being" or "be made." On occasion, when the referent is a human being or some other sentient creature, *ginomai* can of course mean "be born," since being born is, in our experience, invariably how humans and other sentient creatures "come into being." But when *ginomai* means that, the meaning is generally obvious from the context.[23] And in any case, the much more usual word in connection with birth is not *ginomai* at all, but *gennaō*—which Paul himself uses elsewhere in Galatians (three times) when he speaks of the birth of Ishmael,[24] and also in Romans when he speaks of the births of Jacob and Esau.[25] In other words, *gennaō* is apparently the word that normally occurs to Paul when he is speaking of birth.

Why, then, does he here use a different word? Was the choice significant? Jerome evidently thought it might be, since he translated each of Paul's two uses of *genomenos* by Latin *factum*, "made." King James' translators apparently thought the same since they too rendered *genomenos* by "made." Could they have been right? More precisely, if Paul did have some notion of Jesus' virginal conception in the back of his mind, even though he had no intention of dwelling on it or even stating it, might that have been a reason for him not to use the usual verb for "to be born"? One is not suggesting that such a change would have been necessary. The two NT writers who are generally understood to affirm Mary's virginal conception, namely Matthew and Luke, do still use the ordinary word *gennaō* in referring to Jesus' birth. But, as Crean points out, changing to *ginesthai* would certainly be *a* way of affirming the vital truths of Jesus' real humanity and Mary as his mother, while at the same time abstracting those truths "from the specific way in which this happened, namely, by conception and birth."[26] The fact that Matthew and Luke did not choose that way does not mean that Paul could not have chosen it.

Crean, however, takes us a step further, pointing out that

> the common fact of 'coming from,' and indeed of 'being made from' rather than 'being born from,' is sufficient to ground a rather significant parallel, a parallel that the early church certainly perceived, and upon which it was commenting as early as Justin Martyr and Origin: the parallel between the two couples Adam-Eve and Jesus-Mary. In each case, there is a man and woman, and there is a miraculous procession of the one entirely from the other: Eve comes from Adam alone, and Jesus (in regard to his humanity) from Mary alone.[27]

Such a view of the matter, though not necessarily in the forefront of Paul's mind at Galatians 4.4, might nonetheless have influenced his choice of expression. The possibility that Paul might have been aware of this parallel is evidenced, Crean suggests, by another passage, namely, 1 Corinthians 11.11-12:

> Nevertheless, in the Lord woman is not independent of man or man independent of woman. For just as the[28]

> woman is from the man, thus also the man is through the woman; but all things come from God.

It must be at once said that this is part of one of the most obscure passages in the entire NT. I have yet to read or listen to any discussion of 1 Corinthians 11.2-16 that I find entirely satisfactory. That granted, without solving or even attempting to solve the problems presented by the passage as a whole, there are at least some things about it that are reasonably clear. Paul has just said, "For man is not made from woman, but woman from man. Neither was man created for the sake of woman, but woman for the sake of man."[29] Commentators of most schools agree that Paul is here referring to the creation of Eve out of Adam in Genesis, and to the reason given for it: "And YHWH God said, 'It is not good for the human to be alone.'"[30] Whatever Paul may have meant by what he says next—"For this reason a woman ought to have a symbol of authority on her head, because of the angels"—it seems that he still has Adam and Eve in mind as he then continues: "Nevertheless, in the Lord woman is not independent of man or man independent of woman."[31] In other words, despite the apparent superiority of man in being the source of woman, they still need each other—a reasonable enough statement of the biological reality! Paul goes on to say, "For just as the woman is from the man, thus also the man is through the woman; but all things are from God."[32] What does he mean by that? Most commentators suggest something to the effect that Paul is trying to compensate women for the apparent male superiority involved in a man being the source of the first woman by pointing out that male humans are all born now of women.[33] Obviously, however, such a "solution" does not serve at all to restore the balance between the two sexes. As Crean points out,

> Commentators seem to have overlooked the fact that not only does each man have a mother, but so also does

> each woman. In the coming forth of Eve from Adam, the woman is wholly dependent on the man: this fact is not balanced adequately by the fact that both women and men are also dependent on women in order to be born—not to speak of the fact that they are also dependent on men in order to be in a position to be born.[34]

A better solution, Crean suggests, is to understand that Paul is still thinking about the first man and the first woman, whom he sees as *parallel* to Mary and Jesus—the latter, we note, Paul elsewhere characterizes as "the last Adam." Hence Paul's statement, "For just as the woman is from the man, so the man is through the woman," is not in reference to ordinary births, but to Genesis' account of the creation of Eve out of Adam and the virginal conception and birth of Jesus out of Mary. We should then unpack 1 Corinthians 11.12 as,

> For just as the Woman *Eve* is from the Man *Adam (without the involvement of any woman)*, so the Man *Jesus* is through the Woman *Mary (without the involvement of any man)*.

In short, "As Eve is of Adam, so is the second Adam by the second Eve."[35] This *would* restore the balance—even, arguably, tip it in favor of women!

So—do we have here anything like clear evidence that Paul *did* believe in the virginal conception of Jesus? I doubt we can go as far as that. We have noticed that some of his expressions, hard to explain in themselves, would be explicable if he held to such a belief. To strengthen our case (if we propose to make one), we might point to three other things: first, that there is nothing in Paul's teaching that would deny such a belief;[36] second, (as we have already noted) that it is perfectly understandable that such a belief, even if held, would not have been a part either of his basic public preaching or of his letters to young churches; and third, that however peripheral or tangential Jesus' virginal conception may have been to the earliest preaching of the gospel, it seems nonetheless to have been generally accepted without question or controversy by the church of the second generation onward—as is witnessed by its general presence in confessions and symbols, unemphasized but perfectly clear, wherever Jesus' birth is mentioned, as well as in later non-canonical texts such as the mid-second-century *Protevangelium of James*. That fact must be accounted for somehow, and it seems likely that an origin deeper in the church's psyche than the creativity of Matthew and Luke in the seventies and eighties is needed for that.

2

MARK

Mark's gospel contains no account of the events surrounding Jesus' birth. But quite early in his narrative Mark does introduce a scene involving Jesus' family, including his mother.

> **Then he went home; and the crowd came together again, so that they could not even eat. When his family heard it, they set out to take control of him, for people were saying, "He has gone out of his mind."**
>
> **And the scribes who came down from Jerusalem said, "He has Beelzebul, and by the ruler of the demons he casts out demons."…**
>
> **Then his mother and his brothers came; and standing outside, they sent to him and summoned him. A crowd was sitting around him; and they said to him, "Your mother and your brothers and sisters are outside, asking for you." And he replied, "Who are my mother and my brothers?" And looking at those who sat around him, he said, "Here are my mother and my brothers! Whoever does the will of God is my brother and sister and mother."** (Mark 3.19b-22, 31-35)

This is the earliest example in Mark's gospel of a narrative technique that he uses several times elsewhere and to great effect: the sandwiching or bracketing of episodes so that they reflect and resonate with each other. His most dramatic and memorable use of the technique is surely in the passion narrative: the bracketing of the account of Peter's denial by episodes describing Jesus being examined by the Sanhedrin (Mark 14.53-72).

In the example before us we have an opening section wherein Jesus' **family**[1] is seeking **to take control of him**[2] on the grounds that he has **"gone out of his mind."** This leads on to a central section wherein there is opposition to Jesus by **scribes... from Jerusalem**, but now on the much more serious and sinister charge that he is possessed by **Beelzebub** and **casts out demons** by demonic power. Then Mark returns to Jesus' family, who arrive at the place where he is teaching but remain outside and **summon** him to come out to them: the section concludes with Jesus' response.

That there was a degree of family hostility to Jesus' mission during his lifetime is something to which witnesses other than Mark also testify (cf. John 7.1-5). This is, indeed, an element perceived traditionally in the life of the righteous sufferer:

> I have become a stranger to my kindred,
> an alien to my mother's children.
> It is zeal for your house that has consumed me;
> the insults of those who insult you have fallen on me.
> (Ps. 69.7-9)[3]

—a psalm that the fourth evangelist will find it natural to apply to Jesus (John 2.17). Yet it is entirely possible that the reminiscence in Jesus' case also has some basis in history. It hardly takes a massive effort of imagination to perceive possible reasons for such hostility. The family's exercise of its craft will perhaps have been regarded as a role of honor in Nazareth. Jesus' abandonment of the place thereby accorded to him in his society—a place entitling him and his family to a certain degree of respect—might well have been a cause of family opposition. Again, his simply making a name for himself could have been a source of irritation.

Whatever our view of the precise biological relationship between Jesus and his "brothers (*adelphoi*)"—whether we follow the opinion often attributed to Helvidius (they were the natural children of Joseph and Mary, who consummated their marriage following the birth of Jesus), of Epiphanius (they were Joseph's children by an earlier marriage) or of Jerome (they were Jesus' cousins, perhaps the sons of Mary's sister)[4]—such reactions and interactions among family members are entirely plausible. If, as I think, the Epiphanian view is correct and those named here as Jesus' siblings were Joseph's children by an earlier marriage and Joseph was dead, then presumably the eldest of the brothers was now head of the household—he and, indeed, his brothers all senior in the family hierarchy to Jesus and, of course, to his mother. Given which, one might argue that it would be surprising if Jesus' making a name for himself were *not* a cause for irritation.

And that is all we can say. Mark, for his part, does not show any interest in these questions or in related questions as to what may or may not have been Mary's role in this family dispute—or, still less, in questions about the virginal conception of Jesus or Mary's perpetual virginity. Whether or not Mark was aware of such questions or traditions is impossible to say, but they are in any case clearly not what this section of his narrative is about. His purpose here he surely makes abundantly clear: it is to ask the question that Jesus asks and indeed answers. "**Who are my mother and my brothers?**" As we might put it, "What makes us truly members of Jesus' family?" The answer that Mark's Jesus gives to that question is also clear. It is not physical kinship at all. Looking at those who are seated "**around him**"—and Mark surely intends us to notice the contrast between these and his family who are "**outside**"—Jesus says emphatically, "***Here***[5] **are my mother and my brothers! Whoever does the will of God is my brother and sister and mother.**"

Mark refers a second time to Jesus and his family, including his mother, in chapter 6.

> **He left that place and came to his home town, and his disciples followed him. [2] On the sabbath he began to teach in the synagogue, and many who heard him were astounded. They said, 'Where did this man get all this? What is this wisdom that has been given to him? What deeds of power are being done by his hands! [3] Is not this the carpenter, the son of Mary and brother of James and Joses and Judas and Simon, and are not his sisters here with us?' And they took offence at him. Then Jesus said to them, 'Prophets are not without honor, except in their home town, and among their own kin, and in their own house.' And he could do no deed of power there, except that he laid his hands on a few sick people and cured them. And he was amazed at their unbelief.**
> (Mark 6.1-6)

This episode in Mark is generally referred to by commentators as "The Rejection at Nazareth" or some such title. It shows Jesus, who has performed miracles and taught with great success elsewhere in Galilee, causing astonishment that devolves into hostility when, presumably responding to an invitation, he begins to teach in the synagogue in his home town.[6] Here, it seems, we have the very opposite of the return of the "favored son" or civic pride in the "local boy" who makes good. Why, in Mark's view, does this happen? The Nazarenes seem to admit that Jesus speaks with "**wisdom.**" They do not deny that he does "**deeds of power.**" Why then do they object to him? According to Mark, their objection has to do with his role as a craftsman and their knowledge of his family. "**Is not this the carpenter (*tektōn*[7]), the son of Mary[8] and brother of James and Joses and Judas and Simon, and are not his sisters here with us?**" (6.3)

But what did they mean by that? Or at least, what did Mark think they meant? The emphatic "**this** (*houtos*)"—"Is not *this* the carpenter?"—with which their objections begin is initially surprising, since Jewish tradition generally honored working with one's hands, and did not share Hellenistic snobbery about manual work and manual workers. On the contrary, it conceded with great realism that,

> Without them no city can be inhabited,
> and wherever they live, they will not go hungry,

for "they maintain the fabric of the world" (Ecclesiasticus 38.32, 34a). In other words, unlike those of us who sit around writing books or articles for journals that few people read, people who work with their hands actually do something useful! By contrast, such snobbery was not only clearly expressed in the second century by Celsus, the opponent of Christianity, but also, equally clearly, was *shared* by Christianity's defender Origen.[9] Jewish tradition did concede, however, that teaching Torah and being a carpenter, however honorable either may be, do not easily go together.[10] So the point being made by **"Is not this the carpenter?"** is perhaps that it is this particular craftsman, who has abandoned his craft and now presumes to teach, who is scorned.

What of "**son of Mary**"? Was such a reference to Jesus as son of his mother rather than son of his father likely to be insulting? Does it even reflect a claim that Jesus was illegitimate?[11]—a claim that was certainly made later. And if so, is it indirect evidence of his virginal conception—inasmuch as belief in Jesus' illegitimacy and belief in his virginal conception have in common the view that Joseph was not Jesus' father?[12] Or was it simply natural and normal to use the matronymic where someone's father had already had children by an earlier marriage, so that Mark may have been indicating that that was the case here?[13] While commentators tend to one side of the question or the other, most concede that certainty is not possible: Mark simply does not tell us.

What Mark does tell us is the name of Jesus' mother—providing us, incidentally, with the earliest text in the New

Testament to do so[14]—and the names of other members of his family. The information, minimal though it is, is by no means without significance. Mary (i.e., Miriam) was at the time the single most popular female name among Jews of Judea—as distinct from Galilee—being borne by approximately one women in four.[15] Through its Greek forms Maria, Mariam and Mariamme, it derives from Miriam the sister of Moses. Its popularity among Judeans in the time of Jesus has been connected with the Hasmonean princess Mariamme, whom Herod the Great married and later murdered.[16] Was Mary then remembered as having Judean connections? Mark gives us no further hint of that, but we shall find evidence that she was so remembered when we examine Luke's account of her. For the present, suffice it to note that *all* the other names of family members specified by Mark—that is, James (i.e., Jacob), Joses (i.e., Joseph), Judas (i.e., Judah, Jude) and Simon (Simeon)[17]—are biblical, the names of patriarchs, Jacob and his three sons: which seems to suggest a family marked not only by a craft but also by piety.

But how does all this lead to hostility? Indeed, if the precise terms of Mark's account are correct, to something worse than hostility: "**And they took offence at him**" (6.3b). The word rendered "**took offence**" by the NRSV is *eskandalizonto*, and to be a *skandalon* implies far more than that one is merely irritating or annoying. A *skandalon* is a rock over which one falls, a stumbling block to faith. Mark's choice of word about the Nazarenes' reaction to Jesus implies essentially what Paul spelled out about unbelievers:

> They have stumbled over the stumbling-stone, as it is written,
> "See, I am laying in Zion a stumbling block, a rock of offence (*petran skandalou*)." (Rom. 9.32b-33a)

M. Eugene Boring does not state the matter too strongly when he points out that what Mark is saying is that their reaction to Jesus has hardened them in unbelief.[18]

So, our question remains, only becoming more acute as we realize the gravity of Mark's assertion: what brings Jesus' fellow townsfolk to this? The only grounds Mark offers is that they believe they *know* Jesus, "**the carpenter, the son of Mary.**" We may then cite our own proverb—"familiarity breeds contempt"—and Mark offers us some support for this, since he has Jesus quote a proverb that makes somewhat the same point: "**Prophets are not without honor, except in their home town, and among their own kin, and in their own house**" (6.4).

Whatever more there is to be said about why Jesus' fellow townsfolk took offence at him, Mark does not say it. He only tells us what followed: "**And he could do no deed of power there, except that he laid his hands on a few sick people and cured them. And he marveled at their unbelief**" (6.5-6)—an account so embarrassing that Matthew alters "**could do**" to "did" (Matt. 13.58) and Luke omits it altogether.

What does Mark understand by all this? Or expect us to understand? He seems at least to be indicating that the sheer humanity of the Son of God means that his glory does not necessarily impress itself on us. Indeed, it is not necessarily discerned at all. It is veiled. As Alan Richardson said, citing this very passage, "The divine splendour is at once veiled and revealed in the flesh which Christ took from the Virgin Mary his mother." Hence men and women "in every generation since his own (cf. Mark 6.2f.) have looked upon him as merely one of themselves and have failed to penetrate the *incognito* which he had assumed."[19]

That, I suspect, is more or less the point that Mark thought was made by his narrative at 6.1-6. But we should admit that the passage is puzzling, and it may be that Mark, though he faithfully handed on what he had received, found it puzzling too. We shall have cause to reflect again on these events when we examine Matthew's version of them. We shall there, I believe, perceive further hints as to what might lie behind the resentment and hostility that Jesus seems to have engendered amongst those with whom he had grown up.

3

MATTHEW

Matthew opens his gospel[1] with a statement that at once makes clear his intention in writing at all. "**A Book of Genesis**[2] **of Jesus Christ, son of David, son of Abraham**" (1.1)—a statement which Jerome regarded as the author's title for the whole work. Jerome was probably right. As such, following biblical and other precedents, it indicates the content of what is to follow.[3]

"*Genesis*" (that is, "origin, source, beginning") had already, before Matthew's time, become recognized by Greek-speaking Jews as a title for the first book of Torah, and Matthew's reference to "**a Book of Genesis** [*biblos geneseōs*] **of Jesus Christ**" would likely put them in mind of that. Now they might expect to hear a fresh story of "**genesis**"—the origins of the one who as "**son of David**" would fulfil the promises made to David's heirs in 1 Samuel 7 and who as "**son of Abraham**" would be a true Israelite.[4]

Matthew's book proper then begins with a patrilineal genealogy that runs from Abraham to David, from David to the Babylonian captivity and from the Babylonian captivity to Jesus "**who is called the Messiah**"—each section alleged by Matthew to be through fourteen generations:

> **Abraham was the father of Isaac, and Isaac the father of Jacob, and Jacob the father of Judah and his brothers, and Judah the father of Perez and Zerah *by Tamar*, and Perez the father of Hezron, and Hezron the father of**

> **Aram, and Aram the father of Aminadab, and Aminadab the father of Nahshon, and Nahshon the father of Salmon, and Salmon the father of Boaz *by Rahab,* and Boaz the father of Obed *by Ruth*, and Obed the father of Jesse, and Jesse the father of King David.**
>
> **And David was the father of Solomon *by the wife of Uriah*, and Solomon the father of Rehoboam, and Rehoboam the father of Abijah, and Abijah the father of Asaph, and Asaph the father of Jehoshaphat, and Jehoshaphat the father of Joram, and Joram the father of Uzziah, and Uzziah the father of Jotham, and Jotham the father of Ahaz, and Ahaz the father of Hezekiah, and Hezekiah the father of Manasseh, and Manasseh the father of Amos, and Amos the father of Josiah, and Josiah the father of Jechoniah and his brothers, at the time of the deportation to Babylon.**
>
> **And after the deportation to Babylon: Jechoniah was the father of Salathiel, and Salathiel the father of Zerubbabel, and Zerubbabel the father of Abiud, and Abiud the father of Eliakim, and Eliakim the father of Azor, and Azor the father of Zadok, and Zadok the father of Achim, and Achim the father of Eliud, and Eliud the father of Eleazar, and Eleazar the father of Matthan, and Matthan the father of Jacob, and Jacob the father of Joseph *the husband of Mary*, of whom Jesus was born, who is called the Messiah.** (Matt. 1.2-16)

Ancient genealogies invariably have a purpose—usually, to establish connections[5]—and Matthew's is no exception. It connects Jesus firmly to the history of Israel. The number "**fourteen**" is clearly regarded as significant—the author going out of his way to draw our attention to it even where it appears, even by his own account, to be incorrect:

> **So all the generations from Abraham to David are fourteen generations; and from David to the deportation to Babylon, fourteen generations; and from the deportation to Babylon to the Messiah, fourteen generations.** (1.17)

Matthew's genealogy does indeed present fourteen generations from Abraham to David, and another fourteen from David to the Babylonian captivity (1.2-11). But from the captivity to Jesus, there are only thirteen (1.12-16)—hence the schoolboy joke (and no doubt schoolgirl, too, but I attended a boys' grammar school) that the reason Jesus summoned Matthew from being a tax collector was that Matthew couldn't count. The number and the variety of attempts to explain or explain away this discrepancy (such as that a name has dropped out; or that Mary should be counted in addition to Joseph; or that Jesus in his first Advent is the thirteenth and in his second as the Christ will be the fourteenth; or that, in addition to those named, there is a rapist who got Mary pregnant and is therefore the un-named biological father of Jesus[6]) serve perhaps chiefly to indicate that none has been found convincing.

The most obvious reason for Matthew's insistence on his fourteens is that in gematria the numerical value of the Hebrew name "David" is fourteen.[7] The rounding off into three fourteens—that is, six sevens, so that the birth of Jesus begins a seventh seven, seven signifying perfection[8]—is surely taken to imply that the Messiah, the son of David, has come "in the fulness of time" (just as Paul had put it a generation earlier). We are to understand that through Abraham, through David and through all Israel's history[9], its highs and its lows, God has been working the divine purpose—all leading toward the coming of the Anointed One, the Messiah.[10]

And yet—and this is the point at which the genealogy becomes of particular interest to us in relation to Mary the mother of Jesus—and yet, this carefully worked out patrilineal arrangement is five times disturbed by the introduction of women, as I have indicated by highlighting them in italic type in the version above. These women are, moreover, hardly the women we might have expected to stand alongside Israel's patriarchs and kings. We are not presented with Sarah or Rebekah or Rachel, or even righteous Asenath who, though a foreigner, according to tradition became a proselyte and for her piety was called "daughter of God."[11] Instead, the chosen women are Tamar, widow of Judah's son Er, who disguised herself as a harlot so that she might conceive sons for Er by her father-in-law Judah;[12] Rahab, the harlot of Jericho, who with her family was saved from Jericho's destruction because she aided Israel in its moment of need;[13] Ruth the Moabite, a foreigner who joined herself to Israel and ultimately through her marriage to Boaz became the great-grandmother of David; Bathsheba, wife of Uriah the Hittite—referred to by Matthew simply as "**her of Uriah** (*tēs tou Ouriou*)"—with whom David committed adultery, to which crime he then added murder in an attempt to cover it up (2 Sam. 11-12); and finally Mary, who was joined to David's line through her marriage to Joseph.

It is a strange group, with little apparently in common. Rahab and Ruth were gentiles, which is to say they were by definition not part of Israel at all. Tamar and Rahab were prostitutes. Bathsheba's union with David involved adultery and murder.[14] None of them and none of their unions would seem, on the face of it, likely candidates to be part of the divine plan. Indeed, that is something they do have in common: that in furthering the divine purpose through them, God was by no means working through what might be described as "established channels." And that, of course, is also true of Mary. It is evident that in her union, too, Matthew perceives elements that are surprising and irregular.[15] So irregular, indeed, that he is led to make another exception to all that has gone before. Mary's is the only union of which he does not say that the male was father of the son. Indeed, he goes out of his way *not* to say that. He speaks instead of "Joseph, the husband of Mary, from whom Jesus called 'Messiah' was born" (1.16): words which do not in themselves affirm virginal conception,[16] but in their setting surely imply that Joseph was not the child's biological father.

But there is more that should be said. I have already mentioned Elizabeth Schussler Fiorenza's dictum that in patriarchal narrative, the presence of women will as a rule only be mentioned "when women's behavior presents a problem or when women are exceptional individuals."[17] The four women from Israel's scriptures referred to in Matthew's genealogy have that in common, too: they are all exceptional and they all present a problem. More precisely, following up on insights offered by Beverley Roberts Gaventa, we may say that they are exceptional and problematic in that they all, in one way or another, *at once threaten and are threatened by* what surrounds them.[18] Tamar is a threat because she exposes Judah's hypocrisy; but she is threatened because in order to do so she risks being stoned as an adulteress. Rahab is a threat because at the crucial moment a word from her would expose Israel's spies to their enemies; but she is threatened because finally she must depend for her life on their faithfulness and goodwill. Bathsheba is a threat because her beauty leads David to adultery and murder; but she is threatened because she could find herself condemned as adulteress. Ruth is a threat for several reasons—because she determines to stay with Naomi rather than doing what is normal and returning to her own people, and because she takes the initiative in going into Boaz's fields to glean; but she is threatened because her loyalty to Naomi could leave her childless and husbandless, a foreigner in a foreign land, because her going alone to glean could lead to her being raped (as Boaz is evidently aware [Ruth 2.9]), and finally because her going to Boaz at night could lead to her being treated as a harlot if he refused to fulfil his obligations to her as kin.

So much for the four women from Israel's Scriptures. How then does Mary the mother of Jesus fit into this company? We have already noted how Matthew's genealogy hints that she has a degree of irregularity in her union with Joseph that is in common with them. But is she, like them, also at once a threat and threatened? To consider that question, we must turn to the next part of Matthew's narrative.

> **Now the genesis of Jesus the Messiah took place in this way.** (1.18a)

In my rendering of Matthew 1.18a, it will be seen that I have transliterated Greek *genesis* rather than translating it as do most English translations.[19] My purpose is to make plain the verbal link between the genealogy with which Matthew began his gospel and the story he is about to tell now. Both, he says, are concerned with aspects of Jesus' "**genesis**": the former, as we have seen, with his place in the entire history of Israel, the latter, as we shall now see, with the peculiar circumstances of his birth.[20]

The evangelist begins with a summary of the story that he is about to tell:

> **When his mother Mary had been engaged to Joseph, but before they lived together, she was found to be with child from the Holy Spirit.** (1.18b)

To understand the circumstances Matthew refers to here, we need to know something of Jewish marriage customs. These are spelled out in later rabbinic materials but appear to be implicit in our narrative. A betrothal was arranged by elders of the family, the parties to it being very young by modern Western standards: the rabbis specify as a minimum age for the male thirteen and for the female twelve. The ceremony—wherein the groom presented the bride and her father with marriage contract and bride-price—took place at the home of the bride's father. There she would then normally remain until the time came for her to transfer to her husband's home or to that of his father. This might happen one or even several years after the betrothal. During the period between the two events, although the marriage was yet to be consummated, the woman was regarded as legally married, and the cancellation of her marriage would require the formality of divorce.[21]

This then was the situation in which Joseph found himself when, "**before they came together,**" Mary was "**found with child from the Holy Spirit**" (Matt. 1.18-19). Matthew evidently provides this preliminary note for the sake of us, his audience, so that we may be clear from the start that whatever has happened here, God has been the moving and creative power behind it. Here, as Wilfred Harrington puts it, we are given "the clue to the mystery of Mary's pregnancy that Joseph must face."[22] Matthew is, however, also saying important things about his own view of Mary and of Jesus. On the one hand, he regards Jesus as conceived in Mary: in accordance with which, although he will never once call Joseph the father of Jesus, he will not hesitate to refer repeatedly to Mary as Jesus' mother (1.18; 2.11, 13, 14, 20, 21; 12.46; 13.55). On the other hand, it is clear that he regards the conception of Mary's child as in a special sense the work of God, "**from the Holy Spirit**" (1.20). Although we should not, at least in Matthew's thinking, give this expression such force as it might have in later trinitarian theology, still we should not give it less than it has in Israel's Scriptures, where it invariably speaks of God's acts of creation and new creation (Gen. 1.2; Ezek. 37).[23] Matthew's Mary is the locus of God's peculiar creative grace in "**the genesis of Jesus the Messiah**": which is to say, God has chosen her to play a pivotal role in the drama of salvation.

We are not, of course, to suppose that at this point Joseph himself is aware that Mary's pregnancy is a work of God's Spirit, or of the special grace that is at work in Mary.[24] Indeed, it immediately becomes very clear that he is not.

> **Her husband Joseph, being a righteous man and unwilling to expose her to public disgrace, planned to dismiss her quietly.** (1.19)

The story continues from Joseph's point of view. What has happened to Mary looks to him like the case described in Deuteronomy 22.23-27, where a betrothed woman has sexual relations with a man other than her husband either in the town or in the country: if in the town, both must be stoned to death, if in the country, only the man. In either case, the man has "violated his neighbor's wife." We do not know how inflexibly such punishments were meted out in Galilee at this period, but in any case, Joseph's decision not **"to expose her to public disgrace"** but merely **"to dismiss her quietly"** appears as a decision not to invoke against Mary the full provisions of the Law. Rather than that, Joseph will serve her with a "certificate of divorce": a written notice signed by two witnesses that he has divorced her and that she is now at liberty to marry someone else (cf. Deut. 24.1).[25]

So the narrative very directly places Mary in the company of those other women in Matthew's genealogy to whom we referred earlier—*women who were at once threats to the normal order of things and themselves threatened by that order.*[26] Mary is a threat to the normal order of things because she has become pregnant outside of her society's normal parameters for pregnancy. And by that fact she is also threatened, since society, naturally assuming that the child with whom she is pregnant was conceived illegitimately, will likely inflict upon her humiliation and disgrace—a humiliation and disgrace that will only marginally be alleviated by Joseph's decision, **being a righteous man and unwilling to involve her in public disgrace,** to treat her more leniently than the Law required and "**to divorce her quietly** (*lathra*[27])."

> **But just when he had resolved to do this, an angel of the Lord appeared to him in a dream**[28] **and said, "Joseph, son of David, do not be afraid to take home Mary your wife, for the child conceived in her is from the Holy Spirit. She will bear a son, and you are to name him Jesus, for he will save his people from their sins."** (1.20-21)

As Joseph is in the midst of making his decision, the angel of the Lord makes known to him God's will. "All our righteous deeds are like a filthy cloth," says the prophet,[29] and there is surely irony in that Matthew, having presented Joseph as one whose very *righteousness* would lead him to go "**quietly**" against the will of God, now shows us that same Joseph learning that only by abandoning his own righteousness can he truly experience the gracious presence of God, which is coming to him in and through the child being carried by Mary. Karl A. Plank states the issue powerfully: "Mary, in her difference, brings to the world of Joseph the surprising presence of God. Remaining estranged from her, Joseph would stand alone in his purity, joined perhaps by moral peers but alienated from the God whose presence he would protect."[30]

The angel's announcement, coming with the customary angelic "**Do not be afraid,**" affirms first the Davidic lineage of Joseph, so establishing that Jesus, when accepted and named by Joseph as his own[31] will likewise legally be of Davidic lineage, a "**son of David**" as well as a "**son of Abraham.**" Next Joseph learns—and we hear for the second time—that he is in the presence of a miracle: namely, that "**the child conceived in her,**" rather than being the result of fornication, *ek porneias*, as Joseph had supposed, is actually "**from the Holy Spirit:** *ek pneumatos* *estin hagiou.*"[32] Joseph is to name the child, by which act he will be accepting the child as his own: as it was written, "I have called you by name, you are mine" (Isaiah 43.1). The name **"Jesus"** (Hebrew "Joshua" [*Yēšûa*]), which he is directed to give and which in popular etymology is associated to Hebrew *yš* ['to save']) will reflect who the child is and what he will do.

Such is the angel's message. But what does it mean, especially in terms of Israel's story with which the evangelist was so careful to begin? Matthew now brings before us the first in a series of ten so-called "formula" quotations which mark his gospel. Each (in effect) is an editorial comment on the narrative. Each cites Scripture (nine times the prophets, once the psalms). And each is preceded by some version of the formula "all this came to pass to fulfil."[33]

> **All this took place to fulfill what had been spoken by the Lord through the prophet:**
> **"Look, the young woman** (NRSV **the virgin**[34]) **shall conceive and bear a son,**
> **and they shall name him Emmanuel,"**
> **which means, "God is with us."** (1.22-23 citing Isaiah 7.14)

All this—all the events of which we have just heard—were, the evangelist tells us, in fulfilment of prophecy. Centuries earlier, the prophet Isaiah had assured another "son of David," Judaea's King Ahaz, appalled and intimidated by foreign threats, of God's continuing favor and presence. In a very short time, Isaiah declared, the power of those who threatened Israel would wane, with the result that a woman then pregnant (medieval Jewish exegesis suggests that it may have been the prophet's wife[35]) would triumphantly name her newborn "*immanu el*," that is, "God is with us."[36] So Ahaz should abandon thought of any hasty policy decisions he might be about to make, and proceed trusting in God's favor. Matthew sees all this brought to new fulfillment in the angel's word to Joseph, appalled and intimidated as he is by the unexpected pregnancy of Mary. He, too, is assured of God's continuing favor and presence. He, too, should abandon thought of any hasty decisions he might be about to make, such as to divorce Mary. He, too, should proceed trusting in God's favor—something that Matthew emphasizes by drawing his audience's attention to the significance of the name Emmanuel, "**which means, 'God is with us.'**" This promise of divine favor and presence in and through the person of Jesus will be touched on elsewhere in the gospel (18.19-20, 26.29) and emphatically at the conclusion when the Risen One, now holding "all authority in heaven and on earth," will declare to those with him, "See! I, even I,[37] am with you always, to the end of the age."[38]

> **When Joseph awoke from sleep, he did as the angel of the Lord commanded him; he took home his wife but had no marital relations with her until she had borne a son; and he named him Jesus.** (Matthew 1.24-25)

Joseph completes his marriage with Mary, so removing from her the threat of humiliation and disgrace. At the same time, Matthew is careful to inform us that Joseph "**had no marital relations with her until she had borne a son**": which is to say, the evangelist definitely affirms that Jesus was not and could not have been Joseph's biological child.[39] By then *naming* Mary's son, however, Joseph thereby also *accepts* the child as his own, and so removes any legal barrier to Jesus being of the house of David, for as the Mishnah would later put it: "If a man says, 'This is my son,' he is believed.'"[40] By sealing Jesus' membership of the house of David, the evangelist also confirms him as an appropriate candidate to be the Messiah.[41] Perhaps needless to say, the removal of formal, legal barriers with regard to Jesus' status would not therefore necessarily mean an end of the matter as far as inuendo or attitudes were concerned, in the first century any more than it would in the twenty-first. What may have been personal *attitudes* to one about whose birth status there was inevitably *some* kind of question is a matter to which we shall need to return.[42]

So much, for the moment, for Mary and Joseph. But now the scene changes:

> **After Jesus was born in Bethlehem of Judea in the days of Herod the king, Magi from the East came to Jerusalem, asking, 'Where is the one who has been born king of the Jews? For we saw his star at its rising and have come to pay him homage.** (2.1-2)

We move abruptly from the affairs of a single Jewish family to the court of a king and visiting gentile sages. To be sure, Bethlehem was the birthplace of King David, so Matthew is continuing the "son of David" theme from his earlier narrative. And at the same time, since the Magi are gentiles,[43] he is also continuing his earlier "son of Abraham" theme, since in Abraham "all the families of the earth are to be blessed."[44]

> **When King Herod heard this, he was disturbed, and all Jerusalem with him; and calling together all the chief priests and scribes of the people, he inquired of them where the Messiah was to be born. They told him, "In Bethlehem of Judea; for so it has been written by the prophet:**
>
> **'And you, Bethlehem, in the land of Judah,**
> **are by no means least among the rulers of Judah;**
> **for from you shall come a ruler**
> **who is to shepherd my people Israel.'"**
>
> **Then Herod secretly called for the Magi and learned from them the exact time when the star had appeared. Then he sent them to Bethlehem, saying, "Go and**

> **search diligently for the child; and when you have found him, bring me word so that I may also go and pay him homage."** (2.1-8)

The rabbis would later say, "As the first redeemer was, so shall the latter Redeemer be" (*Kohelet Rabbah* 1.9), and it accords with such a view that Matthew now introduces us to a Jesus who is not only son of David and son of Abraham but also *like Moses*. As was the case with the birth of Moses as described in the Scriptures and also in later versions such as those by Pseudo-Philo and Josephus, so Jesus' life will be threatened by a wicked ruler who decrees that he and all male children of his age shall be killed. Like Moses, Jesus will have to flee. And like Moses, only after the ruler's death can he return.[45]

What of King Herod? As portrayed by Matthew, he is certainly not dissimilar to what we know of the Herod of history. As Dorothy Sayers said, "This man was not called 'Herod the Great' for nothing."[46] He was a brilliant soldier and a wily and successful politician, but his achievements were marred by paranoia and cruelty. When news came to him of one "**born king of the Jews,**" Matthew tells us that he was "**disturbed**."[47]

Why might Herod have been so concerned about an event involving an infant? Did Herod himself have Messianic pretensions? No contemporary source speaks of him in that way, but he appears to have gained the title later, at least in the eyes of some. Epiphanius and Jerome speak of those whom Mark calls "Herodians" (Mark 6.3, 12.13) as Jews who revered Herod as Messiah.[48] Tradition suggested two possible roads to such recognition.[49] One was to be of the house of David, which Herod the Idumean certainly was not. The other was to show your eligibility by doing things that were prophesied of the king messiah, such as rebuilding the temple.[50] That, Herod did do.

Acting ruthlessly to eliminate possible rivals is certainly how Herod was remembered. According to the *Testament of*

Moses, probably composed only decades after his death,[51] he was spoken of as one who would "kill both old and young, he will not spare."[52] So Matthew's Herod, after hearing prophecies of a new king to be born in Bethlehem (2.5-6), takes counsel with the Magi "**secretly** (*lathra*)" (2.7)—use of the word "secretly" making sure that Herod's action resonates for us with Joseph's earlier proposed action in divorcing Mary. As that action threatened Mary and her child, so does this. Herod says that he wishes to see the child so that he too may "**pay him homage.**" But we know very well that he intends no such thing.

The Magi, however, go on their way.

> **When they had heard the king, they set out; and there, ahead of them, went the star that they had seen at its rising, until it stopped over the place where the child was. When they saw that the star had stopped, they were overwhelmed with joy. On entering the house, they saw the child with Mary his mother; and they knelt down and paid him homage. Then, opening their treasure-chests, they offered him gifts of gold, frankincense, and myrrh.** (2.9-11)

This part of the narrative centers on the Magi and their gifts. But Mary is present. Indeed, she is very much present. I cannot agree with Brown's suggestion that her role in Matthew's narrative is "minor" or with Gaventa's comment that she "almost fades from our view."[53] It is true that she remains silent, but our reaction to that perhaps says more about our own activity-ridden culture than it does about Matthew's portrait of Mary. We are, I suspect, in danger of confusing quietness (Isaiah 30.15!) with absence or insignificance. What is it that the Magi *see* when they enter the house? It is "**the child, with Mary his mother**" (2.11). First Jesus, then Mary *with* Jesus: *those are the centers of attention.* There is no mention of Joseph. Could the picture of a caring mother—and I trust we may assume Matthew granted that attribute to Mary?—*ever* imply anything but presence in relation to her newborn? To be sure, Mary—and indeed Jesus—are silent. But they are so as the still center of a turning world. That is how poets and painters over centuries—da Fabbiano, Lippi, delle Notti [see Frontispiece], Botticelli, da Vinci, Rubens, Rossetti and countless others—have shown us the scene. One suspects the poets and painters perceive something the commentators have missed.[54]

> **And having been warned in a dream not to return to Herod, they [the Magi] left for their own country by another road. Now after they had left, an angel of the Lord appeared to Joseph in a dream and said, "Get up, take the child and his mother, and flee to Egypt, and remain there until I tell you; for Herod is about to search for the child, to destroy him." Then Joseph got up, took the child and his mother by night, and went to Egypt, and remained there until the death of Herod. This was to fulfil what had been spoken by the Lord through the prophet, "Out of Egypt I have called my son."** (2.12-15)

Far from allowing Mary to fade from our view, in the next part of the story, Matthew now speaks repeatedly of "**the child and his mother**"—"**the child**" being not mentioned without her. Joseph, of course, is seen as more obviously *active* than Mary—as men tend to be in a patriarchal society. Yet what Joseph does—the flight into Egypt—is entirely in relation to Mary and her son, and is an act of obedience. Indeed, throughout the entire story, Joseph's only action on his *own* initiative—his initial proposal to divorce Mary—is also his only action that is potentially disastrous, so that he has to be turned from it.

It is not, of course, that the evangelist despises initiative. The Magi certainly take initiative. They have been active from their first appearance: honest seekers after truth who are not afraid to admit what they do not know, they follow their curiosity and are rewarded. The scene at the court of Herod turns into a striking reversal of the "Jewish faith outsmarts gentile wisdom" tradition found elsewhere in Scripture.[55] Here, the gentiles have certainly been obliged to turn to Israel for the knowledge that they need, but now it is they, not those to whom they have turned, who believe.[56] Warned of God "**not to return to Herod,**" they listen and obey—and so avoid becoming a threat to Mary and her child. It is hard to suppose that Matthew sees no connection between them and the promised gentile believers with whom his gospel will end.[57]

> **When Herod saw that he had been tricked by the Magi, he was infuriated, and he sent and killed all the children in and around Bethlehem who were two years old or under, according to the time that he had learned from the Magi. Then was fulfilled what had been spoken through the prophet Jeremiah:**
>
> **A voice was heard in Ramah,**
> **wailing and loud lamentation,**
> **Rachel weeping for her children;**
> **she refused to be consoled,**
> **because they are no more.**
>
> (2.16-18)

Of every character in the action, the one who most clearly takes initiative and is prepared to act is the evident villain of the piece: initially in his questioning of the Magi, and now when he finds they have frustrated him. Here, Herod the man of action plays his part, and we are left in no doubt as to how deadly he would have been to Mary and her child, if Joseph and then the Magi had not listened to God's word. So, from the beginning of the gospel, death is not far from Jesus.

> **When Herod died, an angel of the Lord suddenly appeared in a dream to Joseph in Egypt and said, "Get up, take the child and his mother, and go to the land of Israel, for those who were seeking the child's life are dead." Then Joseph got up, took the child and his mother, and went to the land of Israel. But when he heard that Archelaus was ruling over Judea in place of his father Herod, he was afraid to go there. And after being warned in a dream, he went away to the district of Galilee. There he made his home in a town called Nazareth, so that what had been spoken through the prophets might be fulfilled, "He will be called a Nazorean."**
>
> (2.19-23)

Joseph's final act in this narrative is another act of obedience: he takes "**the child and his mother**" back to the land of Israel. As regards the situation in Judaea following the death of Herod, Matthew appears to be accurately informed: Archelaus seems to have been as cruel as Herod though lacking Herod's competence.[58] So Joseph took his family not to Judea, where Archelaus "**was ruling,**"[59] but to Nazareth. Thereby, he set the stage for the son of David to begin his messianic task as prophesied: which seems—although no one is quite sure—to be the intended implication of Matthew's reference to "**the prophets**" and the word spoken through them, **"He will be called a Nazorean."**[60] Of Mary we learn only the one continuing fact, to which Matthew again twice draws our attention: she remains with her child. Apropos of which, having referred earlier to poets and painters, one might consider the imaginative reflection of a novelist on this continuing bond between Mary and her son that Matthew's text will not allow us to forget:

> She had thought in the conception to have ended all things. She had only begun them. The conception meant

> the birth and the birth meant the death and in between was the important thing. The oneness of her and the child, drawing the milk of her flesh into his blood of his: that cord she could not cut, ever. She had started what she could not control; what she could not name or finish. The carrying him in simplicity had seemed like enough. It was not enough. She was tired already. She would be tired for a long time… She could not understand, she only knew that there was more to come. Her body had thought the conception a beginning the birth an ending. It was not an ending, just another beginning. (Sara Maitland, *Daughter of Jerusalem*)[61]

I am by no means claiming that Matthew appreciated all that is expressed in that passage—I suspect that no male writer could or can. But we should know by now that all that a text can mean is not confined to what its author intends or understands. What Maitland spells out is arguably implicit if not expressed in the one fact to which he repeatedly draws our attention: the fact of **"the child and his mother."**

There are two more references to Mary in Matthew's gospel. Both result from his following Mark. The former involves Jesus' relationship to his family:

> **While he was still speaking to the crowds, his mother and his brothers were standing outside, wanting to speak to him. Someone told him, "Look, your mother and your brothers are standing outside, wanting to speak to you." But to the one who had told him this, Jesus replied, "Who is my mother, and who are my brothers?" And pointing to his disciples, he said, "Here are my mother and my brothers! For whoever does the will of my Father in heaven is my brother and sister and mother."** (Matthew 12.46-50)

Comparing this with Mark's account, we see that Matthew has softened the dispute between Jesus and his family by omitting the suggestion that they think he is mad. In Matthew's version, they merely come to speak to him. The effect of this is to make the evident point of the story—to ask the question "Who is truly a member of Jesus' family?"—clearer than it is in Mark's version, since we are not distracted by other issues.

The second additional Matthean reference to Mary involves Jesus' relationship with his fellow townsfolk:

> **When Jesus had finished these parables, he left that place and came to his home town and began to teach the people in their synagogue, so that they were astounded and said, "Where did this man get this wisdom and these deeds of power? Is not this the carpenter's son? Is not his mother called Mary? And are not his brothers James and Joseph and Simon and Judas? And are not all his sisters with us? Where then did this man get all this?" And they took offence at him. But Jesus said to them, "Prophets are not without honor except in their own country and in their own house." And he did not do many deeds of power there, because of their unbelief.** (Matthew 13.53-58)

Matthew here follows Mark closely and does not tell us anything about Mary that we have not been told elsewhere. Taken in the context of his entire gospel, however, he perhaps offers us grounds for the hostility of Jesus' townsfolk to his success that are not offered by Mark's more concise but therefore more limited narrative. We have noted how Joseph's receiving Mary into his home and accepting her child as his own will have removed from Mary's son any *legal* barrier to his being of the house of David and hence an appropriate candidate to be the Messiah. But of course the removal of formal, legal barriers would not therefore necessarily be an end of the matter apropos personal attitudes toward one about whose birth status there was some kind of question. There can be no doubt that opponents of Christianity would subsequently declare that Jesus' conception was illegitimate.[62] Matthew, by contrast, declared that, though Joseph was not Jesus' biological father, nevertheless, Jesus' conception was "of the Holy Spirit." As Leslie Stemp, a barrister friend of mine, pointed out to me many years ago, when people are in dispute, there is a very good chance that anything they agree on—the element that neither side denies—is actually the case. And there was here agreement on at least one thing: *that the circumstances of Jesus' birth were not normal.* And that fact alone, regardless of what lay behind it, meant that in the traditionally patrilineal society into which Jesus was born, in which women belonged in their husbands' or their fathers' households, *Jesus' own status was questionable.*[63] There was a flaw, an irregularity, in his kinship, which made him unsuitable for betrothal and marriage.[64] Indeed, all Christian tradition is clear that Jesus did not marry and did not raise a family.[65] Was that because he honored the law as it was understood by Judaean authorities?[66] Possibly. But in any case it surely meant that in the eyes of some he achieved less than full manhood.[67] In that light, not only his "brothers" but any "proper" male in the village that was Nazareth (we are talking of a community of probably less than 500 people[68]) might have regarded themselves as better than he. Did that superiority afford *rational* grounds for their taking "offence" at his being recognized as having "wisdom" or performing "deeds of power"? Of course it did not, any more than Caucasians have ever had any rational grounds for calling clever or successful Africans "uppity", or males generally any rational grounds using the same kind of language about clever and successful women. That, however, does not mean that such things did not happen, in the ancient world as in ours. What is more—and we here revert to Mark's version of the story—we may perhaps detect awareness of that and the mindless prejudice that lies behind it in the weary reaction that Mark ascribes to Jesus: "and he marveled at their unbelief."[69]

4

LUKE

In the prologue to his gospel (Luke 1.1-4), Luke[1] indicates his intention to conform in some measure to the literary conventions of Hellenism—perhaps not, as is sometimes suggested, to the conventions of Hellenistic historical writing, but rather to the conventions of serious Hellenistic correspondence, wherein the writer indicates that he has researched his subject carefully and undertakes to provide reliable information. As Loveday Alexander has shown us, in style and vocabulary Luke's prologues are not so much academic as businesslike, finding their closest parallels in official reports and letters, and in a broader area of literature which she characterizes as "the scientific tradition."[2]

Following his prologue, Luke gives us two full chapters of narrative about the circumstances surrounding Jesus' origins, mostly about his birth but including, unique in the New Testament, two narratives about his infancy and boyhood. As with Matthew's birth narratives, opinions differ as to the sources and origins of these traditions. What is not in doubt is the extraordinary care and artistry that has gone into Luke's presentation of these "intricately organized"[3] narratives. He parallels his account of Jesus' birth with an account of John the Baptist's birth, in such a way that the forerunner and the one to whom he points are linked even before either is born. The narratives, so arranged, take the form of a triptych:

Two Annunciations (A1, A2) (1.5-38)
  Visitation (B) (1.39-56)
Two Births (C1, C2) (1.57-2.20)

Then follow the two boyhood narratives to which we have referred:

> An episode from Jesus' infancy: the Presentation (2.22-40)
> An episode from Jesus' boyhood: Jesus and the doctors (2:41- 52)

The whole has provided material and inspiration for artists and writers over millennia.

Once they have been introduced to us, the most prominent figures in the two opening narratives (1.5-38) are evidently the two mothers, Elizabeth and Mary. Of these the greater by far is evidently Mary, in that not only is she to play a prominent—indeed, pivotal—part in the action, but we are also offered insight into what she is thinking and feeling: not at all a common feature of such narratives.

Let us consider each of the elements of Luke's triptych in more detail, and particularly as they bear on our subject—how the church remembered the mother of Jesus.

Two Annunciations

The rabbis would later observe that "wherever [in Scripture] it is written, She was barren, it means that she would bear"[4]—such are the births granted to Sarah (Gen. 16.1), Rebecca (Gen. 25.21), Rachel (Gen. 30.1), the (unnamed!) mother of Samson (Judges 13.2) and Hannah (1 Sam. 1.2), *and always they are for Israel's deliverance*.[5] It is evident that Luke wants his hearers to have such Biblical traditions in mind as he gives his account of the angelic message that precedes the birth of John the Baptist. He even switches his style of writing from the Hellenistic Greek of his prologue, educated but workmanlike, to a plausible imitation of the Septuagint.[6]

He provides us with a narrative that we may conveniently divide into six stages, each of them echoing Scriptural traditions:

(1) *The Angelic Visit*: Zachariah and Elizabeth are barren and elderly (Luke 1.7).[7] While serving in the Temple, Zachariah has a divine visitation (Luke 1.11).[8]

(2) *Disturbance and Doubt*: Zachariah is disturbed by the visitation and receives angelic reassurance (1.12-13a).[9]

(3) *The Promise*: Zachariah is told that his prayers have been heard and Elizabeth will have a son who will be a great prophet in the spirit of Elijah (Luke 1.13b-17).[10]

(4) *The Question*: Zachariah asks how he can know this, since he and Elizabeth are old (Luke 1.18).[11]

(5) *The Confirmation*: The angel identifies himself as Gabriel and announces that there will indeed be confirmation: Zachariah will be dumb until the birth of his son, because he did not believe Gabriel's word (Luke 1.19-20).[12]

(6) *What Happens Next*: Following the vision, Zachariah comes out of the Temple (according to custom, it would have been in company with other priests). He is, however, unable to speak. Therefore, he cannot take part in the Aaronic blessing which they would customarily give[13] but can only make signs (1.21-23).[14]

Luke's narrative of the annunciation of the birth of John the Baptist complete, he then brings Mary onto the scene. Again, there will be an annunciation story in six stages, exactly as in the annunciation of the Baptist. At each stage, there will be an evident parallel in content with the Annunciation to Zachariah. But the parallelism will be "step-parallelism," that is, what Joseph A. Fitzmyer describes as "parallelism with one-upmanship. The Jesus side always comes off better."[15] The effect of this at each stage will actually be to make us aware of *differences* between the two narratives, and always in such a way that, great though God's grace is as manifest in the birth of John, God's grace manifest in the birth of Jesus is infinitely greater.

Let us then consider each in turn of the six stages:

(1) *The Angelic Visit*

> **In the sixth month the angel Gabriel was sent by God to a town in Galilee called Nazareth, to a girl engaged to a man whose name was Joseph, of the house of David. The girl's name was Mary. And he came to her and said, "Rejoice (**NRSV: **Greetings), favored one! The Lord is with you."** (Luke 1.26-28)

The "**sixth month**" is evidently the sixth month of Elizabeth's pregnancy: by which reference Luke ties his two annunciation stories together. At the same time, he also faces us with a striking change of atmosphere. The annunciation to Zachariah was set amid the rituals of the Jerusalem temple. What more fitting place could there be for God to reveal the divine purpose? The annunciation to Mary, however, begins with the angel Gabriel[16] "**sent by God**" not to Jerusalem or anything like it but "**to a town in Galilee called Nazareth**"—a town just about as obscure and unlikely as a center for divine revelation as it is possible to imagine (see John 1.46!).[17]

Gabriel is sent, moreover, not to a priest whose advanced years and the barrenness of his wife have been stressed, but "**to a girl**" (1.27). NRSV has "to a virgin"—yet again,[18] a rendering of Luke's Greek *parthenos* that no doubt reflects concerns that Christians have brought to this text over centuries, but surely does not at all reflect the way in which ordinary persons in Luke's own day, listening to his account for the first time, would have heard it. The feminine form of Greek *parthenos* will have been understood as refering to a young woman of marriagable age, with or without focus on viriginity.[19] It is not that Luke does not believe in Mary's virginity—he does, and he will come to it later. But not yet! Rather than thinking of such matters at this point, we do better to adapt ourselves to the frame of mind in which we hear the lyric "Fear no more the heat o' the sun" in Shakespeare's *Cymbeline*. When the poet says,

> Golden lads and girls all must,
> As chimneysweepers, come to dust,

our thoughts on hearing "golden lads and girls" are surely not of virginity or of its lack, but rather of youth and promise and hope as opposed to the old age, death and despair that are implicit in "dust." This is how Luke's *parthenos* will have been heard by his audience, standing as it does in contrast to the elderly, barren couple of whom we have just been hearing. This is a young woman in the bloom of her youth. Greek *parthenos*, like English "girl," may or may not imply virginity, *but it always implies youth, and at this place in Luke's narrative, that is the point.*

This girl is, moreover, "**engaged to a man**"[20]—the mention of new marriage offering yet another sign of youth and promise and hope. The man's name, Luke adds, "**was Joseph, of the house of David,**" and the girl's name "**was Mary**" (1.27). The mention that Joseph was a descendant of David, for those with any knowledge at all of Israel's traditions, would certainly be a hint—if the sending of an angel were not hint enough!—that something special was happening here. It is true that the scene in a home in Nazareth of Galilee stands in sharp contrast to the traditions and rituals of the Temple amid which the angel came to Zachariah. But then, was not David himself something of an outsider? Did not he, too, come onto the scene apart from what might have been seen as "normal channels"—the normal, proper channels of God's working? Such thoughts may occur briefly to us, but are at once dismissed, for the center of the following action is the **girl**: we have already been told that she, not Joseph, is the one to whom the angel was sent. Her name "**was Mary**"—a name, as we have already noted, hallowed in Biblical tradition as that of Moses' and Aaron's sister, Miriam (Exod. 2.4-7, 15.20, Micah 6.4).[21]

To Zachariah there merely "appeared an angel of the Lord, standing at the right side of the altar of incense": a silent manifestation of divine power, presence and authority. By contrast, Gabriel now comes to the place where Mary is—presumably, her home—and *addresses* her: addresses her, moreover, in terms that are both formal and deeply respectful.

The address itself, "**Rejoice**! (Greek: *chaire*)"[22] is a little surprising. We might have expected "Peace! (Greek: *eirenē*)." But we can see at least two reasons why Luke might have chosen *chaire*—first, because it was a word used more than once in his Greek Bible when God spoke words of salvation and hope to Israel:

> Rejoice (*chaire*) greatly, O daughter Zion,
> Proclaim, O daughter Jerusalem,
> Behold, your king comes to you,
> just and salvific is he,
> meek and riding on a beast of burden and a young foal.
> (NETS Zach. 9.9)[23]

As L. T. Johnson puts it, "Mary has the Lord 'within her' even as the eschatological Zion would have the presence of the Lord within it." Therefore, "Not for the last time, Mary represents Israel."[24]

And second, Luke may have liked *chaire* because it resonated with his following word, *kecharitōmenē*: the perfect passive feminine participle of the verb *charitoō*, which means "to bestow *charis*." Throughout our English New Testaments, the Greek word *charis* is variously translated "grace"[25] or "favor."[26] Similarly the participle that Gabriel uses in his address to Mary is translated either by "favored,"or "highly favored" (KJV, NRSV, NAB, REB) or else by "full of grace," "endowed with grace" (D-R following the Vulgate; *GAGNT* 171). How would Luke have expected his hearers to understand *charis*?[27] How might he have intended it? As numerous commentators point out, in this entire section Luke is clearly imitating the style and idioms of the Septuagint, where *charis* seems generally to be understood *as a gift or benefit bestowed by God*. So the Psalmist declares that God "gives *charis* and glory to those who walk uprightly."[28] The only other use of the verb *charitoō* in the New Testament—Ephesians 1.6—clearly understands *charis* in this way too, when it speaks God's "glorious grace (*charitos*) that he freely bestowed on us (*echaritōsen hēmas*) in the Beloved"—or, as Ernest Best more literally but really rather effectively renders it in his commentary on Ephesians, "the glory of his grace, with which he graced us in the Beloved."[29] And that, surely, is how we are to understand *charis* and *charitoō* here. However we choose to translate Luke's Greek—whether we choose to speak of God's "favor" or of God's "grace"—the angel's address to Mary declares first and foremost God's *gift* to her: it is *God's* "favor" and it is *God's* "grace" that she receives, springing from God's love.

The Angel's immediately following words begin to tell her what this gift means: **"The Lord is with you"** (1.28). With just such a declaration, the hero Gideon is greeted in Israel's Scriptures.[30] And the Lord's presence is surely a gracious and a *saving* presence,[31] for do not the Scriptures themselves say so?

> YHWH is near to all who call on him,
> to all who call on him in truth.
> He fulfils the desire of all who fear him;
> he also hears their cry and saves them. (Ps. 145.18-19)

(2) *Disturbance and Doubt*

> **But she was deeply troubled by his words, and pondering what sort of greeting this might be. The angel said to her, "Do not be afraid, Mary, for you have found favor with God."** (1.29.30)

As invariably with divine visitations in Scripture, Zachariah found the appearance of the angel troubling, and so does Mary. Zachariah was "troubled (*etarachthē*)," and Mary is "*deeply* troubled (*dietarachthē*)."[32] Both—as again is usual with divine visitations in Scripture—will soon receive assurance.[33] But even before that assurance is given, there is a difference in their reactions. Of Zachariah, we are told that the effect of his being troubled was that "fear overwhelmed him" (an old man's reaction?). Of Mary, we are told of a much more interesting, positive and perhaps youthful reaction. Despite being "deeply troubled," she is also *curious,* pondering "**what sort of greeting this might be**"—a winsome curiosity wonderfully caught, for this viewer at least, in the *quizzical* Mary of Henry Ossawa Tanner's *L'Annonciation* (see Figure 2). C. F. Evans suggests that in Luke's account, "Mary is depicted as more intellectual than Zachariah. Her reaction is not one of fear but of extreme perplexity at the angel's statement (*logos*) and of pondering its implications."[34] I think I would say, "more intelligent" rather than "more intellectual," but otherwise I find the idea interesting. I find, moreover, something immensely amiable—even endearing—about a curiosity that cannot be quenched by fear. One of my favorite moments in Linda Woolverton's version (created for Disney) of Jeanne-Marie Leprince de Beaumont's *La Belle et la Bête* occurs as Beast in gruff tones introduces Belle to the rules of her new home and says, "You're free to go anywhere you like… except the West Wing." Belle, though obviously still terrified, *cannot* prevent herself asking, "Why, what's in the West…?"and

Figure 2. Henry Assawa Tanner, *The Annunciation*. Philadelphia Museum of Art

we know at once that, despite Beast's immediate roar, "IT IS FORBIDDEN!", it will only be a matter of time before our heroine will feel obliged to investigate. Mary's "pondering" at the archangel's word has a touch of this, and Gabriel's "**Do not be afraid**" to her is thereby much more a matter of formality—of what is *normal* in accounts of such visions—than was his use of the same words earlier to the terrified Zachariah. And while the basis of his comfort to Zachariah was simply "your prayer has been heard," for Mary, he has a word of grace that goes far beyond that, picking up on God's gift to her already promised in the *kecharitōmenē* of his initial salutation, which now he unpacks: "**for you have found favor (***charis***) with God**"—a Semitism found frequently in the LXX that, as François Bovon puts it, "does not at all describe the result of human activity, but rather expresses God's gracious election."[35] But election for what? The angel proceeds to tell her.

(3) *The Promise*

> **And lo,[36] you will conceive in your womb and bear a son, and you will name him Jesus. He will be great, and will be called the Son of the Most High, and the Lord God will give to him the throne of his ancestor David. He will reign over the house of Jacob forever, and of his kingdom there will be no end.**
>
> (1.31-33)

Like Zachariah, Mary is told that she shall have a son, and how he shall be named. But there the parallels end. Zachariah is being told that his prayer has been heard, and that he and Elizabeth will have a son who will be a prophet (1.15-16). The announcement to Mary begins with the solemn Septuagintism "*kai idou*," which I have rendered "**And lo,**" surely indicating that something of great importance is about to be said: and indeed, the angel is about to promise for Mary's child a destiny far greater than that promised to Zachariah's and Elizabeth's child. Zachariah and Elizabeth's child will be a prophet. Mary's child will be Messiah and Son of God. Mary will conceive in her womb "**and bear a son,**" and "**will name him Jesus**" (1.31). Unlike Matthew, Luke shows no sign of knowing the meaning of this name, but from his reading of the LXX he surely knows who the first "Jesus" was—that is, Joshua (cf. Hebrews 4.8)—and what he did for the deliverance and settlement of Israel. What then of this new "Joshua"? The angel continues, "**He will be great… Son of the Most High… the Lord God will give to him the throne of his ancestor David… He will reign over the house of Jacob forever… and of his kingdom there will be no end.**" Here, we have a loose bringing together of ideas extracted from 2 Samuel

7, Psalms 2 and 89 and prophetic passages such as Isaiah 9.5-7, and their implication is clear. Mary's child is destined by God to be the anointed descendant of David and to fulfil the promises associated with David's kingship.

(4) *The Question*

> **And Mary said, "How shall this be, since I am a virgin?"** (Luke 1.34)

Zachariah raised an objection to the angel's message, and so now does Mary. So far our two narratives again run parallel. At first glance, moreover, the two objections seem, as Raymond Brown put it, "not noticeably different" from each other.[37] But that is at first glance. They are in fact by no means the same objection, nor are they made for the same reasons, nor do they manifest the same spirit.

Zachariah was being promised precisely that for which he and Elizabeth had prayed: a son. His objection was essentially a request for proof, "How will I know that this is so?" It reflected his own doubt—"How will I know?"—as to whether God could or would actually respond to their prayer for something that, though by no means impossible, would be surprising, "for I am an old man, and my wife is getting on in years."

What then of Mary's objection?

"How shall this be," she asks, **"since I am a virgin?"**

In my rendering of her words at this point, I follow the NRSV. Luke's Greek reads literally, "since I do not know a man (*epei andra ou ginōskō*)?"—using the verb "know (*ginōskō)*" in the sense of "to have sexual relations with," as it is used in the Greek Bible[38] and elsewhere in Greek literature.[39] *Pace* Fitzmyer, there is nothing in the least "vague"[40] about Mary's words here. The only vagaries are to do with finding an English equivalent. Manifestly *incorrect* is RSV's "I have no husband," which is not only euphemistic and prudish, but also, given the understanding of "betrothal" in that culture, simply wrong. Correct translation choices are either to render Mary's words literally: "I do not know a man" (as, in effect, KJV, D-R and RV); or else, given that in normal English usage, the verb "know" is not generally used of sexual intercourse, to paraphrase: "I am a virgin" (so, in effect, NRSV, NEB, NAB REB, TOB and TILC).

While of course we cannot judge the psychology of the "historical Mary," we can say something about Luke's Mary, the Mary of the narrative. The present tense of the verb with which she speaks of her virginity—"*andra ou ginōskō*"—tells us *why* she questions the angel's promise. She evidently understands Gabriel to be saying that her pregnancy will come about in the near future, *before she goes to live with Joseph.*

Here, certainly, is a matter of honor and also perhaps of life itself. However much Mary may have found "**favor**" with God, however great the promised child may be, its conception in such circumstances faces her, as we have seen in regard to Matthew's account, with a likely charge of adultery and whatever shame or punishment might follow from that.[41]

Even this, however, is not the whole matter. As Mary, if no one else, is presumably in a position to know, in human terms what the angel promises is not merely *unlikely*, as is Elizabeth's pregnancy, but *impossible.* So—**"How shall this be?"** Her question, in sharp contrast to Zachariah's unbelief, is therefore also *fides quaerens intellectum*: faith in quest of understanding and, to that extent, is of a piece with her initial curiosity and "pondering" about the angelic greeting.[42]

(5) *The Confirmation*

The angel said to her, "Holy Spirit will come upon you, and the power of the Most High will overshadow you; therefore the child to be born will be holy; he will be

> **called Son of God. And now, your kinswoman Elizabeth in her old age has also conceived a son; and this is the sixth month for her who was said to be barren. For no word from God shall be powerless."** (Luke 1.35-37)

Gabriel gave Zachariah the confirmation for which he asked, but it was in the form of a punitive miracle: he was to be struck dumb until the birth of his son because "he did not trust." The angel (and presumably therefore the evangelist) evidently regard Zachariah's doubt as what Bovon calls "culpable unbelief."[43]

The confirmation that Gabriel offers to Mary is of quite another order. Indirectly, the angel affirms her understanding of his message. She is correct. She is indeed to conceive before Joseph has taken her into his home. At the same time, it also affirms that she has been faithful to her vows and to her husband. It does all this by assuring her that the birth of the promised child will not be a result of human intercourse at all, but an act of God: "**Holy Spirit will come upon you, and the power of the Most High will overshadow you.**"

Here is an element in the annunciation story that has *no* parallel in accounts of angelic visitations and promises elsewhere in Scripture.[44] It does, however, have parallels in accounts of other creative and redemptive acts of God. At the beginning of creation God's Spirit "hovered over the face of the waters" just as a nurturing mother eagle "hovers" over her young (Gen. 1.1-2 cf. Deut. 32.11). When the prophet Samuel anointed David, the Spirit of the Lord "came mightily upon David from that day forward" (1 Sam. 16.13). At the birth of the church, the Holy Spirit will, in Luke's phrasing, "come upon" the gathered followers of Jesus (Acts 1.8). So now, the Holy Spirit will "**come upon**" Mary, and "**the power of the Most High**" will "**overshadow**" her (1.35), as the cloud indicating the divine presence will "overshadow" the disciples at the Transfiguration (9.34). The birth of the child will be a miracle, an act of new creation. Early Christian understanding found Jesus to have been "declared to be Son of God with power according to the spirit of holiness by resurrection from the dead" (Rom. 1.4). The tradition handed on by Luke drives back the divine appointment of Jesus as Son of God to his conception in Mary's womb.[45]

From a literary standpoint, we may note that this is the climax of the first part of Luke's carefully constructed birth annunciation narratives. We have noted how he parallels each part of the one with the matching part of the other, always so as to show that John the Baptist is great, but that Jesus is greater. So here, he finally caps the *improbability* of the barren and elderly Elizabeth's conceiving a child with the *impossibility* of Mary who **"does not know a man"** conceiving one.

"And now," says the angel, **"your kinswoman Elizabeth in her old age has also conceived a son; and this is the sixth month for her who was said to be barren."** Just as in the past, other recipients of divine promise were given a sign—we might point to the stories about Moses at the bush (Exod. 3:1-12) or Gideon threshing wheat (Judges 6:11-21)—so now is Mary: it is already **"the sixth month"** in the pregnancy of her kinswoman Elizabeth, **"who was called barren."** So again Luke again links his two narratives. Fulfilment of the merely *unlikely* promise to Zachariah and Elizabeth will be a sign to Mary that the *impossible* promise to her will also be fulfilled. Here also, we note, is confirmation of what we surmised as possibly implicit in Mark—that the memory of Mary included a tradition that she had family connections in Judea.

"For no word from God shall be powerless." As commentators have long noted, Gabriel's final word of reassurance to Mary is an evident echo of YHWH's word of promise to Abraham at Genesis 18.14.[46] Luke has, however, made a change that is theologically important. Genesis 18.14 says that "for YHWH" ("with God" in the LXX) no word shall be impossible. Luke 1.37, however, says that "**no word** ***from God***" shall be impossible.[47] The effect of this is that, whereas in the Genesis narrative Abraham is being reminded of God's power (cf. Rom. 4.20-21), in the gospel the angel is reminding Mary not only of God's power but also of God's faithfulness. What she has heard is a word *from God*, and God does not utter words that God will not fulfil.

> For as the rain and the snow come down from heaven,
>   and do not return there until they have watered the earth,
> making it bring forth and sprout,
>   giving seed to the sower and bread to the eater,
> so shall my word be that goes out from my mouth;
>   it shall not return to me empty,
> but it shall accomplish that which I purpose,
>   and succeed in the thing for which I sent it.
> (Isa. 55.10-11)

(6) *What Happens Next*

> **Then Mary said, "Here am I, the slave (NRSV** servant[48]**) of the Lord; let it be with me according to your word."** (1.38)

So we are brought to the final move in this, the last stage of the two annunciations. Whereas the parallel scene with Zachariah concluded with Zachariah struck dumb because he did not believe, the scene with Mary concludes with her joyful affirmation and acceptance. Every word in this affirmation is important.

"Here am I: *idou*!" Throughout the Greek Bible, with this and similar words, other saints of God in Israel's history had placed themselves at God's disposal. The patriarch Abraham, whom God called in order "to test him" replied with same word, and so did Isaiah in the Temple, hearing the divine need for a messenger.[49] So Mary, too, now places herself at God's disposal.

Mary does this, moreover, claiming for herself nothing but the very humblest of roles: "*hē doulē kuriou*: **the slave of the Lord**" (1.38a). Such a role is inferior even to "*pais*" ("child" or "servant") for, in the Law, "*doulos / doulē*" was a role in the households of Israel that even a *gentile* might fill, but was too lowly for an Israelite (LXX Lev. 25.44).

That granted, we need also to recognize that Luke has Mary speak thus in a society and culture in which some slaves actually found the system working to their advantage. Slaves or freed persons of the Emperor would be people of no significance in themselves, but in certain circumstances such a person might give orders to a patrician and expect to be obeyed. As Dale B. Martin points out,

> Though the institution of slavery was severely oppressive, some slaves were able to manipulate it to become rather powerful persons with a certain degree of informal status in society, compared, at least, to the majority of the people of the empire, who were, though free, poor and powerless. For this small but significant minority of slaves, slavery represented an avenue to influence and was therefore, remarkable as it usually sounds to modern ears, a means of social mobility.[50]

The key was to be in a favorable relationship with the *right* master or mistress. Hence, though slavery was usually a metaphor for drudgery, it could also be a metaphor for salvation—as it clearly was on occasion for Jew and pagan alike.[51] The operative question is therefore: To whom or to what will you belong? Thus, as Gaventa points out,

> By claiming for herself the title "slave of the Lord," Mary claims that her honor derives from God, not from any of

> the normal indicators of status that operated in the first-century Mediterranean world.[52]

In accepting for herself this role, Mary says, **"let it be to me according to your word"** (1.38b). The angel's "word" is, of course, God's word. As we hear Mary say this, faced as she is with an uncertain future, surely we are struck by a degree of resemblance between her consent to God's will now, and her son's consent when faced with the cross: "Father, not my will but yours be done" (22.42). In this respect, as in others, the Son of God is remembered as also the son of his mother.

But of course resemblance does not mean identity, and the situations are by no means the same. They differ as does Christmas from Good Friday, and Soares Prabhu has rightly complained about translations of—and, I would add, commentators on—the annunciation story who suggest a *merely* resigned and submissive acceptance by Mary, rather than joy and eagerness.[53]

The contrast between the two narratives and the two expressions of consent is indicated by, among other things, a particularly striking nuance in Luke's Greek. In the passion narrative, the verbal form of Jesus' "not my will but yours be done (*ginesthō*)" is a simple imperative: indicating acceptance, but certainly not a wish. As Bovon says, "no human being, full of plans and wishes, wants to cease to exist"[54]—and indeed, Jesus has just expressed his own wish quite clearly: "if you will, let this cup pass from me!" Here, to quote Bovon again, "Jesus unequivocally displays his membership in the race of mortals."[55]

Mary's words to the angel, however, stand in sharp contrast. Her **"let it be** (*genoito*)" is in the *optative* mood, expressing not merely acceptance or submission, but *desire*, "used here to express a prayer."[56] Mary not only obeys and is faithful, she is interested and even eager. It is of a piece with Gabriel's greeting "Rejoice!" It is also of a piece with Mary's own earlier optimistic curiosity. Nowhere in Israel's entire Scripture and records of God's servants is there an acceptance quite so powerful and unqualified as this.[57]

And the angel departed from her.

So ends the first section of Luke's triptych.

The Visitation

> **In those days Mary set out and went with haste to a Judaean town in the hill country, where she entered the house of Zechariah and greeted Elizabeth.** (Luke 1.39-40)

Luke does not tell us why Mary sets out so quickly—"**in those days**"—and travels "**with haste** (*meta spoudēs*)." But perhaps he does not need to? Of course we must not psychologize the Lucan Mary, and the expression in itself only speaks directly of the manner of her departure, not her feelings. Yet neither should we treat her as an automaton. Manner is not unrelated to mind, and it will accord with what Luke has already told us that young Mary (as we might say) "cannot wait" to find out the truth of the angel's words and to share with her kinswoman the news of her own pregnancy, and that she is eager and diligent in pursuing those ends.[58] That is not, of course, to say that Luke wishes us to see nothing more here than teenage excitement—or, to put it another way, we are not denying that this particular teenager does have a profound reason to be excited. We might, indeed, compare Mary's behavior to something that is still to come in our narrative—the shepherds who, having received the message of Christ's birth, will come "with haste/*speusantes*" to Bethlehem to find the holy family (Luke 2.16). All of which is to say that the work of God, once perceived, leads to a positive urgency that does not willingly brook delay. Such a sense of urgency and hence of eager diligence (though words for "haste" and "hasten" are not directly used) is implicit in Jesus' own parables of the Hidden Treasure and the Pearl of Great Price (Matt. 13.44-46): an awareness of something so precious as will lead one to put aside or give up everything one has to obtain it.

I confess I am baffled by the reasoning of those commentators who, in discussing these narratives (even intending to praise Mary), speak *only* of her "submissiveness," "gentleness" and "mildness."[59] Of course it is true that in the Annunciation scene that precedes our present passage we have seen her submissive: to the will of God! Even then, however, hers was a submissiveness that did not prevent her from challenging Gabriel when his words did not seem to her to be making any sense. Ann Loades surely has a point:

> A woman who will quiz an archangel, give her (rapturous? enthusiastic?) assent, or agreement to the divine spirit working within her, risk scandal and single parenthood is, one might think, something of a risk-taker, and by no means a model of submission, subordination and passivity.[60]

And it is surely a young woman who is at the very least "something of a risk-taker" whom the evangelist now shows us. Indeed, in the present narrative, Mary is totally active, the subject of every verb. Newly pregnant, she "**set out**" and "**went with haste**"—going "adventurously across the mountains" as René Laurentin puts it.[61] To be precise, Luke portrays her undertaking a journey that, from Nazareth to an unspecified town in the Judean hill country, has to be in the region of 165 kilometers.[62] Apparently she does this alone. *Pace* Hospodar ("there is a probability that Joseph escorted his betrothed"[63]), the omission of any mention of Joseph is precisely what makes it *im*probable that Luke envisaged him accompanying Mary. (In exegesis of texts, as in other kinds of detection, it is often silence, the omission of the expected, *the dog who does not bark,*[64] that points us to the path we need to follow.) That is not to say the evangelist will not have assumed for Mary such attendance as would be normal for any respectable young woman travelling in that society,[65] but it remains, in marked contrast to narratives that will come later—the presentation in the Temple and the family's visit to Jerusalem (2.1-52)—that Joseph is not mentioned. That, if Luke understood him to be present, would be very surprising.

Her journey completed, Mary "**entered the house of Zachariah**" (that is the only mention of him in the episode; what follows will be entirely between the two women) and "**greeted Elizabeth**" (1.40).

> **And it came to pass, when Elizabeth heard Mary's greeting, the child leapt in her womb. And Elizabeth was filled with Holy Spirit and exclaimed with a loud cry, "Blessed are you among women!"**
>
> (1.41-42a)

Luke does not tell us the content of Mary's greeting, but he does tell us what follows—introducing it with a solemn, biblical-sounding "**And it came to pass** (*kai egeneto*[66])" that is regrettably omitted by NRSV, REB and NAB—I say "regrettably" since Luke's formality is clearly deliberate. It has the effect of slowing down the action and warning us that we are about to learn something of special significance. It is a formality, moreover, that is sustained by the solemn repetition of proper names in what follows: "**when *Elizabeth* heard *Mary's* greeting... *Elizabeth* was filled with Holy Spirit**"[67]—where it might be argued that for conveying the sense, pronouns alone would have sufficed.

What then is this thing of special significance that we are to learn? It is that when Elizabeth heard Mary's salutation, her own child "**leapt in her womb**" (1.41). In other words, already the Baptist begins his life's work as Jesus' forerunner![68] Elizabeth herself, "**filled with Holy Spirit,**" then speaks prophetically: "**Blessed are you among women!**" At the annunciation, Gabriel called Mary "favored one" or "graced one"; now Elizabeth calls her "**blessed**"—*eulogēmenē*[69]—which, in effect, complements her being "favored," for the passive "**blessed**" also speaks of the act of God, the ultimate bestower of favor and grace.

> **And blessed is the fruit of your womb! And why has this happened to me, that the mother of my Lord comes to me? For as soon as I heard the sound of your greeting, the child in my womb leapt for joy. And happy is she who trusted that there would be a fulfilment of what was spoken to her by the Lord.**
>
> (1.42b-45)

Elizabeth herself now begins the work of her son (so that he too will in this respect be the child of his mother) by declaring "**blessed**" not only Mary but also her unborn child, whom she calls "**my Lord.**" In doing so, she poses a question—"**Why has this happened to me?**"—which she at once qualifies by telling Mary what the evangelist has already told us: "**For as soon as I heard the sound of your greeting, the child in my womb leapt for joy.**" Yet her next words—and we must remember that she is still speaking "**filled with the Holy Spirit,**" which means (among other things) that her words are to be trusted—are not directly about the child at all, but about Mary herself: "**And happy**[70] (NRSV "blessed") **is she who trusted**[71] (NRSV "believed") **that there would be a fulfilment of what was spoken to her by the Lord.**" Elizabeth makes clear that it is not the physical fact of Mary's motherhood that is the *essential* element in her happiness, precious, of course, though that is. The *essential* element is Mary's faith: "**happy is she who *trusted***"[72]—a sharp contrast to

Zachariah, who must remain dumb until the birth of his son "because you did not trust."[73]

Not surprisingly, in connection with Elizabeth's word to Mary, commentators have referred to Jesus' conversation later in the gospel with a woman who cries out to him,

> "Happy is the womb that bore you and the breasts that nursed you." But he said, "Yes, rather (*menoun*), happy are those who hear the word of God and obey it!" (Luke 11.27-28)

The occurrence of such references does not mean, however, that the commentators are always correct in their understanding of the two episodes. Luke does not, as some have suggested, here present Jesus speaking dismissively of his mother, nor are his words a dismissal or rebuke of the person who has cried out. The element of correction or adjustment implied by Jesus' word "*menoun* (yea rather)" is *not* to say that the woman is wrong about the privilege she has spoken of for Jesus' mother, but to direct her to the deeper gift *which she herself is now manifesting*—as, of course, Jesus' mother had done at the right time—namely, *to be able to hear God's word and accept it.* In other words, far from rebuking the speaker, Jesus is praising her for her attitude to him, an attitude that stands in marked contrast to others in the same section of narrative who have spoken before her (11.14-26). Here, then, is a striking challenge to patriarchal values. Bovon—citing Rachel C. Wahlberg—sums up the issue: "the supreme honor of a woman… is therefore no longer a matter of maternity, but rather of living as a believer in the presence of God."[74]

Elizabeth began by asking a question: **"Why has this happened to me, that the mother of my Lord comes to me?"** In response, in the hymn that church tradition has come to call *Magnificat*, Mary cries out, as G. B. Caird put it, "as though she were herself the daughter of Zion,"[75]

> **My soul magnifies the Lord,**
> **And my spirit has rejoiced in God my Savior.**

or, as the REB paraphrases rather well,

> **My soul tells out the greatness of the Lord,**
> **my spirit has rejoiced in God my Saviour!** (1.46-47)

In other words, Mary's is a prophetic joy that cannot be contained or delayed. That is the answer to Elizabeth's question. Why has the mother of the Messiah come to her? She has come, and come **with haste**, to share her joy with her kinswoman.

In Mary's *Magnificat*—as, incidentally, also in the *Benedictus* and *Nunc Dimittis* (1.68-79, 2.29-32)—Luke gives us examples of what ancient rhetoricians and grammarians would have called *prosōpopoiía*: a form of composition not meant to be regarded as verbatim reporting of what was said on a particular occasion, but rather as faithful representation of what a particular person in a particular situation will have intended to say.[76] Luke is not, indeed, the only writer in the New Testament to make use of *prosōpopoiía*. Origen, in his commentary on Romans, recognized that Paul also made use of it in his Letter to the Romans, in his portrayal of the frustrated sinner who feels that one's very knowledge of God's Law—of what one *ought* to do—is precisely what influences us to do exactly the opposite! This portrayal leads to the desperate cry, "Wretched person that I am, who shall deliver me from this body of death?"—a cry that Paul then answers in his own person from the gospel of Jesus Christ (Rom. 7.14-8.2).[77]

In composing the *Magnificat*, there can be no doubt that Luke took much of his verbal inspiration from the Song of Hannah in 1 Samuel 2.1-10. But the actual content of the *Magnificat* was surely not based on Hannah at all, but on Luke's understanding of Mary and her intentions, gained, of course, like all his material, from those in the church whom he had consulted (Luke 1.1-4). The resulting song transcends the earlier at every point.

It falls into three parts.

The first part is, as we have already seen, a direct response to Elizabeth's question. It speaks of Mary's joy and of the reason for it:

> **for he has looked with favor on the lowliness of his slave.**

For a second time in the narrative, Mary declares herself to be not, as our English versions have it, "servant" but "**slave** (*doulē*)" of the Lord: a title that she wears as a badge of honor. So she declares—prophetically and truly—

> **Surely, from now on all generations will call me happy!**

Our English versions, again, generally say "call me blessed," but the verb in Greek—*makariousin me*—is a cognate of *makarios*, which generally means "blessed" in the sense of "fortunate," "happy" or even "privileged."[78] And the reason for her happiness? The mark of God's "**favor**" to her? It is the miracle that Elizabeth has already discerned, the miracle growing within her womb, to which she now refers with reverent periphrasis—

> **for the Mighty One has done great things for me—**

an affirmation which at once leads her to praise and sanctify the Name of God:[79]

and holy is his name.

Or perhaps, again with REB, we might render "**whose name is holy,**" echoing the Psalmist: "holy and awful is His Name" (111.9b). Like the psalmist, Mary speaks in virtually the same breath both of God's generosity and God's awful holiness—the paradox of grace unforgettably described by third Isaiah:

For thus says the high and lofty one
  who inhabits eternity, whose name is Holy:
I dwell in the high and holy place,
  and also with those who are contrite and humble in spirit,
to revive the spirit of the humble,
  and to revive the heart of the contrite. (Isa. 57.15)

I do not understand how C. F. Evans (and he is by no means alone in his judgment) can consider the *Magnificat* to be "only loosely attached to the narrative, which would not be disturbed by its removal."[80] Is it not rather the case, as generations of readers and hearers have understood by simply *listening* to Luke's account, that *Magnificat* responds to the question that Mary has just been asked (which without *Magnificat* would remain unanswered), and the narrative would be gutted without it? How is it that commentators fail to see what has seemed obvious to many? I find myself reminded of Helena's frustration at her lover Demetrius' apparent inability to see her beauty: "He will not know what all but he do know!"[81] Evidently it is not lack of learning that leads to this. It is, perhaps, an unwillingness to use—even, perhaps, a fear of using—a little imagination.

The grace of which Mary speaks is not, of course, for her alone, nor the particular right or possession of any individual or time, but rather for all who will accept it in every age, as she at once goes on to acknowledge as she moves to the second part of her hymn:

> **His mercy is for those who fear him**
> **from generation to generation.**

God's particular option is, moreover, for the poor and weak—of whom Mary, given the power structures of her society, simply by the fact of being young and female is an apt representative:

> **He has shown strength with his arm;**
> **he has scattered the proud in the thoughts of their hearts.**
> **has brought down the powerful from their thrones,**
> **and lifted up the lowly;**
> **he has filled the hungry with good things,**
> **and sent the rich away empty.**

It is by no means without justification that commentators have linked this passage to the revolutionary spirit of liberation theology. Indeed, there is about the Magnificat more than a hint of the Catonsville Nine in the nineteen-sixties[82] or Greenham Common in the nineteen-eighties and nineties.[83] François Bovon cites Gustavo Guttiérez's understanding of a new "spirituality of liberation"—that is,

> a concrete manner in which to live the gospel: inspired by the Holy Spirit, and in solidarity with all people before the Lord. In this sense the Magnificat is a pattern for every prayer, every praise of God; at the same time it is onc of the New Testament texts with the most strongly political and liberating content. It calls on us to take the words totally concretely and to fight against oppression in order to take seriously the Lord of history.[84]

But if God's mighty act towards Mary is grace not merely for her but for all who will trust in him, then of course it will also be a mark of God's faithfulness toward Israel. So Mary comes to the third part of her hymn, in which she speaks finally of the specific grace promised to God's covenant people—

> **He has helped his servant Israel,**
> **in remembrance of his mercy,**
> **according to the promise he made to our ancestors,**
> **to Abraham and to his descendants forever.**

And surely the promised grace to *all* who will believe fulfils the promise to Abraham, for that promise was from the beginning that in Abraham's seed not only Israel but "all nations" (Gen. 12.3) were to find blessing.

This, then, is Mary's word of prophecy for the "**generations**" without limit of whom she has already spoken, all those of all nations who in ages to come shall call her "**happy.**" How, then, shall we summarize that prophecy and Luke's portrait of the woman who utters it? Literary critic C. S. Lewis compared its rhetoric to that of Jesus himself, which, though essentially "good news for the poor," is certainly remembered as at times severe. "No one who puts a hand to the plough and looks back is fit for service in the kingdom of God" (Luke 9:62). How far, Lewis asks, in this aspect as in others, is it not true that Luke shows us a Jesus who "was His Mother's own son"?

> There is a fierceness, even a touch of Deborah, mixed with the sweetness in the *Magnificat* to which most painted Madonnas do little justice; matching the frequent severity of His own sayings. I am sure the private life of the Holy Family was, in many senses, "mild" and "gentle," but perhaps hardly in the way some hymn writers have in mind. One may suspect, on proper occasions, a certain

> astringency; and all in what people at Jerusalem regarded as a rough north-country dialect.[85]

Precisely. The dramatist Dorothy Sayers grasped the point entirely; the voice of the actress playing Mary must be "sweet but not sugary; and there must be no trace of any kind of affectation. A very slight touch of accent—perhaps a faint shadow of Irish quality—would be of assistance."[86] Personally, I've always imagined Mary with a very slight Yorkshire accent. But then, my own mother came from Beverley in the East Riding.

Yet Mary's *Magnificat* is also, first and last and throughout, an act of praise, a sanctification of the Name. And thereby she shows herself a true daughter of Israel.[87] I am struck by Herbert McCabe, O.P.'s observation:

> A philosopher once complained about a lot of philosophical theology: he said it was nothing but paying metaphysical compliments to God. But when you come to think of it, what more authentic human activity is there than paying compliments to God? All our doctrines about God are nothing but an interpretation of our need to worship him, to pay him compliments.[88]

Again—precisely.

> **And Mary remained with her for about three months and then returned to her home.**

Mary stayed with Elizabeth "for about three months"—in other words, until it was time for Elizabeth to bear her son—"**and then returned to her home**". She will by then, of course, have been about three months into her own pregnancy. Again, granted we may assume she had some attendance, there is no hint of any presence by the male members of her household.

Luke speaks of her return as he spoke of her departure: alone. A strong, brave young woman has accomplished what she intended to accomplish. She has consulted with an elder woman of her household, and together, guided by God's Spirit, they have faithfully discerned God's purposes: an encounter powerfully—and for me, iconically—depicted in Pontormo's *Visitation* (see Figure 4).

Figure 4. The Visitation: Painting by Pontormo (1494-1557) in the Church of San Francesco e Michele, Carmignano.

Two Births

As with the two annunciations, the two birth narratives follow each other. The birth of Elizabeth's child is described briefly and without preamble, as is the rejoicing of her family and the child's circumcision on the eighth day (Luke 1.57-59a). This last, however, is enriched by the linked narrative of the naming of the child—"His name is John"—announced by Elizabeth. Following his consent to that name, Zachariah's tongue is loosened and all around them are filled with awe (1.59b-66). Zachariah, filled with the Holy Spirit, proclaims in the hymn we call *Benedictus* the coming greatness of the child who will be a prophet and witness to the Lord's salvation (1.67-79). Finally, the evangelist affirms that the boy indeed "grew and became strong in spirit, and he was in the wilderness until the day he appeared publicly to Israel" (1.80)—an affirmation that may well be seen as supporting the entirely plausible suggestion that John the Baptist passed some of his early years with the Essenes.[89]

The birth of Mary's child is narrated at much greater length and with considerable preamble. Luke begins by setting the event in time, indeed, in the history of the world:

> **In those days a decree went out from Emperor Augustus that all the world should be registered. This was the first registration and was taken while Quirinius was governor of Syria.** (2.1-2)

We need not concern ourselves with attempts to justify the exact details of this account or harmonize it with Josephus' *Antiquities*.[90] Suffice it to say that, under Augustus, population registrations did indeed take place. Hence, as François Bovon says, Luke may indeed be "mistaken in literal terms, but he does correctly capture the historical tendency of the time, and of the emperor, in historical and popular terms."[91] These registrations were of two types: citizen registration (*census populi*), useful for purposes of taxation and military service, and census of provincial inhabitants (*incolae*) who were not Roman citizens. Presumably the "**registration**" referred to here (apropos of which Luke uses the word *apographē*[92]) would be of the latter type.

> **All went to their own towns to be registered. Joseph also went from the town of Nazareth in Galilee to Judea, to the city of David called Bethlehem, because he was descended from the house and family of David.** (2.3-4)

What are the implications of this narrative?

On the one hand, a decree of the emperor himself, the most powerful man on earth, appears not as a mighty act of the supreme ruler but as merely as part of the scenery, an element in the divine providence.[93] By means of it, the pregnant mother of God's Messiah is brought to Bethlehem, the city of David, which is where the Messiah ought to be born.[94] Augustus by his victories had ended the terrible wars that had ravaged the empire. He was with some justice celebrated as bringer of peace, and an *Ara Pacis Augustae*—Altar to the Augustan Peace—stands in Rome to this day as a monument to that.[95] But, as Luke is about to show us, the Messiah that is to be born will bring about a peace far greater than Caesar's, for he is to bring about the true peace which only God can give.

On the other hand, Galilee was a client state of the Empire, but by that very fact technically and legally not part of it. Therefore, there was no *need* for Mary and Joseph, whose place of residence was Nazareth in Galilee, to return to Bethlehem and take part in a Roman census merely because Joseph was of Davidic decent, *unless he chose deliberately to associate himself with Roman* imperium.[96] But that, Luke says, is precisely what he did do.[97]

> **He went to be registered with Mary, to whom he was engaged and who was expecting a child.** (2.5)

Even at that, however, there is still a problem: for there would have been no need for Mary to travel with him for the registration. The head of the household could register himself and his family.[98] The shocking fact of Mary, while in an advanced state of pregnancy, accompanying Joseph on the approximately 150-kilometer journey from Nazareth through Samaria to Bethlehem will have been just as evident to the evangelist and his original audience as it is to us. Why would this have happened? Why would they have undertaken such a thing?

If Luke had intended by his description of Mary at this point **"expecting a child"** to offer an *explanation* for her accompanying Joseph—and the construction of his sentence could certainly be taken as implying that[99]—then perhaps he had in mind—and even expected us to remember?—a point on which he had already touched earlier in his narrative: that Mary had *relatives* in Judaea, that is, the family of Zechariah and Elizabeth.[100] We are perhaps to understand that she and Joseph intend the birth to be with Mary's family, where they will meet what Kelley Nikondeha describes as "the warmth of expected hospitality."[101] What then happens?

> **While they were there, the time came for her to deliver her child. And she gave birth to her firstborn son and wrapped him in bands of cloth, and laid him in a manger, because there was no place for them in the inn.** (2.6-7)

With justice, Luke Timothy Johnson describes this passage as "one of the most overinterpreted in the New Testament."[102] Certainly commentators have found much about which to be uncertain and many questions to ask. We probably do best as interpreters of Luke to focus on what is *clearly* said.

The evangelist begins by saying that while Joseph and Mary were in Bethlehem, **"the time came for her to deliver her child."** For all the miraculous work of God's Spirit in this pregnancy, for all Mary's and Elizabeth's prophetic testimony to that work, the pregnancy itself comes to term like any other pregnancy. Are we to understand that Mary came to term earlier than expected? Perhaps. That would certainly make sense in the context of the narrative as a whole. Be that as it may, Luke maintains the picture of Mary that he has already drawn for us—active, energetic, and faithful—by giving us three verbs, each of which has Mary as its subject: "**she gave birth to her firstborn... wrapped him in bands of cloth... laid him in a manger**" (2.7).

The first verb, "**She gave birth to her firstborn son**" is a necessary prelude to the second and third. Yet it is also important in itself. Jesus is born—as Paul puts it, "born of a woman"—as are we all. The Scriptures defined "**firstborn**" as "whatever is the first to open the womb" (Exod. 13.2), and its use here makes clear that Mary had no children before she bore Jesus.[103]

Second: Mary then "**wrapped him in bands of cloth**"—in itself so utterly normal a practice as to be, as Gaventa observes, "hardly worthy of notice."[104] Yet Luke *does* notice it and will notice it again before his story is told. At the very least, it is surely a sign of Mary's care, even her love: "in swaddling clothes was I nursed, and with care," says Solomon, according to tradition.[105] What is more—and perhaps even more to the point in terms of character—it shows Mary as competent, caring and coping, even in the midst of what must be strange and new to her: the mere fact of motherhood, let alone *this* motherhood! Joseph, at this point, has faded from our view or, at most, stands supportively in the background.

Third, Mary "**laid him in a manger.**" The word here traditionally rendered into English as "**manger**"[106] is *phatnē*, generally used of a feeding trough for domesticated beasts,[107] suggesting indeed a barn, cave or "stable place" just as Christina Rossetti and Christian tradition generally have it.[108] Apropos Mary laying her baby in such a place, we are at once offered an explanation: "**because there was no place** (*topos*[109]) **for them in**

the inn" (2.7)—an "explanation," however, that raises as many questions as it answers. The noun translated "**inn** (*kataluma*)" was used both of a place for lodging within a building, and of an open area—a campsite—where travelers and their animals could spend the night.[110] Luke himself will later use the word to refer to the "guest room" (NRSV) where Jesus and his disciples will eat the last supper (22.11). Given this breadth of possibility, how should we understand it here? "Inn" has long been the accepted English rendering (KJV and Douay-Rheims[111]) and I have followed it in my own version. Given, however, the breadth of possible meanings available, it may be that Luke's sense would be better caught by some vaguer term such as Brown's "lodging" or Johnson's "lodging area."[112] Perhaps I retained "inn" for no better reason than that I am used to it. Be that as it may, one should at least be aware that the word the evangelist used scarcely carried the nuances of warmth, good food and comfort traditionally associated with an English inn.

So when Luke speaks of the "**inn**" where there was no "**place**" for Mary and Joseph and of the "**manger**" where she laid "**her firstborn son**," what is he actually saying? Luke Timothy Johnson (here succumbing, perhaps, to the very tendency to overinterpretation to which he has himself pointed) suggests that we are to see Mary and Joseph as "transients, equivalent to 'the homeless' of contemporary city streets."[113] Fitzmyer, with less evident political relevance but perhaps more common sense, given what Luke actually tells us, suggests that in the crowded conditions (presumably caused by the census—cf. 2.3!) "there was simply not space enough for all."[114] In which case, far from seeing Mary and Joseph as equivalent to modern "transients" or "homeless," we might even understand Luke to imply that they were treated rather kindly. There being no place suitable for the girl to deliver her child in the crowded general lodging area, the little family are afforded a space that at least offers Mary some measure of privacy.

By telling us how Mary then lays her child "**in a manger**" because there is "**no room**" elsewhere, the evangelist shows her not only competent and caring, but also making use of what is available to her. It is entirely of a piece with the strong, active and intelligent young woman whom he has already shown us.

The picture of Mary laying the child in an improvised crib thus fixed in our minds, Luke with a masterly narrative stroke then cuts to another scene entirely: a field, perhaps one or two miles outside of Bethlehem.[115]

> **In that region there were shepherds living in the fields, keeping watch over their flock by night.** (2.8)

Traditional interpretation immediately—and rightly—adverts to the fact that proclamation of the Messiah's birth begins, according to Luke, not with the great, rich or powerful, nor with the pious or learned, but with humble folk doing what they have to do to earn their bread:[116] "**living in the fields**"[117] and "**keeping watch over their flock by night**"—literally, "watching the watches of the night." Luke probably means that different members of the group were taking turns to watch.[118]

> **Then an angel of the Lord stood before them, and the glory of the Lord shone around them, and they were terrified. But the angel said to them, 'Do not be afraid.** (2.9-10a)

The shepherds' fearful reaction is, of course, the normal reaction throughout Scripture of human beings to angelic visitations, as is the angelic reassurance, "**Do not be afraid.**"

> **for see—I am bringing you good news of great joy for all the people: to you is born this day in the city of David a Savior, who is the Messiah, the Lord. This will be a sign**

> **for you: you will find a child wrapped in bands of cloth and lying in a manger.** (2.10b-12)

Specifically, the angel brings good news for Israel. The expression "**all the people,**" given that it is uttered in connection with the Messiah in the city of David, evidently means "all Israel," and "**this day**" states that what has hitherto been a promise for the future is now present. The Savior is born. Strikingly, the "**sign**" that will greet the shepherds is not some marvel, but precisely the simple picture that we have already seen: a child, "**wrapped in bands of cloth and lying in a manger.**" One thinks of Christina Rossetti's

> In the bleak midwinter a stable place sufficed
> The Lord God Almighty, Jesus Christ.

Evidently, Rossetti's words owe much to later theology, but the paradox that she presents is in essence already implied by Luke.

> **And suddenly there was with the angel a multitude of the heavenly host, praising God and saying,**
> **"Glory to God in the highest heaven,**
> **and on earth peace among those**
> **on whom his favor rests!"**[119]
>
> (2.13-14)

The message of the angels balances, and indeed trumps, the message of Caesar concerning "the whole world" with which this section of Luke's narrative began. In the age of "Augustan peace" (*pax Augusta*), a child has been born who shall bring "**on earth**" an even greater **peace;** this peace will be the gift of God's free and unearned grace (that is, God's "**favor** [*eudokia*]") toward humankind.

> **When the angels had left them and gone into heaven, the shepherds said to one another, "Let us go now to Bethlehem and see this thing that has taken place, which the Lord has made known to us."So they went with haste and found Mary and Joseph, and the child lying in the manger.** (2.15-16)

Invariably, when Luke tells us something three times, he intends us to notice it. So in Acts we have three versions of St Peter's vision that leads him to eat with gentiles, and three versions of St Paul's call. Similarly here, the shepherds' arrival at Bethlehem is marked by their finding Mary and Joseph and "**the child, lying in the manger**"—for a third time mentioning the manger! Clearly, we are to remember that although Jesus' birth is in certain respects miraculous, his is still a birth like other births.

Mention of the "**manger**" and the fact that it is humble shepherds who are there to see it rather than the wise or the noble may also remind us that a part of what will be going on throughout this story is that the most surprising people will seem to see and have some understanding of what is happening, whereas those whom we would expect to understand—indeed, those such as priests and scholars who might be foolish enough to imagine that they have something of a corner in understanding—will not seem to understand at all! As Jesus himself will be remembered saying later in the gospel: "I thank you, Father, Lord of heaven and earth, because you have hidden these things from the wise and the intelligent and have revealed them to infants."[120]

At Luke's mention of "**a manger** (*phatnē*)," his first hearers may well have recalled Isaiah's prophetic words as rendered by their Greek bibles:

> The ox knows its owner,
>   and the donkey its master's crib (*phatnē*),
> but Israel has not known me,

> and the people have not understood me. (NETS LXX Isaiah 1.3)

Such an association has, indeed, long been implicit in Christian tradition, for the familiar scene of ox and ass present at Christ's birth surely owes at least as much to Isaiah 1.3 as to the evangelist. Implicit in their inclusion in the traditional Christian picture of the "master's crib" is surely belief that even the beasts, after their degree and in their own way, understand what is happening. As for the shepherds,

> **When they saw this, they made known what had been told them about this child; and all who heard it were amazed at what the shepherds told them. But Mary used to treasure up all these words, pondering them in her heart.** (2.17-19)

Luke gives us a picture of general surprise at the shepherds' story: "**all who heard it were amazed.**" But then his depiction of Mary's response sets her somewhat apart from this. She "**used to treasure up** (*suneterei*[121]) **all these words, pondering** (*sumballousa*[122]) **them in her heart.**" In my translation I try to capture what seems to me a rather striking change (not at all reflected in the NRSV or REB) from the simple past with which Luke speaks of reaction to the shepherds' tale—"**all...were amazed**"—to the imperfect tense with which he speaks of Mary's reaction: "**she used to treasure up... pondering,**" the implication being that this was something that became habitual for her.

It is not usual in the gospel narratives—as, indeed, it is not usual in Graeco-Roman "lives" generally—for us to be told a character's thoughts. Usually we are told what people say and do and what happens to them, not what they are thinking or feeling.[123] Why, then, the exception in Mary's case? One possibility is that the evangelist is hinting at the source of the traditions he is handing on—a suggestion that I would not dismiss so lightly as some; it would entirely be congruent with his claim to have investigated "everything carefully from the very first" (1.3). Jane Schaberg surely points correctly to the most likely origin of nativity traditions in the family of Jesus, "probably from Mary or from the brothers and sisters of Jesus rather than from Joseph, who does not appear in any story of the ministry."[124] Families being what they are, however, I do not have the least difficulty in reconciling such a view with "the evidence we have that the family of Jesus was not among his followers during his ministry."[125]

Along with this, however, Luke may also intend to point to something special about Mary herself. According to Bovon, "Mary, the paragon of faith, must understand… and interpret… correctly." Hence, in Bovon's view, "**pondering**" here implies "the clear and correct interpretation of divine intervention. Mary understands what she has seen and heard."[126] I cannot agree. Luke's use of the same verb elsewhere, where it does not involve actual physical confrontation or conflict, invariably involves *some measure of perplexity or uncertainty*. Hence I think it more likely that, as Gaventa suggests, Luke intends us to perceive in Mary an element of perplexity. She is a paragon of faith *not* because she is able to understand and interpret everything correctly, but precisely because she remains faithful and obedient even when she does *not* understand (cf. Romans 8.24!).[127] Once again, I find helpful the novelist Sara Maitland, as she seeks to explore the mind of Mary:

> She looks again at the baby and realises that the beginning is now. In the glorious moment of her assent, in the rich song of praise that flowed from her in the arms of her cousin Elizabeth, in that moment she had thought to end it all. Had thought the moment would be total.… But the spiral was started: she was returned

> to where she had begun. Virginal, alone, complete, she was now bound inextricably to the product of that perfection—and on what strange routes would this boy drag her? With what sword would he pierce her heart? (*Daughter of Jesualem*)[128]

Precisely.

> **The shepherds returned, glorifying and praising God for all they had heard and seen, as it had been told them.**

Witness, however humble and simple, to the birth of God's Messiah is the occasion for true joy and the praise of God. One is somewhat reminded of the spirit in which Luke will conclude his narratives of the Messiah's passion, resurrection and exaltation: the disciples "returned to Jerusalem with great joy; and they were continually in the temple blessing God."[129]

Luke has, however, one more thing to say about the birth of Jesus.

> **After eight days had passed, it was time to circumcise the child; and he was called Jesus, the name given by the angel before he was conceived in the womb.**

In contrast to the narrative of the Baptist's birth, here is no grand prophecy of the future, no great moment of reconciliation. But that, of course, is because these things are not needed. Mary, unlike Zachariah, has believed from the beginning. And in the hymn we call *Magnificat,* she gave prophetic witness to her Son before he was even born, thereby showing herself to be in every sense the bearer of God's Word to Israel. Nevertheless, the narrative of Jesus' naming is important: it shows Mary and Joseph continuing to be obedient to Torah. In the fulness of time the Son of God was sent, "born of a woman, born under the Law," Paul said. And that is precisely what Luke shows us happening.

So ends Luke's triptych about the Birth of the Messiah. But the evangelist has two more stories to tell about Jesus' early years: one of Jesus' presentation in the Temple, the other of a boyhood visit to Jerusalem. The central concern of both—as, indeed, of Luke's whole narrative—is Jesus, who he is and what he will do. From the viewpoint of our present study, however, they are interesting in that both also involve Mary, and in rather striking ways.

The Presentation of Jesus in the Temple

> **When the time came for their purification according to the law of Moses, they brought him up to Jerusalem to present him to the Lord (as it is written in the law of the Lord, "Every firstborn male shall be designated as holy to the Lord"), and they offered a sacrifice according to what is stated in the law of the Lord, "a pair of turtledoves or two young pigeons."**

Strictly speaking, of course, it is only the mother who requires purification under the Law,[130] and nowhere is such a rite referred to as "presentation" of the newborn. Perhaps Luke made a mistake when he said, "***their*** **purification**."[131] More probably, one suspects he simply regarded the little family as a unit: what is required of one is, in a sense, required of all, since the family as whole is not living according to the law until the requirement is fulfilled. As for their bringing the child to the Temple in order to "**present him to the Lord**," it is possible—indeed, likely—that Luke had in mind the story of Hannah's presentation of the infant Samuel.[132] As Luke Timothy Johnson has reminded us, while in many respects Luke is indeed a Hellenistic author, "the symbolic world he himself inhabits and the traditions he exploits are those of Torah. The events of Israel's past, and the language used to describe those events, shape his own narrative."[133] Thus René Laurentin suggests that Luke's account may also have been colored by reminiscence of Malachi's prophecy that the Lord would visit his Temple.[134] That seems entirely possible, and the church, historically, has certainly made such a connection, as witness its lectionaries.[135]

In any case, Luke is clear that there were those, guided by the Holy Spirit, who saw this bringing of Jesus to the temple as a moment of supreme significance in God's dealings with Israel.

> **Now there was a man in Jerusalem whose name was Simeon; this man was righteous and devout, looking forward to the consolation of Israel, and the Holy Spirit rested on him. It had been revealed to him by the Holy Spirit that he would not see death before he had seen the Lord's Messiah. Guided by the Spirit, Simeon came into the temple.** (2.25-27a)

The central concern here is Simeon's prophetic witness to Jesus' role in salvation—the salvation not only of Israel, but also of the Gentiles. Luke marks this witness by a threefold reference to the presence of "**the Holy Spirit.**" In other words, by assuring us that what Simeon says is to be believed.

> **And when the parents[136] brought in the child Jesus, to do for him what was customary under the law, Simeon received him in his arms and praised God.** (2.27b-28)

The old man Simeon then, guided by the Spirit, meets the couple with their baby. There follows one of the most beautiful scenes in all Scripture. Unfortunately, in rendering it, our English versions somewhat let us down—and have done, since Wycliffe. For Luke does not say that Simeon "took" the child, as KJV, DR, and our modern versions have it, but that he **"received"** him—*edexato*[137]—implying Mary and Joseph's permission, and even perhaps their invitation. Quite often, stained-glass windows will portray Mary handing the child into Simeon's arms: it is an instance of the artist perceiving something that translators seem to have missed. Luke implies that Mary initiates the action, and Simeon responds. It is of a piece with her initiative at earlier points in the narrative. She perceives in Simeon something or someone important and hands the child to him.

Simeon, then, "**receives**" the child "**into his arms**," and so the Spirit's promise to him that he would not die until **he had seen the Lord's Messiah** is fulfilled—and more than fulfilled. For Simeon not only sees him: he touches him, holds him, embraces him; and given that Jesus comes to Simeon in the weakness of babyhood, for this moment Simeon actually carries him, as the stronger carries the weaker. Simeon has waited faithfully upon God, and the reward of his faithfulness is that for a moment he becomes *christopheros*—a bearer of Christ. In that moment of joy, Luke places on Simeon's lips the third of the prophetic hymns that mark the opening chapters of his gospel.

Like the other two hymns, Zechariah's *Benedictus* and Mary's own *Magnificat*, Simeon's hymn speaks of the fulfilment of God's promised salvation. Simeon's, however, is briefer than the others. It is the word of one on the threshold of death, about to be dismissed "**in peace.**" Yet it is confident, joyful, and full of hope: "**for my eyes have seen your salvation.**"[138] Luke quite frequently uses the word "**salvation** (*sōtērion*)" and its cognates to speak of God's work,[139] but perhaps nowhere does he make clearer than here that Jesus is that work. Simeon has seen the Lord's Messiah, as he was promised; he has seen Jesus, as Mary and Joseph have placed the baby in his arms; and therefore he has seen God's salvation. Luke's Christology is also his Soteriology. It is no wonder that the church has for centuries chosen to use the canticle *Nunc Dimittis* at Evening Prayer and in Compline, as it marks the end of the day and prepares for the night and for sleep, which is indeed a kind of death—"death's counterfeit,"[140] as Shakespeare and others remind us.

> **And the child's father and mother were amazed at what was being said about him. Then Simeon blessed them and said to his mother Mary, "This child is destined for the falling and the rising of many in Israel, and to be a sign that will be opposed, so that the inner thoughts of many will be revealed—and a sword will pierce your own soul too."** (2.33-35)

Even as Mary and Joseph are marveling at Simeon's words, even as he blesses them, he utters an aside that is directed to Mary alone—Luke is very specific about that. This is a much darker word that stands in tension with what has gone before. The image of falling and rising reminds us—and Luke surely intends it to remind us—of Isaiah 8.14-18, where the prophet and his children are set for "signs and portents" in Israel, at which some will stumble, and others gain new strength. That meant suffering for the prophet and his family, and it will mean suffering for Jesus. And Mary his mother will share in that suffering: "**a sword will pierce your own soul also.**" Matthew tells of Jesus himself saying, "Do not suppose that I have come to bring peace to the earth. I did not come to bring peace, but a sword" (10.34). Not surprisingly, then, the sorrows of Mary have over the centuries become an element in Christian devotion,[141] sometimes portrayed literally in the light of Simeon's metaphor as swords piercing her.[142]

> **There was also a prophet, Anna the daughter of Phanuel, of the tribe of Asher. She was of a great age, having lived with her husband for seven years after her**

marriage, then as a widow to the age of eighty-four. She never left the temple but worshipped there with fasting and prayer night and day. At that moment she came and began to praise God and to speak about the child to all who were looking for the redemption of Jerusalem. (2.36-38)

Luke likes to pair men and women,[143] and Simeon does not have the stage to himself. On comes Anna, an elderly woman who is also a prophet and a worshiper of God. We are told quite a lot about her—her family, her age, her life story: virgin, wife, widow. In some ways she balances Simeon, but Luke is far too good a storyteller to have her merely repeat or reinforce what Simeon has done. So, although he presents the two figures in a way that is somewhat symmetrical, he also gives them different functions.

Simeon has pointed to the gospel story in its *entirety*; he has spoken of what is to come, and of its effects. Anna acts with a focus that is narrower, but therefore more precise. Luke says of her that she "**began to praise**" God—at least, that is what our English versions have her do, though the expression Luke uses—*anthōmologeito*—says rather more than that. It implies *publicly* confessing or acknowledging something.[144] So we need to note that Anna "openly and publicly gave thanks" to the Lord, and spoke "**of him**" to all in that place who were looking for "**redemption**"—the "**redemption of Jerusalem**"—which of course means, by extension, "all of God's people, Israel."[145] The word "**redemption** (*lutrōsis*)" and its cognates is very specific in Luke's usage, and indeed in the Bible generally; it speaks of *release*, whether legal (Ruth 3.3.12-4.14), or salvation-historical (Isa. 45.13; 52:3).[146] So the very simplicity of what is said by Anna directs us to the point. We have already noted the possibility that in composing these narratives, Luke had the prophecy of Malachi in mind: "The Lord, whom you seek, will come suddenly into his temple." Arguably, the essence of what Anna says is, *Here He is!* Yet again, it is clear that the church has made the connection. An eighteenth-century *Painter's Manual* has Anna standing next to Joseph, and in her hand is a tablet with the inscription, "This child has created heaven and earth."[147] Of course Luke himself was not making such a claim as that, but his narrative was certainly moving in that direction.

> **The child grew and became strong, being filled with wisdom; and the grace of God was upon him.** (2.40)

Much the same was said of the Baptist, but the expressions regarding Jesus are stronger. "**Being filled with wisdom**"—the present participle, "*being* filled (πληρούμενον)," standing for a process and indicating growth—points already to Jesus' ministry as Luke understands it.[148] The **"grace of God** (*charis theou*)" (NRSV "favour of God") that is upon him resonates back to the "grace" of which the angel assured Mary at the Annunciation (*kecharitōmenē … Mariam, heures gar charin para tō theō*) and forward to the "words of grace" that will go forth from him as he begins his ministry to the amazement and dismay of his fellow townsfolk.[149]

The Boy Jesus in the Temple

> **Now every year his parents went to Jerusalem for the festival of the Passover. And when he was twelve years old, they went up as usual for the festival.**
>
> (2.41)

Unique among the evangelists, Luke offers this vignette of the early adolescence of Jesus. As always, its focus is clearly on Jesus himself. It is something of a staple in Graeco-Roman "lives" for the author to provide a vignette from childhood or youth that hints broadly as to what this person shall be.[150] This is certainly true of the present narrative. The passage begins with the observation that Mary and Joseph went up "**every year**" to Jerusalem for Passover—confirming, in other words, that they are pious and keep the Law.

> **When the festival was ended and they started to return, the boy Jesus stayed behind in Jerusalem, but his parents did not know it. Assuming that he was in the group of travelers, they went a day's journey. Then they started to look for him among their relatives and friends. When they did not find him, they returned to Jerusalem to search for him. After three days they found him in the temple, sitting among the teachers, listening to them and asking them questions.**
>
> **And all who heard him were amazed at his understanding and his answers.**
>
> (2.43-47)

In other words, the child is shown as father to the man. The reaction of the bystanders is also somewhat standard—"**they were amazed.**"

> **When his parents saw him they were dumbfounded (NRSV astonished); and his mother said to him, "Child, why have you treated us like this? Look, your father and I, in anguish, have been searching for you."**
>
> (2.48)

The focus is on the child Jesus but, as in the narrative of the shepherds, the reaction of Mary—in this case, of Mary and Joseph—is much more striking than that of unspecified bystanders. Jesus' "**parents**" were, says Luke, "**dumbfounded/** *exeplagēsan*"—the word is very strong.[151] And so is the word that

Mary then uses—"*odunōmenoi*: **in anguish**"—to describe their searching for their son.[152] Certainly what happens in this episode does not by any means exhaust what is implied by Simeon's "**sword**" of 2.35. That granted, it seems perverse not to see here—or to imagine that Luke did not intend us to see here—Mary's first glimpse of the suffering that she must indeed experience in witnessing the life and work of her son.[153]

> **He said to them, 'Why were you searching for me? Did you not know that I must be in my Father's house (*en tois tou patros mou*)?' But they did not understand what he said to them.**
>
> (2.49)

Mary and Joseph, in the fact that "**they did not understand**" what Jesus said[154] certainly have plenty of company, for those who comment on Luke's text have also found Jesus' words enigmatic. His expression *en tois tou patros mou* (literally, "in the things of my father") could be understood as traditionally in the English versions "**in my Father's house**"; or it could be understood as "concerned with the affairs of my Father"; or even (taking *tois* as masculine plural) "among my Father's people," i.e., the teachers of the Law, where indeed she and Joseph have just found him. And, of course, such meanings by no means exclude each other. Two things, however, are not enigmatic or in doubt. One is the "**must** (Greek: *dei*)" with which Jesus speaks of his actions—for, in Luke, *dei* seems invariably to involve not merely necessity, but God's saving will.[155] The other is the reminder to Mary—in direct response to her "**your father and I**"—that the "**Father**" with whom her son must be involved is not Joseph. At this point, as Bovon aptly notes, "the door to the Christological mystery has briefly cracked open."[156] Mary does not understand, and neither does Joseph (2.50). As always, the mark of grace in her will not be that she understands God's purposes, but that she continues to trust God. It should not be necessary to say—but perhaps it *is* necessary—that in biblical understanding generally, the opposite of faith is not doubt. The opposite of faith, actively speaking, is unfaithfulness; passively, it is refusal to trust. (2.51)

> **Then he went down with them and came to Nazareth, and was obedient to them. His mother used to treasure all these things in her heart. And Jesus increased in wisdom and in years, and in divine and human favor.**
> (2.52)

The mark of grace in Mary is she continues be faithful and to trust despite her uncertainties. She "**used to treasure all these things**"—these very puzzling things—"**in her heart.**" The imperfect tense of the verb—again ignored by the NRSV translation—indicates what became habitual for Mary. (Is Luke again hinting at the source of the story he tells?) In that household, in obedience to Mary and Joseph, Jesus grew. We do not need to engage ourselves in debates about what exactly is meant in Jesus' case by "**divine and human favor**"; the point being made—and it is the second time Luke has made it (cf. 2.40)—is that Jesus, like any other human being, had to grow. It is of a piece with his being born of a woman and needing to be swaddled as a baby. He did not begin by being six feet tall, nor did he start his life completely wise or knowing everything without being told. Like all of us, he had to learn what it is to be human; and like all of us he will have learned much of that from his mother. If we are offended by this, then we are not defending Jesus' divinity. We are simply denying the incarnation.

Account of the Apostolic Community in the Book of Acts[157]
(about thirty years later than the preceding)

Then they returned to Jerusalem from the mount called Olivet, which is near Jerusalem, a sabbath day's journey away. When they had entered the city, they went to the room upstairs where they were staying, Peter, and John, and James, and Andrew, Philip and Thomas, Bartholomew and Matthew, James son of Alphaeus, and Simon the Zealot, and Judas son of James. All these were constantly devoting themselves to prayer, together with certain women (*sun gunaixin*[158]), including Mary the mother of Jesus, as well as his brothers.

(Acts 1.12-14)

A striking thing about Luke is that after his stories of Jesus' birth and childhood, he has never actually mentioned Mary by name again[159] until after the resurrection. Now, suddenly, he tells us that she is in the upper room, praying, in company with the eleven and the faithful women and the other disciples. Other people have played active roles in Jesus' story—people like Mary of Bethany, Mary of Magdala, Peter and John—but of Mary we have heard nothing. And yet at this point she is again mentioned—mentioned, indeed, rather casually, in the middle of the list, as if her presence with the others was not something surprising, but rather something we ought to be taking for granted. The point, in a storyteller as accomplished as Luke, is surely clear enough.

When the day of Pentecost had come, they were all together in one place. And suddenly from heaven there came a sound like the rush of a violent wind, and it filled the entire house where they were sitting. Divided tongues, as of fire, appeared among them, and a tongue

> **rested on each of them. All of them were filled with the Holy Spirit and began to speak in other languages, as the Spirit gave them ability.** (Acts 2.1-4)

Mary, who manifested trust and obedience at the Annunciation, has continued to trust and obey, even though she was not center stage. Now offering neither threat nor problem, she has therefore—in the manner, of course, of patriarchal narrative[160]—been ignored. Quietly and without fuss she has endured the promised sword thrust into her soul. In her earlier trust and obedience she bore the Word of God in her own flesh. Now she will be present and will partake when the Spirit is given to the church and tongues of fire will come to rest on each (2.3, cf. 2.17). *That* is Mary's story, as Luke tells it.

5

JOHN

John's treatment of Mary at once strikes us as different from treatment of her in the other three gospels—as, of course, is also true of his treatment of Jesus. To begin with, John never calls her "Mary." In his role as author, he normally refers to her as "the mother of Jesus" (2.1, 3) or simply "his mother" (2.5, 12; 19.25, 26), and has Jesus himself address her as "*gunē*" (2.4, 19.26)—in our English versions, generally, "woman"—a mode of address that we shall need to consider in its place.

John, like Mark, has no nativity stories involving Mary. What he does have, however, is his Prologue (1.1-14), which plays in his gospel something of the part that the annunciation and birth narratives play in Matthew and Luke, together with two narratives in which the mother of Jesus figures quite prominently: the Wedding at Cana in Galilee (2.1-12) and her presence at the cross (19.25-27). None of these has any clear parallel in the other three gospels.

The Prologue

> **In the beginning was the Word, and the Word was with God, and the Word was God. He was in the beginning with God. All things came into being through him, and without him not one thing came into being.** (1.1-3)

The Prologue begins by speaking of God's "**Word** (*logos*)," by which the evangelist surely intends at least all that the Scriptures of Israel mean when they speak of God's creative Word. John's

"**In the beginning was the Word**"—or, as the NEB and REB have it, "**In the beginning, the Word already was**"—affirms God's eternal Word beyond and transcending the creation. It thus accords perfectly with the opening to Genesis, where the Hebrew text that is normally rendered into English as "In the beginning God created the heavens and the earth" could and probably should be rendered "When God began to create the heavens and the earth": the effect of the whole being to remind us that what was "in the beginning" for us and the created universe was by no means "in the beginning" for God.[1] Hence one ought in this connection to use words such as "beginning" and even more such evidently temporal expressions as "before" and "after" with extreme caution, if at all; for, as the Genesis language implies, time itself is a part of the created order: "God said…And God called…And it was evening and it was morning, first day… second day…" and so on (Gen. 1.3, 5, 8. Alter's translation). Thus, in Judeo-Christian terms, the pagans' question "What was God doing before creation?" is, as Augustine pointed out, meaningless, since time itself is a part of the created order:

> You [O God] made that very time, and no time could pass by before you made those times. But if there was no time before heaven and earth, why do they ask what you did "then"? There was no "then," where there was no time. (*Confessions* 11.13).

While, of course, one must not tie theology to the conclusions of modern science (or, indeed, do the opposite, as some Christians are tempted to do), it is worth noting that this seems to sit well enough with modern physics' notion of space-time as an inseparable whole and essentially *physical*, so that the beginning of the physical universe was also the beginning of time. Asking "What was God doing before creation?" is like asking "What is north of the North Pole?" It is not that there *is* nothing beyond or transcending the earth's North Pole, but that one cannot appropriately use "north-south" language to speak of it.

Following assertions of the role of God's Word in creation (1.2-5) and John's role as witness (1.6-8), we come to the Word's role in salvation history:

> **He came to what was his own, and his own people did not accept him. But to all who received him, who believed in his name, he gave power to become children of God, who were born, not of bloods, nor of the will of the flesh nor of the will of a man, but of God. And the Word became flesh and lived among us, and we have seen his glory, the glory as of a father's only son, full of grace and truth.** (1.11-14)

The passage at once confronts us with several questions.

First: do "**He came to what was his own**" and the expressions that follow refer to the coming of Word to Israel throughout her history?—to the prophets and to Israel's repeated rejection of the prophets?—so leading up to "**And the Word became flesh**" and the Incarnation? This seems to make good sense in the ordering of events. Or do these expressions actually refer to the ministry of Jesus himself, in which case the following **"And the Word became flesh"** must be seen as an encapsulation and summing up of what has gone before. Commentators are evidently divided on this.[2] My own view is that both sides tend to be right in what they affirm and wrong in what they deny. The presence of the God's Word and Wisdom in the world and the manner of their reception throughout Israel's history are indeed affirmed here; but they are encapsulated and in a sense *repeated* at the coming of the Word made flesh: something that will become apparent as the gospel story unfolds.[3]

A second question (obviously related to the first, and directly related to our particular inquiry) is, how seriously should we take the very poorly attested alternative reading, "who *was* born not of blood or of the will of the flesh or of the will of man, but of God"?[4] If we were to accept this reading, we would have an evident additional Scriptural witness to the virginal conception of Jesus. The unanimous witness of the Greek manuscripts has led textual critics[5] to conclude that the plural reading must be correct, and what the evangelist intended. Even so, a surprising number of modern commentators have continued to argue for the singular reading,[6] which was actually adopted in the first JB (1966).

Further questions arise from that fact that the meaning of text itself is not entirely clear: **"not of bloods** (*ex haimatōn*)" (**"bloods"** is in the plural) seems most likely "intended to exclude birth as a result of sexual congress, through the joining of two bloodlines";[7] there are no known parallels to this usage, but it does seem to have been how Augustine understood it.[8] Nevertheless, it is a strange expression. Next, "**nor of the will of the flesh**" seems to refer to what we might call "ordinary carnal desire," bearing in mind the distinction we noted earlier: that for John the word "flesh (*sarx*)" does not denote something sinful, but rather what is merely natural, and therefore weak in comparison with what is divine. Finally, "**nor of the will of a man** (*andros*)" probably means "of a husband." So, as John McHugh sums it up,

> The three negatives thus affirm that the birth of believers comes not through sexual congress, nor from those natural urges that lead to sexual congress, nor from the desire of a husband, here considered as the one who initiates the move towards physical union.[9]

All of which, however, taken as a whole, constitutes a further problem: why on earth is it necessary, in speaking of "**the power to become children of God**" to exclude notions of physical begetting at such length and so unequivocally? Who ever imagined that becoming **children of God** was a matter of human sexuality anyway? If, however, the singular form of the text *were* original—so that this was an assertion of what was true about the birth of Jesus—then this would make sense: which brings us back to our originally stated dilemma.

Granted the two things that appear to be most evident about this passage, namely, (1) that the original text clearly referred in the plural to *all* who are "children of God" and (2) that it has nonetheless chosen to use language that can hardly be heard by those who know the tradition of the virginal conception of Jesus *without* putting them in mind of it, we should perhaps ask whether that coincidence is entirely accidental? Possibly the evangelist *did* have in mind traditions of the virginal conception of Jesus but shared the early church's reticence (to which we have already referred in our discussion of Paul) in regard to it. Is the evangelist, while saying nothing about the tradition directly, yet reminding us that *all* who have **"believed in his name"** and been given **"power to become children of God"** are, by that very fact, in some sense—and arguably the deepest sense—children of miracle, virginally conceived? As C. K. Barrett put it, "it remains probable that John was alluding to Christ's birth, and declaring that the birth of Christians, being bloodless and rooted in God's will alone, followed the pattern of the birth of Christ himself."[10] Precisely. And that, of course, is how it has been with the coming of the Word to the people of God throughout her history from Abraham onwards.

So, however we view the precise intention or relationship to each other of the various elements in the passage, we come to what is quite evidently its climax: **"And the Word became flesh."**

The **"And,"** as Westcott pointed out, comes as the triumphant conclusion to a perfect sequence: **"In the beginning was the Word … and the Word was God … And the Word became flesh."**[11] St Augustine famously wrote in the seventh book of his *Confessions* that in studying the works of the Platonists,

> Again, I read there that the Word, God, "is born not of the flesh, nor of blood, nor of the will of a man nor of the will of the flesh, but of God". But that "the Word was made flesh and dwelt among us I did not read there." (Henry Chadwick, transl.)[12]

Christian familiarity with John's claim can perhaps shield us from its sheer audacity—an audacity that Augustine saw very well. While, as we have said, "**flesh**/*sarx*" does not for the Fourth Evangelist carry the taint of corruption and sin that it has for Paul, it does stand for what is physical and mortal. It is transient: "a wind that passes and does not come again" (Ps. 78.39). It is surely therefore everything that the divine, the holy and the transcendent are not:

> All flesh is grass, and all the goodliness thereof as the flower of the field. The grass withers, the flower fades, because the breath of YHWH blows upon it. The grass withers, the flower fades, but the Word of our God shall stand for ever. (Isa. 40.6-8)

Even so, John does not say that the Word assumed flesh or borrowed it or wore it—like an actor putting on a costume—but that the Word "**became**"[13] it.[14] At which point, this passage becomes directly relevant to our concerns. Just as in Paul's "born of a woman, born under the Law," so here there lies behind the text something that is not explicit but absolutely necessary if what *is* explicit is true. Just *where* did the Word "**become flesh**"? Whose flesh or what flesh did the Word "**become**"? There is only one possible answer to those questions. In terms of the name by which others speak of her, **the Word became flesh** in Mary's flesh, the womb of Mary. In John's own terms, **the Word became flesh** in the flesh of her whom he will consistently call "the mother of Jesus."

The Word, moreover, **"dwelt[15] among us,"** so fulfilling God's promise to "dwell among the children of Israel." Human beings are by nature, as Aristotle famously observed, social beings.[16] We cannot be human alone, and we learn how to be human by being with others, especially those who first care for us. If the Word **dwelt among us**, then here too the mother of Jesus must take her place. Hers the first face he saw, the first words he heard (hence we speak of someone's "mother tongue"), the first love he knew. This means, as Sara Maitland reminds us, that,

> To put it bluntly, the eternal Logos, whose glory we beheld and from whom we have received grace upon grace, was potty trained—and presumably rather well potty-trained, since he did not grow up seeking consolation by conquest, affirming his masculinity over the mother's ownership of his bodily production by despising women, nor having a cringing fear of those in authority.[17]

But given John's own terms, we anticipate. Let us now turn to the scene in which he brings "the mother of Jesus" onto his stage as a visible participant in the action.

The Marriage at Cana

By way of clearing the ground, we should at once note that the center and focus of this narrative, as of all Johannine narratives, is Jesus. In this respect, indeed, the narrative itself might mislead us, since it begins with Mary, and only then—as if as an afterthought!—brings Jesus onto the scene.

> **On the third day there was a wedding in Cana of Galilee, and the mother of Jesus was there. Jesus and his disciples had also been invited to the wedding.** (2.1-2)

But we do not have to look far to see that this is a technique that John uses elsewhere, bringing first onto the scene a character who will indeed play a role in what is to follow, but always subordinate to Jesus' own role. So it is with Nicodemus (3.1), with the "royal official" (4.46b), and with the raising of Lazarus (11.1-2). That granted, let us nonetheless be wary lest we pass *too* quickly over this reference to "**the mother of Jesus**," which serves indeed, if we allow it, to remind us of something of great importance. The evangelist has already pointed us to what is involved in the person of Jesus: he is the Word made flesh—not any word but, as we have already said, "the Word of our God" which "shall stand for ever" (Isa. 40.6-8). So he fulfilled God's promise to "dwell among the children of Israel" (Exod. 29.45). And now the evangelist's simple reference to "**the mother of Jesus**" reminds us—in case we were so overawed by the majesty and glory of this mystery as to be in danger of forgetting or overlooking it—just how God brought this about. Like every other human being, *Jesus had a mother*. The Word became flesh through the particular biological functions of a particular woman, at a particular time and in a particular place. The very title "**mother of Jesus**"—regardless of whether or not John knew the birth narratives of Matthew and Luke, or his attitude to them if he did—*implies* a birth story of some kind and is nonsense without one: as indeed is the case when we introduce anyone as someone's mother. Set alongside the "the Word became flesh and lived among us" of John 1.14, "**mother of Jesus**" declares, first, that *none the less* Jesus is also a human being who is, like every other human being, born of a woman; and second, that she who approaches him is the one who stands in that unique relationship to him.

John does not ever name the mother of Jesus. Why? The question is an obvious one; it is also impossible to answer. In John's case, as in Paul's at Galatians 4.4, I find it hard to imagine that he did not know it—indeed, even harder. What one does notice, however, is that reticence over naming is also the case in the evangelist's treatment of another character in the narrative who is clearly important to him—I mean the one who is at times referred to (perhaps reflecting his own modesty?) simply as "the other disciple"[18] and at other times (perhaps reflecting his community's special pride in him) as "beloved" by Jesus.[19] Given John's gospel also expresses awareness of a special relationship between this disciple and Jesus' mother,[20] perhaps we need look no further for a reason for the evangelist's reticence in this respect.

This account of "**a wedding in Cana**" is to be a story of how Jesus "**revealed his glory**," and the centrality of Jesus is quickly made clear. "**Jesus and his disciples**" are also guests at the wedding, and when Jesus' mother is made aware of a problem, it is to her son that she brings it.

> **When the wine gave out, the mother of Jesus said to him, "They have no wine." (2.3)**

So far, all is clear. Jesus' reply, however, raises problems.

> **And Jesus said to her, "Woman, what concern is that to you and to me? My hour has not yet come." (2.4)**

One problem with this is in Jesus' mode of addressing his mother. The other is in what he then says to her.

Of these, the former is easily understood, even if not—so far as English renderings are concerned—so easily solved. In koine Greek of the period Jesus' word, "**Woman** [*gunai* (vocative of *gunē*)]" is an entirely normal, polite way of addressing a woman. Jesus is shown so addressing various women in John and in the other gospels,[21] and we should hear in it absolutely no sense of rebuke, disrespect, distancing, or lack of affection. It is only somewhat unusual in that it is used here and at 19.26, without qualification, as a form of address by a son to his mother, but even at that, it certainly is not discourteous.[22] Why, then, is there a problem? Not because the sense of the Greek is difficult, but simply because there is no good equivalent for it in modern

English, or indeed, so far as I can see, in modern French, Italian or Spanish. "Madam" or "Lady," in the senses in which they were used in the seventeenth century, would get it quite well. Thus, Shakespeare's Juliet seems quite naturally to call her mother "madam," and Romeo uses "lady" to address the girl with whom he is in love (*Romeo and Juliet* 1.2.1; 3.5.69; 2.2.107). By contrast "**woman,**" as *gunai* is commonly rendered in our English translations, does not get it at all, since such an address in modern English is both abrupt and discourteous.

So much may be said for Jesus' mode of address. The issue is, however, altogether more difficult when we come to his following words: "**What concern is that to you and to me? My hour is not yet come.**" Here, there really *is* a problem, plainly illustrated by the varied ways in which different English versions render these expressions: from the (possibly somewhat plaintive?) "what do you want from me?" (NJV), through the (somewhat cold?) neutrality of "that is no concern of mine" (REB), to the downright hostile "you must not tell me what to do" (TEV). Certainly we are here dealing in John's Greek with a Semitism—a Hebrew expression that may be rendered literally as "What to you and to me?" It is an expression that in Israel's Scriptures invariably indicates unwillingness to be involved in something, but with different implications: sometimes implying a sense of injury, sometimes hostile refusal—a nuance that is generally indicated by the context.[23] What is the nuance here? That is the problem—there is no indication from the context. If only—as a Spanish-speaking friend of mine observes[24]—we could hear Jesus' tone of voice! We cannot. We can only observe that Mary is pointed towards an "hour" that is still to come—also as yet unexplained.

Does Mary's response to Jesus' words indicate that, for her part, she thinks that her son has agreed to help? There are certainly commentators who believe that it does. "Clearly," wrote C. K. Barrett, "Jesus' mother does not regard his words as a direct refusal of the favour she has implicitly asked."[25] But *is* it clear?

Thomas Aquinas presents Mary as understanding her son's words in precisely the opposite way: "Now although his mother was refused, she did not lose hope in her Son's mercy."[26] The fact is, we are not told how Mary understands her son's response. What we *are* told—and it is especially significant for the subject of our present study—is what she does.

> **His mother said to the servants, "Do whatever he tells you."** (2.5).

As Westcott puts it, her command "is wholly unlimited: all is left to Christ."[27] Mary makes way for whatever her son will do and, insofar as she appears to carry some authority, has others do the same. No more than that, but no less. If this is not a mark of faithfulness and trust—*pistis* in its fullest sense, even though the word does not occur in the narrative—it is hard to know what that would be. As for what might have led to that faithfulness and trust, perhaps no more need be said than this: that having watched his growing from babyhood into manhood, the evangelist imagined not unreasonably that she knew her son.

There follows a somewhat oddly constructed narrative:

> **Now standing there were six stone water-jars for the Jewish rites of purification, each holding twenty or thirty gallons. Jesus said to them, "Fill the jars with water." And they filled them up to the brim. He said to them, "Now draw some out, and take it to the chief steward." So they took it. When the steward tasted the water that had become wine and did not know where it came from (though the servants who had drawn the water knew), the steward called the bridegroom and said to him, "Everyone serves the good wine first, and then the inferior wine after the guests have become drunk. But you have kept the good wine until now."**

To begin with, we are told very precisely of Jesus instructing servants to fill "**six stone water-jars for the Jewish rites of purification,**" each holding the equivalent of about 40 liters. This, the servants do, filling them "**up to the brim.**" We are told of Jesus' instruction to draw from the jars and take what they have drawn to the "**chief steward,**"[28] which they do. But then we learn only obliquely—backed into the narrative, so to speak, from the chief steward's own comments—that a miracle has taken place. Somewhere in the process the water has become wine—and not merely wine, but apparently a vast quantity of *good* wine, better than any that has been served before! Other things that seem to be hinted at—such as the significance of the "**hour**" to which Jesus has referred; the significance (if there is one) of "**water,**" "**wine**" and "**wedding.**" All these elements occur elsewhere in Scriptural portrayals of God's mighty acts. Are they then symbolic here, and if so, of what? The significance of its being "**water for purification**" according to "**Jewish rites**" that is transformed for the revelers; the significance of the apparently enormous amounts of "**wine**" that are involved—all these things remain enigmatic and unexplained. We are simply told in conclusion that,

> **Jesus did this, the first of his signs, in Cana of Galilee, and revealed his glory; and his disciples believed in him.** (2.11)

So we are brought abruptly to the climax and purpose of the narrative: "**his disciples believed in him.**" It is, as Barrett points out, "implied that the disciples believed because of the manifestation of the glory of Jesus in the sign."[29] Perhaps also implied—albeit very gently—is a distinction between the faith of the disciples and the faith of Jesus' mother. She believed even before the sign and despite the cryptic nature of her son's response to her. She witnessed to that faith by her words: "**Do**

whatever he tells you." The disciples, by contrast, needed also "**the sign**" that "**manifested his glory**" before they could come to faith in him.

> **After this he went down to Capernaum with his mother, his brothers, and his disciples; and they remained there for a few days.** (2.12)

Commentators seem regularly to be in controversy or otherwise exercised by this closing note, expressing concerns about its geography,[30] its source,[31] and its relationship to the synoptics.[32] It is unlikely that any such concerns were in the mind of the evangelist or those who worked with him. Westcott makes the only point that was, I suspect, intended: "As yet the family life was not broken." The verse provides an entirely appropriate narrative pause—a "beat," in the literary jargon with which I am most familiar—before we turn to the tension and drama of the next section of the story, which will be Jesus' visit to Jerusalem. Luke, strikingly, provided a similar "beat" at the conclusion of his pericope about the teenage Jesus going missing on a visit to Jerusalem.[33]

Jesus and Abraham

A later passage in the gospel does not directly mention Jesus' mother but may have a bearing on the evangelist or others' attitude to her. It occurs as a part of what is possibly the most bitter debate in the gospel between Jesus and those whom the evangelist calls "*hoi Ioudaioi*"—"the Jews" (NRSV), or perhaps better, "the Judaeans."

> **They answered him, "Abraham is our father." Jesus said to them, "If you were Abraham's children, you would be doing what Abraham did, but now you are trying to kill me, a man who has told you the truth that I heard from God. This is not what Abraham did. *You*** (*humeis*)

> **are doing what your father does." They said to him, "*We* (*hēmais*) are not illegitimate (*ek porneia*) children; we have one father, God himself."** (John 8.39-41)

Of possible interest to us for our present study is the statement by "*hoi Ioudaioi*" that "***We***"—the grammatically unnecessary use of the pronoun makes this emphatic—"***We* are not illegitimate children**" (literally, "were not born of fornication"). Certainly this may be understood as a straightforward response to Jesus' assertion that Abraham is not their true father and that they are illegitimate children. But the emphatic "**we**" (in response to Jesus' emphatic "**you**") could also be understood as hinting at questions about Jesus' own legitimacy. As C. K. Barrett puts it, they "find a fresh way of turning the argument against Jesus. The implication (especially of the emphatic *hēmeis*) is that Jesus was born of *porneia*."[34] Such an intention by the evangelist would be of a piece with the possible awareness of questions surrounding Jesus' birth that we noted in considering his expressions at 1.12-13.

The Cross

At least one of the questions posed by the story of the Marriage at Cana finds a degree of solution toward the end of the gospel. When comes the "**hour**" of which Jesus speaks to his mother at the wedding at Cana? It comes, we will learn (12.26, 17.1), when Jesus is brought to the cross. Strikingly, it is at the cross that the mother of Jesus again appears.

> **Meanwhile, standing near the cross of Jesus were his mother, and his mother's sister, Mary the wife of Clopas, and Mary Magdalene. When Jesus saw his mother and the disciple whom he loved standing beside her, he said to his mother, 'Woman, here is your son.' Then he said to the disciple, 'Here is your mother.' And from that hour the disciple took her into his own home.** (John 19.25-27)

Familiar though the image of Mary at the cross is through both art and hymnody, John is the only evangelist to place her there.[35]

The scene, at least in the modern era, is marked by persistent and apparently contradictory traditions of interpretation. Some commentators emphasize its symbolic nature. For Rudolf Bultmann, "the mother of Jesus, who tarries by the cross, represents Jewish Christianity that overcomes to offence of the cross. The beloved disciple represents Gentile Christianity, which is charged to honor the former as the mother from whom it has come."[36] For Raymond Brown, Jesus' mother was "symbolically evocative of Lady Zion who, after the birth pangs, brings forth a new people in joy."[37]

C. H. Dodd, by contrast, regarded the narrative as unconnected with Johannine theology, claiming it rather as a version of the historical tradition, devoid of symbolism.[38] The most he would go beyond that was to note that in this episode the evangelist does turn our attention from what is happening in the present of his narrative to what will happen afterwards, to the future life of the church, in which Mary's motherhood—necessarily a symbolic motherhood—was understood as having a continuing role.[39] Similarly, in Ernst Haenchen's view, the episode shows how in his passion "Jesus savours the proximity of those close to him." The meaning of Jesus' words to his mother and to the beloved disciple is indicated in 19.27b: "And from that hour the disciple took her into his own home." In other words, the beloved disciple "has taken over the care for Jesus' mother." Of course Heanchen too is aware of later symbolic interpretations of the narrative, "but," he points out, "there is nothing in the story that points to such a symbolic meaning for these figures."[40]

There is a sense in which both schools of thought are probably right. On the one hand, I doubt that those who first told this story had much more in mind than is indicated by Dodd and Haenchen: a final moment of warmth between Jesus and his mother. On the other, I am by no means convinced that the evangelist himself and his immediate hearers saw no more in it than that. Jesus, in encouraging his followers to pray to God as their *abba* just as he did, had himself implied that they were in his eyes (and therefore God's) his brothers and sisters. His mother was therefore necessarily in some sense their mother.[41] Indeed, might not this dying word of Jesus from the cross, together with all that Jesus had taught them during his ministry about God as their *abba*, have been exactly what led to the evangelist's conviction, expressed from the very beginning of his gospel: that the birth of *all* who "believe on his name" is a miracle, a divine begetting, and God's "nevertheless" to our apostacy?

6

REVELATION, OR THE APOCALYPSE

The document known to us as Revelation, or the Apocalypse, identifies itself as "prophecy" (1.3, 22.6-7, 18-19) and takes the form of a circular letter. Like all New Testament letters—and indeed, like all biblical prophecy—Revelation addresses a specific situation: in this case, Christians in seven identified churches in the Roman province of Asia in the late first century of the Christian Era. The churches are named in the order in which they would have been visited by travelers who used the circular route that went north from Ephesus towards Smyrna and Pergamum, and then turned south to take in Pergamum, Thyatira, Sardis, Philadelphia, and Laodicea (1.4.-22). Like all biblical prophecy, Revelation has, of course, continued to speak to those of other times and places, which is, no doubt, a major reason why we continue to be interested in it.

The prophecy presents visions revealed "in the Spirit on the Lord's day" to someone called John, who further identifies himself as "slave (*doulos*)" of Jesus Christ (1.1). These revelations came to him, he says, while he was on the island of Patmos "on account of the word of God and the testimony of Jesus" (1.9)—which might refer to judicial banishment (*relegatio in insulam*) by Roman authority or might mean simply that he had gone there to preach. In form, the letter has much in common with the Book of Daniel, which John of Patmos will surely have regarded as a prophetic book. Like Daniel, Revelation presents a series of visions whereby the seer finds himself, as he believes, enabled to perceive the reality of God's activity in history—a history seen, however, not from the human point of view but the viewpoint of eternity.

At the very center of Revelation—what would have been its literal, physical center, if the text is thought of in its probable original form as a scroll on two cylinders[1]—is a set of visions that is extraordinary even standing as it does among visions that are generally extraordinary: a passage that perfectly exemplifies Andrew R. Guffey's astute observation that "Revelation is not merely a text, not merely a composition, but also a work of visual imagination."[2]

The passages begin with the sounding of a seventh (and last) trumpet proclaiming God's enthronement and heavenly voices proclaiming the union of heaven and earth: which is to say, proclaiming the consummation and perfecting of that divine-human union promised time after time in Scripture—in Eden, in the call of Abraham, in Solomon's temple, and by the prophets—and time after time wrecked by human folly. Now, however, John of Patmos hears it declared that the promise is at last fulfilled. **"The kingdom of the world has become the kingdom of our Lord and of his Messiah, and he will reign for ever and ever"** (11.15b). In Jesus, the longed-for union of God and humankind has come about. Even though it was brought to the cross, that union did not fail, and human folly was not able to destroy it.

> **And the temple of God in heaven was opened, and the ark of his covenant was seen within his temple; and there were flashes of lightning, rumblings, peals of thunder, an earthquake, and heavy hail.** (11.19 cf. Ps. 2.2 especially LXX)

In the earthly temple, no one might enter the holy of holies save the high priest, and he only once a year on the day of atonement.

Now, however, John of Patmos sees heavenly Temple, the true Temple, open to all. In the earthly temple, the Ark of the Covenant, the sign of God's presence, had long disappeared—delivered by Jeremiah, according to one tradition, to a cave on Mount Sinai where it would stay hidden until Israel was finally restored and God's glory would appear (cf. 2 Macc. 2.4-8). Now, however, in the heavenly Temple, John sees the Ark, sign of God's presence and forgiveness.[3] Here the promises to Israel and her hopes have been fulfilled.

And now, in this setting,

> **A great portent appeared in heaven: a woman clothed with the sun, with the moon under her feet, and on her head a crown of twelve stars.** (Rev. 12.1)

When they heard those words, perhaps some among the seer's earliest hearers in Asia Minor thought initially of Ephesian Artemis, who generally appears with her head wreathed in a nimbus, and whose mythology does include elements that resonate with this woman "**clothed with the sun**," such as pursuit and persecution of a pregnant mother and the birth of a divine child. The parallels are loose, since Artemis herself is not the persecuted mother, yet hearers might experience some echoing of themes or, as Guffey suggests, adaptation of elements in the iconography.[4] Or did early hearers perhaps think of the triumphant goddess Roma, whose servant—the Emperor—had brought peace and justice to the earth? This was the chosen myth of the Empire, and depictions of it will have been all around them: on coinage, in temples, in plaques and dedications. Perhaps that symbol occurred to them for a moment—but again, while there were possible resonances, the woman of whom the seer speaks is evidently *not* the goddess Roma any more than she is Artemis. The most striking way in which she differs from both is, obviously, that she is in the pangs of childbirth:

> **She was pregnant and was crying out in birth pangs, in the agony of giving birth. (12.2)**

At which mention, those among the seer's first hearers who knew the Scriptures of Israel will perhaps have begun to think of Eve: she who was warned, according to Genesis,

> I will greatly increase your pangs in childbearing;
> in pain you shall bring forth children. (Genesis 3.16a)

So is the woman Eve?

Or is she perhaps the "daughter of Zion" as the prophet Micah spoke of her?

> Writhe and groan, O daughter Zion,
> like a woman in labor. (Micah 4.10a).

Both Eve and the daughter of Zion are told of distress to come upon them, yet in neither case is the sentence without hope. In Genesis, God's words to the serpent have already declared the serpent's own doom,

> I will put enmity between you and the woman,
> and between your offspring and hers;
> he will strike your head,
> and you will strike his heel. (Gen. 3.15)

And God's words to the "daughter of Zion" are even clearer in their promise:

> for now you shall go forth from the city
> and camp in the open country;
> you shall go to Babylon.
> There you shall be rescued,

> there the Lord will redeem you
> from the hands of your enemies. (Micah 4.10)

So is the woman Eve?—which is to say, in effect, does she stand for humanity? Or is she the "daughter of Zion"?—which is to say, in effect, does she stand for the people of Israel? The latter is certainly how the earliest patristic exegesis saw her.[5]

Yet even as we pose those questions, the seer draws back further from his scene, widening the picture to include another figure—this time a figure of terror.

> **Then another portent appeared in heaven: a great red dragon, with seven heads and ten horns, and seven diadems on his heads. His tail swept down a third of the stars of heaven and threw them to the earth. Then the dragon stood before the woman who was about to bear a child, so that he might devour her child as soon as it was born.** (Rev. 12.3-4)

As various commentators point out, there are in the literature of the world many tales of a usurper who would destroy the true heir and claim the inheritance.[6] Some of our own most beloved film and pantomime stories—*Snow White*, *The Sleeping Beauty*, *Cinderella*—are versions of them. So, on a larger canvas, are the *Star Wars* movies, each of which—the three original, the three prequels, and the three sequels—has running through it a theme of usurped and oppressive power that brave men and women defy, outwit and finally overcome. By the time the Seer of Patmos wrote, Christianity itself already had one such story of its own: Matthew's account of Herod's attempt to kill the child Jesus, an account that in its telling evidently echoed themes from still earlier traditions of the birth of Moses.

Behind such narratives we may discern human imagination playing upon a myth common to many cultures—the solar myth, wherein the dragon of darkness tries daily to kill the light, only to be killed in turn as the new day dawns, or else tries annually to kill the sun itself, only to be defeated by the return of Spring. The Greeks, the Egyptians, the Celts, the Norse—all knew versions of such a myth, which is to say, of a story told not merely for the joy of a tale (though surely told for that, too) but also as an attempt to make sense of life itself, of death and birth, of the despair and hope that surround us all daily.

The seer, having brought the usurper onto the stage, turns our attention back to the mother:

> **And she gave birth to a son, a male child, who is to shepherd (NRSV "rule") all the nations with a rod of iron. But her child was snatched away and taken to God and to his throne; and the woman fled into the wilderness, where she has a place prepared by God, so that there she can be nourished for one thousand two hundred and sixty days.** (Rev. 12.5-6)

So who is the woman? Now at last, the seer provides us with an allusion that is unambiguous, a psalm whose associations are both royal and messianic: Psalm 2.[7] Elsewhere in his prophecy,[8] he has already associated that psalm and the one who shall "**shepherd the nations**" with Jesus. Given which, the rich feast of images he has given us round the "**woman**" suddenly comes into focus and coalesces in a single figure: the mother of Jesus—Jesus' mother, of course, not as the world will have seen her, but as God will have seen her in her acceptance of her calling to be mother of the Messiah. Mary is the one whose child is the true heir of all things, and in his exaltation we may see the real heir taking his rightful place when, despite all that the dragon can do, **“her child was snatched away and taken to God and to his throne”** (Rev. 12.5). In other words, the basic stuff of the apostolic proclamation: the birth, suffering, death, resurrection, and exaltation of Jesus—the “stuff” that Peter announced at Pentecost (Acts 2.14-36), that Paul “delivered” to his converts at Corinth (1 Cor. 15.1-11) and that Christians rehearse every time they recite the Apostles or Nicene Creed—that “stuff” is the *true* version of the myths of the heir who must be rescued from the usurper. In it, all those other versions find their meaning, their fulfilment and, in that sense, their “end (*telos*),” even as Christ is the “end (*telos*)” of the Law (cf. Rom. 10.4).

Of course, it is true that being seen thus, Mary of Nazareth is not *merely* Mary of Nazareth. We were not wrong to see in the woman crowned with stars the figure of Israel, the Zion of whom Isaiah spoke (Isaiah 66.7-9, cf. 2 Esdras 13.32-38), for the people of God *are* the ones from whom, as Paul had put it, “according to the flesh, comes the Messiah, who is over all, God blessed forever” (Rom. 9.5). As Jesus himself declares by the fourth evangelist, “salvation is from the Jews” (John 4.22). Therefore, in becoming mother of the Messiah, Mary does indeed stand for Israel.[9] Nor were we wrong to connect her with Eve, for whence does God call the holy people, if not from humankind?—the same humankind that stumbled in the Garden, the humankind from whom God called Abraham? So, as daughter of Zion, Mary must also be the new Eve, that is, *woman*, now receiving fulfilment of the promise that was involved even in her curse and the curse of the serpent. To her, God's word was that “in pain you shall bring forth children,” but to the serpent, it was that the woman's offspring “will trample your head, and you will bite his heel”[10] (Gen. 2.15-16).

But none of this means that the woman crowned with stars is not still the woman—the real woman, indeed, Mary of Nazareth—of whom Jesus was born. On the contrary, it is essential to it: for as we have noted more than once, and as the evangelists and Paul are, in their different ways, at pains to make clear, it is in and through Mary's reality and the physical reality of her motherhood, and through nothing else, that God has chosen to bring the miracle to pass, allowing the prophecy, the promise, even the myth, to enter history as a thing that actually happened. That, at least, is the witness of the rest of the New Testament. And that, it appears to me, is what is implicit here. Thus, even that fine exegete G.B. Caird, having *correctly* associated the woman crowned with stars with "the Messianic community," with "prophecy about Mother Zion," and with "the Jerusalem above who is our mother," is nonetheless *wrong* when alongside of that he says of her that she is "not Mary," as if that followed what he had just said[11]—a perfect example of being right in what one affirms and wrong in what one denies.

As is quite often the case, artistic imagination can here work as well—or even better than—written commentary. The East Window of the Lady Chapel in Exeter Cathedral confronts worshipers with a simple, non-dogmatic assertion of the relationship we have been considering, based on five scenes from the biblical narrative that its creator, Dorothy Marion Grant, and the dean and chapter who commissioned it in 1951 evidently considered proper to their honoring of God's grace in Mary.

Figure 5: East Window of the Lady Chapel in Exeter Cathedral, by Marion Grant (1912-1988)

Reading from one's left to right, the scenes are:

First, The unfaithfulness and disobedience of Eve: Eve is tempted by the serpent, while Adam looks on (Genesis 3.1-6).[12]

Second, The faith and obedience of Mary: following her *fiat mihi*, God's Spirit as a dove overshadows her, and Gabriel falls to his knees in adoration of the Word made flesh in her womb (Luke 1.38).

Third, Mary the Mother of God, the center and pivot of the story: Mary with the Christ Child, angels above her, shepherds and magi around her, and even creatures—ox and ass who "know their owner and their master's crib"—adore the Christ child, heaven joined to earth (Matthew 1.25, 11; Luke 2.9-20 cf. Isaiah 1.3).

> *Fourth*, again Mary's faith and obedience: *mater dolorosa* with the beloved disciple at the crucifixion: she looks to the Crucified as he commends the beloved disciple to her care and her to his, appointing her "mother" to the church (John 19.26-27).
>
> *Fifth* and finally, Mary, still clearly the mother of Jesus, but now seen as the seer of Patmos saw her: *regina caelorum*, crowned with stars, robed with the sun, and the moon beneath her feet (Rev. 12.1--5a).

Most strikingly for our immediate concern, the story of Mary is here shown beginning with the story of Eve, "the woman," and the story of Eve is shown concluding with the woman clothed with sun. As Irenaeus puts it, in God's good providence,

> Just as the human race was subject to death by a virgin, it was freed by a virgin, with the virginal disobedience balanced by virginal obedience (*Against Heresies* 5.19.1).

It is a mistake to suppose that a figure who is real cannot or does not also embody or become representative of a value, a group, or an ideal. On the contrary, Qumran's Teacher of Righteousness and the fourth gospel's Beloved Disciple are both in their own ways representative figures: but there is not the slightest reason to doubt that behind those representative figures are real persons who led real lives. As for our not being told their names: it is striking that the Johannine tradition does not name the mother of Jesus any more than it names the disciple whom Jesus loved, although one can scarcely doubt that author(s) of that tradition knew both names—indeed, "the disciple whom Jesus loved" is, after Jesus himself, likely the main direct inspiration behind the gospel. In literature later than antiquity, we might compare the treatment of Beatrice in Dante's *Commedia*. As Anna Maria Chiavacci Leonardi points out, Beatrice is at the same time,

> a historic reality and a symbol ... while representing, as appears unmistakably at the end of the *Purgatorio*, a reality that transcends her, Beatrice never ceases to be herself, moving Dante's innermost being to the same trembling and emotion as in the days when they were in Florence.[13]

All this may, indeed, point to another and not unrelated truth: a certain modesty in iconic sanctity. As Calhoun Walpole points out, "Icons do not seek to gather attention for themselves; rather, they point us to something grander and deeper. Icons ... encourage us to look beyond, and above."[14]

In what follows, the seer draws back still further from his scene and allows us to see it in an even wider context: a vast cosmic struggle—"**war in heaven**"—in which the legions of light, Michael and his angels, are victorious (Rev. 21.7-12). "**The great dragon was thrown down ... he was thrown down to the earth, and his angels were thrown down with him**" (12.9). Who, then, or what is the dragon? Herod the Great? Those who brought Jesus to the cross? John of Patmos identifies it directly with that which brought chaos into God's creation from the beginning: the dragon is, he says, the "**ancient serpent, who is called the Devil and Satan, the deceiver of the whole world**" (Rev. 12.9): which perhaps implies that all or any of us have at times embodied the dragon or represented the dragon or done its work—even Peter, according to Jesus.[15] The dragon's redness surely speaks of violence, bloodshed and war.[16] Its "seven" heads speak of a blasphemous claim to divinity, since seven is the number of divine activity (Rev.1.4, 12-13) and at the same time remind us of the chaos monster, Leviathan, who is overpowered by YHWH.[17]

> **So when the dragon saw that he had been thrown down to the earth, he pursued the woman who had given birth to the male child** (Rev. 12.13).

Alas, the dragon's malice is not finished even when he is defeated, and the true heir has received the honors due him. A whirlpool of images then echoes the *former* deliverance of Israel even as it speaks of the *latter* deliverance of the woman. Of the former it was said,

> As an eagle stirs up its nest,
>   and hovers over its young;
> as it spreads its wings, takes them up,
>   and bears them aloft on its pinions,
> YHWH alone guided them. (Deut. 32.11-12a)

So now it is said of the latter that the woman is safely delivered **"into the wilderness"** by **"the two wings of the great eagle"** (Rev. 12.14a).

As Israel was nourished in the wilderness with manna, so now the woman is **"nourished for a time, two times and half a time"**—that is, following the imagery used by Daniel (12.7), she is nourished throughout the period during which evil is permitted to harass the people of God (Rev. 12.14b).[18]

The evil one spews forth a river of destruction after the woman to sweep her away: but as Israel was enabled to walk in safety amid the waters of the Red Sea, so now the earth itself—as Eugene Boring puts it, "no neutral bystander in this drama"[19]—

> **came to the help of the woman; it opened its mouth and swallowed the river that the dragon had poured from his mouth.** (Rev. 12.16)

In other words, there is in the very ordering of creation itself that which is on the side of the woman.[20]

> **Then the dragon was angry with the woman, and went off to make war on the rest of her children.** (12.17a)

Who are the "rest of her children"? John answers our question immediately: they are **"those who keep the commandments of God and hold the testimony of Jesus**" (12.17b). In other words, they are the church. Naturally, we recall from elsewhere in Johannine literature the scene at the cross: "Woman, here is your son. . . . " "Here is your mother."[21] In the seer's view, however, we have gone a step further. It now seems that not only the beloved disciple but *every* disciple of Jesus is spiritually the child of his mother.[22] It is of a piece with the fourth evangelist's initial affirmation that all believers are in a sense born of a miracle, even as was Jesus himself.[23]

All of which brings the seer's words directly into connection with readers in his own and every age: in short, with us. The seven-headed dragon—the beast pretending to possess divine authority and power—is always with us and continues to threaten "**those who keep the commandments of God and hold the testimony of Jesus**." But theirs also is the privilege of being spiritually a part even of Jesus' earthly family, of calling his mother their mother. Such appear to be the implications of this extraordinary passage in the Revelation to John.

7

MARY AS THE EARLY CHRISTIANS REMEMBERED HER

When I began these reflections on the early church's memory of Mary, I noted an observation by Elizabeth Schüssler Fiorenza: that in patriarchal narrative, the presence of women is usually only mentioned "when women's behavior presents a problem or when women are exceptional individuals." Having looked at the texts referring to Mary in early Christian memory, do we find this observation borne out, and if so, how?

Is Mary remembered as presenting a problem? Evidently, yes. The willingness of this young woman—a girl of probably no more than fourteen or fifteen—to become the mother of a child who is not her husband's at once places her in a situation where she is outside the norms of her society, would appear to have dishonored Joseph, and could even be faced with being put to death. In other words, she presents those around her with a problem. Indeed, she presents *herself* with a problem. This is implicit in Luke's narrative and spelled out especially clearly in Matthew's, wherein Joseph's blundering if well-meaning attempts to rectify the situation must be countered by angelic intervention.

Is Mary remembered as an exceptional individual? Again, evidently, yes. Luke, in particular, presents her as exceptional in several ways: most evidently in the willingness—and even joy—with which she accepts a calling that, as we have just noted, places her in considerable jeopardy. Following that, her trekking across mountains to see her kinswoman Elizabeth, apparently unaccompanied by Joseph or any other of her kin, suggests that she is both adventurous and bold. At the house of Elizabeth, she is presented as prophetic, for there she utters the *Magnificat*, one of the great oracles of Scripture. Perhaps David Brown is correct in his suggestion that the *Magnificat* prophecy assigns "a confidence and certainty to the beginning of Jesus' life, and thus to Mary, that almost certainly was not there."[1] But again, perhaps not. "What we can't show we don't know" is a sword with two edges. It remains unarguable that, for some reason, the prophetic Mary is how she was remembered, and that fact has to be accounted for somehow. That she is subsequently portrayed, in an advanced state of pregnancy, as willing to accompany Joseph on his trek to Bethlehem for the Roman census again reinforces our impression of her courageous spirit.

In the light of which I would again stress a point made earlier in this study—that we must reject the suggestion that Mary's role as she appears in these narratives is only one of "submission and humility" rather than creativity or action. Rather, Ann Loades' comment about her is more to the point:

> I remain entirely at a loss in reading theologians who deny Mary (and by implication, other women) even a shred of creativity in her consent to pregnancy, a pregnancy which might result not only in her abandonment and ostracism, but given the conditions of her time, even in her own death. . . . We must, I think, suppose that Mary was a girl with remarkable courage.[2]

E. L. Mascall—a notable theologian in many ways, but hardly notable as an ardent feminist—made the point some years ago. While granting that Mary's role in the incarnation indeed involved "obedience, trustfulness, and fidelity," it would not, he considered,

> be accurate to describe it as passive, at any rate in the sense which that word usually bears today. It was an act of the most emphatically positive kind, requiring determination, courage and burning self-dedication.[3]

Precisely. And if Jesus was truly human, these aspects of Mary's person—determination, courage, self-dedication—cannot be irrelevant to the person of her son. Our humanity—the particular humanity of each human individual—is shaped by those with whom we have our closest and most significant experiences of being human: that is how human beings become the people that they are. For Jesus, that experience was no doubt to some extent with Joseph. But above all, it has to have been with his mother: hers the first face he knew, the first voice he heard, the first smile he saw.[4] Luke even gives us a glimpse of how the evolution of that relationship was remembered. In his account of "Christ at Twelve Years" (as Albert Huck's *Synopsis* calls the episode[5]), he shows us Mary and Joseph wrestling with the problem Jesus offered them as he entered his teenage years and began (like many of that age) to act in ways they did not expect.

John, in his narrative of the marriage at Cana, offers us a further glimpse as to how their relationship was remembered when Jesus had become a man. At this later stage of her life, the mother of Jesus appears as a figure of quiet insight and authority. She turns to her son in a moment of social and domestic crisis and apparently understands perfectly his somewhat cryptic response when others (including commentators ancient and modern) do not seem to understand it at all. Based on that understanding, she is then willing to give instruction to the household—someone else's household!—on how to deal with the domestic and social crisis facing them: instruction which is, in essence, to listen to her son—an instruction which, it seems, they obey without question.[6] The somewhat Dionysian miracle that follows is, as we noted in our discussion of the passage, virtually backed into the narrative. Clearly, it is not the center of interest. What *is* of interest to the evangelist is that, by this beginning of signs, Jesus has "manifested his glory" and his disciples have "believed in him."[7] Mary, however, needed no such sign; as her actions have made clear, she already believed in her son.

It is, of course, John alone who also presents the mother of Jesus at the cross. Here, she is surely *mater dolorosa*, as the hymn has it, but still a figure of quiet authority to whose care the beloved disciple is commended even as she is commended to his.[8]

All this, though in no way dependent on or even directly connected with the traditions that Luke preserves, is nonetheless entirely consistent with Luke's own final reference to Mary in Acts, praying with the band of Jesus' followers and receiving with them the blessing of the Holy Spirit.[9]

There remains what might be considered the elephant-in-the-room, which for some is a—or even *the*—major question. Did the early Christians remember Mary as the *virgin* mother of Jesus? Clearly, this was not an element in early public Christian proclamation, so far as we can reconstruct it[10]—nor, it seems to me, given its nature as a claim deeply personal to his mother and her family, would we have expected it to be.[11] The heart and center of the church's public proclamation from the beginning was the life, death and resurrection of Jesus Christ the Son of God. Every strand of the New Testament makes this clear. All of which is, again, exactly as we should expect it to be.

What then of the claim that Jesus was conceived illegitimately? Granted agreement that Joseph was not Jesus' biological father, the theory that Jesus was conceived illegitimately stands in relation to belief in the Virginal Conception somewhat as the theory that the disciples stole

Jesus' body stands to belief in the Resurrection. Each is the obvious, non-miraculous, common-sense explanation of what is otherwise a miracle. Each, in its origins, seems to have been proposed by those who were opposed to Christianity.[12] That granted, we should note that the parallel is also *in*exact, since the Resurrection is fundamental to Christian faith as all mainline Christianity—Eastern or Western; Roman Catholic, Protestant or Anglican—has received it. As Paul said, "if Christ has not been raised, then our proclamation has been in vain, and your faith has been in vain." He said no such thing of the Virginal Conception—indeed, there is no clear evidence that he even knew of the tradition, although as we have noted, there is no clear evidence that he did not, and such knowledge *may* lie behind his choice of wording at Galatians 4.4 as well as his (admittedly obscure) remarks at 1 Corinthians 11.11-12.[13]

What is clear is that in the seventies and eighties of the first Christian century, when the witnesses, including those who actually knew Mary of Nazareth, will have been beginning to die—at that point, there appeared in the so-called "birth narratives" of Matthew and Luke two rather striking witnesses to the strange tradition of Mary as *virgin* mother.[14] Subsequently, as we have noted, we have a perhaps deliberately indirect witness in the gospel of John, together with what appears to be a virtually immediate and universal acceptance of the tradition of virgin birth by the early church: facts that in themselves seem to imply an origin deeper in the church's genes than merely Matthew's and Luke's witness in the eighties. I referred earlier to Jane Schaberg's suggestion that the most likely origin of nativity traditions about Jesus is in his own family, a suggestion that appears to me ever more likely to be correct.[15]

The alternative narrative sometimes suggested—that virginal conception was a story created by Christians to defend against the allegation that Jesus was illegitimate—may, I think, be safely dismissed. There was, after all, a much more obvious way for

Christians to deny such an allegation. They had only to point out that *Joseph had accepted Jesus as his own*, and "if a man says this is my son, he is believed" (*Mishnah Bavra Batra* 8.6). The suggestion that, instead of appealing to this, Christians chose to *invent* a story of virginal conception is unlikely, if not absurd. One does not effectively defend oneself against a charge that is plausible by devising a story that is by all normal standards impossible.

So much we may reasonably say of the church's recollections of Mary in her lifetime. Of course, they do not constitute material from which we might create a "life," an account of "the Mary of history." We can claim no more than that we have glimpses of her—"fleeting" glimpses, as Gaventa puts it. But though such glimpses are not enough to lead to an account of her "life and times," they do amount to a picture. Not a detailed photograph, nor even a careful portrait in oils, but at least, let us say, a vivid sketch. Taken together, the witnesses leave us with an *impression*, and we may by no means assume that such an impression tells us nothing of Mary as she actually was. If we thought that, there would be no point in calling witnesses in a court of law.

Moreover, regardless of the precise historical accuracy of any particular word or deed that our witnesses ascribe to her, taken all together—and at this point I mean "all," even the Revelation to John, which evidently makes no claim whatever to tell us about "the Mary of history"—taken all together, even despite themselves, our witnesses tell us two things that may hardly be disputed. They tell us that Mary made an impression. In a society where women, virtually by definition, were expected—and even generally assumed—to make little impression, she was actually *remembered*. For the proclamation of the gospel there was, as is evident from our records, no need for her to have been remembered at all, otherwise than as a cypher—the woman who played a necessary role in the Word being made flesh, born of a woman. Yet she *was* remembered, as a woman and even as an individual. Perhaps even more striking, they tell us that apparently she achieved this without trying for any such thing; while walking, by all accounts willingly and faithfully, entirely in the shadow of her Son.

POSTSCRIPT

THE CONTINUING SIGNIFICANCE OF MARY FOR CHRISTIANS IN THE TWENTY-FIRST CENTURY

When I was a very young curate in the parish of St Mark's, Reigate, in Surrey, I remember Leslie Stemp, the retired barrister in whose house I had the privilege of lodging, finding himself in argument at the front door with a somewhat rabid objector to anything that smacked of what the objector called "Mariolatry." I still recall the sound of their voices.

"I don't see any difference between the Virgin Mary and my mother!" the objector declared fiercely.

Mr Stemp nodded.

"I see," he said. Then, after a brief pause, dryly, "I suppose you would be prepared to concede a certain difference in their sons?"

That, of course, is precisely the point. Jesus is only once called "son of Mary" in the gospel tradition, and Paul's comment about her is brief and indirect.[1] Yet already, each in its own way indicates something that is true of every other element of Marian teaching that we find in the New Testament and every valid element that we find subsequently in the life of the church: which is that they are all necessarily tied to Christology. What we understand of Jesus affects our understanding of Mary. The significance of Jesus requires—indeed, demands—a special significance for his mother. In Kyriaki Karidoyanes FitzGerald's words, Mary is honored "not in isolation but because of her intimate relationship to Christ, the God who became human. . . . Her title, 'Theotokos,' points us to Christ."[2] Thus, at the Council of Ephesus (431) and subsequently the Council of Chalcedon (451), the very title "*theotokos*"—"God Bearer" or "Mother of God"—was affirmed of her, not as a teaching about Mary herself, but as an element of Christology—indeed, an essential element.[3]

God the Word in Jesus Christ became human. As a human being, Jesus knew growth, joy, suffering, death, resurrection and exaltation. And through it all, he remained human and remains human, even exalted to the right hand of the Father. That is Christian and Catholic orthodoxy, Eastern and Western, Anglican, Protestant and Roman Catholic. And just as all humanity without exception is the humanity of our mothers, so Jesus' humanity is the humanity of Mary. As E. L. Mascall put it, "the Holy Ghost made Mary a mother in the fullest physical sense, for it was in her womb, not in the cradle at Bethlehem, that the Word became flesh."[4] And simply in the natural order of things it will have been above all in relationship to her—her looks, her touch, her voice, her manners and values—that the Word-become-flesh became a boy, a youth, a man, growing "in wisdom and in stature," as the evangelist says.

The union of God and humankind in Mary's son provided—and provides—the essential ground for later convictions surrounding the degree to which—while, like all of us, dependent for her salvation upon "God my Savior" who has "looked with favor on the lowliness of his slave"—Mary is seen nonetheless as *uniquely* blessed by that favor.[5] So Christian imagination, working upon what was remembered of her in the Scriptures, seems naturally to have concluded from quite early times that every part of her earthly life should be celebrated, so that alongside festival celebrations of events described in Scripture—her Annunciation (March 25th), her Visit to Elizabeth (May 31st), the Nativity of her son (25th December) and the Presentation of him in the Temple (February 2nd)—it would also celebrate the blessedness and grace that will surely have surrounded other events in her life, such as her conception (December 8th), her nativity (September 8--nine months later, naturally) and her dormition or "falling asleep" (August 15th). These celebrations long preceded—and evidently long managed very well without—the dogmatic assertions and counter-assertions regarding her Immaculate Conception[6] and Assumption[7] (much later and invariably Western) that have come to be associated with them.[8] Presumably, those who instigated these early celebrations were quite well aware that the particular occasions of grace they commemorated were not directly mentioned in Scripture—as was, of course, also true of *homoousion* and *theotokos*. Presumably, however, they also thought that, as with *homoousion* and *theotokos*, they followed from Scripture.

Thus, apropos Mary's conception, Scripture told them that Gabriel called Mary *kecharitōmenē*, "highly favored," or "endowed with grace,"[9] and went on to say that she had "found favor with God" even *before* she had received the angelic message that she was to become the mother of God's son and given her assent to that. Surely mere common sense will have suggested that such grace as fitted Mary for such a role must have been extraordinary?—equal at the very least to that which for the rest of us is granted only through baptism into her son?[10] Are these perhaps notions at which the Fourth Evangelist was hinting in his reference at John 1.12-13 to an evidently spiritualized "virginal conception" that according to him characterizes *all* God's children?

As to the end of Mary's earthly life, while there is no direct testimony to that in the New Testament, the Scriptures as a whole certainly presented our forebears with other instances of those who had followed God faithfully, such as Enoch and Elijah, being drawn at once into the divine presence.[11] Given Mary's unique closeness to and involvement in God's purposes, how could Christians possibly have supposed that she would have experienced anything less? Or that she, too, will not at once have been "promoted to glory" (as our Salvation Army Friends splendidly express the Christian hope)? And indeed, they claimed nothing more thereby than that it was given her to experience at once that which in God's purposes is the true destiny of us all: to be "partaker of the divine nature."[12]

Strange though it may seem, it has been my consideration of the tradition of Jesus' illegitimacy, and even that Mary had been the victim of rape, that has led me to reflect more carefully on what actually might be meant by notions of Mary's perpetual virginity and even her freedom from sin. It is, in my experience, only too easy for piously intended but ill-considered reflection on these things to devalue our own mothers, and all women who are mothers in the usual way.[13] Indeed, I find such reflections can come dangerously close to equating divinely created and divinely blessed gifts of sexual desire and erotic delight with sin. In other words—Manicheism alive and well, only disguised as Catholic devotion![14] Kyriaki Karidoyanes FitzGerald (who firmly holds to belief in the virginal conception of Jesus as historical and that Mary had no other children) provides a healthy corrective.

> The Greek word *parthenia*, virginity, much like the term *Theotokos*, points to more in Greek than the English translation sometimes indicates. Numerous writings of the early desert ascetics reveal to us that the meaning of virginity (*parthenia*), while it certainly includes the keeping of physical chastity, implies something more. This refers to a dynamic process focusing upon purity of heart. Purity of heart may be quickly identified as a kind of unconditional integrity in the presence of the living God. It was the goal of the early ascetics to conquer their selfish desires and develop a pure heart before God.

> This is expressed in the words of the Psalm, "Create in me a clean heart, O God, and renew a right spirit within me" (LXX Ps. 50, MT 51). The title *aierparthenos* (ever a virgin) invites us to reflect deeply on Mary's inner state of integrity before God.[15]

Real *parthenia* is then much as Paul said of "real circumcision": "a matter of the heart—it is spiritual and not literal. Such a person receives praise not from others but from God" (Rom. 2.29). As William S. Stafford has reminded us,

> Outside of Eden, not all are called to human marriage. Yet the marriage of the incarnation is one to which everyone is called, the Beloved who seeks everyone, and is the end of all seeking.[16]

As for "sinlessness"—surely a difficult notion for sinners to grasp at all, if not impossible—Robert Jenson offers an interesting suggestion:

> Jesus' sinlessness is best understood as his unbroken faithfulness to his calling, a faithfulness identical with his reality as the second identity of God. May we say that Mary analogously was at no juncture unfaithful to her calling as Mother of God and archprophet? The anticipation of purpose, by which any human life occurs, was in her case and the case of this purpose unbrokenly coherent. Christ's human will . . . might have broken in Gethsemane or elsewhere; the fact that it did not is the same fact as that his human identity is the second identity of God. May we interpret Mary's assent to the angel's message analogously? And as itself constituting her sinlessness?[17]

To that I would only presume to add—"by whatever means the angel's message may have come to her."

All in all, we are speaking of what Israel's Scriptures called *lev tahor* and the greatest of Welsh hymns calls *calon lân*—a pure heart:

Calon onest, calon lân.
  Calon lân yn llawn daioni.
An honest heart, a pure heart.
  A pure heart full of goodness.

This, it seems, we may all perceive in the grace that filled Mary, regardless of our view of the particular events that may have made up her life.

I have referred in these reflections to Robert Jenson's assertion that, "if one takes John 1 as what it is . . . and inserts Mary explicitly into her place in the story, the Marian doctrines immediately result."[18] In my view, that assertion is correct and even inevitable. It is inevitable, because it is through her freely given response to God's call that God chooses in her womb to become *sarx*—flesh, the stuff of humanity and creation—uniting *sarx* with God's own self in order to redeem *sarx*. And we mean *freely* given response. If the story of the annunciation to Mary is about anything at all, if it is not simply the account of a largely meaningless ritual, then at its heart lies the fact that Our Lady was free. She could have said, "No!" And for whatever time we imagine between the angelic salutation and her response (perhaps the merest fraction of a second), Heaven permitted its own purposes to hang in the balance. Hence she is named at exactly that point in the Apostles and Nicene creeds where the union of God and creation is directly confessed. Christians either, by the "I believe" of the Apostles Creed, confess their *individual* faith in Jesus Christ,

[God's] only son, our Lord,
who was conceived by the Holy Spirit,
born of the Virgin Mary[19]

or else, by the "We believe" of the Nicene Confession, they declare *with the whole church* that the same Lord Jesus is,

the only Son of God,
eternally begotten of the Father,
God from God, Light from Light,
true God from true God,
begotten, not made,
of one Being with the Father.
Through him all things were made.
For us and for our salvation
he came down from heaven:
by the power of the Holy Spirit
he became incarnate from the Virgin Mary,
and was made man.[20]

In both symbols, Mary alone stands at the nexus between God and creation, thereby at that point and in her own person representing all that stood and stands in need of redemption: herself, her people Israel, humankind, and the entire created order—the very insights as to her role in the drama of salvation that we saw reflected in the seer's visions of "a woman crowned with the stars" at Revelation 12. Her claim of "lowliness" and her claim to be a "slave" both speak of her standing before God. As such, they are claims with which every single one of us can and must identify.

These were the truths that the Council of Ephesus grasped and affirmed in 431. No one could pretend that the processes—the debates and politicking—that led to their affirmations were pretty. They were not,[21] any more than were those processes that led to the formulation of the *homoousion*. In both cases, however—as, indeed, throughout the whole history of the people of God as we encounter it in the Scriptures of Israel, the New Testament, and the subsequent story of the Church—God may be understood to have worked through human confusion and even through human sinfulness, enabling that confusion and sinfulness somehow to say what needed to be said. When was it ever true that the business of discerning God's purposes through the morass that is human experience and history was anything but chaotic?

When we have considered and celebrated Mary's role in the drama of salvation through Jesus Christ her son, there remains, however, at least for those brought up in the Christian tradition that nurtured me, a second and direct role for her in relation to us now. *Sancta Maria, Mater Dei, ora pro nobis. Holy Mary, Mother of God, pray for us.* So I was taught to ask for Mary's prayers. And of course that leads in time to a question—a good *Reformation* question!—do we actually *need* anyone other than Christ to pray for us?[22] Do we need someone beside Jesus to be our "intercessor" and "friend of sinners" as the hymn has it? And the answer, once the question is put like that, is obvious. No, of course we do not need anyone else. For, as Paul said,

> If God be for us, who can be against us? ... For I am convinced that neither death, nor life, nor angels, nor rulers, nor things present, nor things to come, nor powers, nor height, nor depth, nor anything else in all creation, will be able to separate us from the love of God in Christ Jesus our Lord.[23]

Certainly nothing more is necessary than that. But then—the irrelevance of that particular objection to our seeking Mary's prayers—or, indeed, the prayers of anyone—is immediately obvious too: and from the same source. For, as Paul draws his letter to a close, he unapologetically asks for "prayers to God on my behalf" from those same Christians to whom he has just written of the all-sufficing love of God in Christ![24] And why not? For whenever did God limit God's gifts to what was *necessary*? Our God is a God of cornucopia. When God prepares my cup, it "overflows." When God gives me a measure, it is "good measure, pressed down, shaken together, and running over." So of course, though more is not necessary, *more is given*. What we are given is what the Apostles Creed calls *communio sanctorum:* the communion or fellowship of the saints.[25] The Scriptures themselves tell us that, from the beginning, apostles and the apostolic faithful prayed for each other and asked and expected others to pray for them.[26] And though, of course, those apostles are long departed this earthly life, we the living still worship and pray in communion with them, "with angels and archangels and with all the company of heaven," as the old Book of Common Prayer had it, precisely because, as Paul said, nothing—including death—can separate us from the love of God in Christ Jesus. So, what could be more obvious and natural than to be taught—as I certainly was from the beginning of my life in the church—that we should continue to ask them to pray for us?—and especially to ask the prayers of her whom the author of Revelation saw crowned with stars, *Regina Caelorum*; who was yet also, from our very earliest descriptions of the church after the resurrection, modestly content simply to be with her fellow disciples in the upper room, "constantly at prayer"?

Now, of course—seventy years later!—I would go further. I would argue that it is the *particular* role of prophets to intercede for God's people, and Mary is surely the arch prophet, who brought the Word of God to us not merely upon her tongue, but in her own flesh. Robert Jenson summed up the matter with his usual precision:

> Mary is the type of the church in that the church is the prophetic community. The Word of the Lord comes

> archetypically to Mary, and what she thereupon brings forth, in the very way of the prophets' forth bringing, is the Word in person: 'The Word became flesh and dwelt among us.' Mary is the arch prophet, the paradigmatic instantiation of the church's prophetic reality.[27]

When therefore we invoke Mary's intercession, we are doing something more than requesting the prayers of a fellow saint, important though such requests are. Mary is not just a fellow saint. She is the mother of Jesus. That is why it is normal in the liturgy, when she is named in company with other saints, that we name her first.

What, then, shall be my own last word as I reflect on my heroine (for that is what she has become for me in the course of these reflections)?

Whatever Mary is, she is by God's grace, and by that grace God chose to work through her the greatest of all miracles: the union of God and humankind.[28] That is the unvarnished testimony of Christian Scripture: "so the Word became flesh and dwelt among us."

In a society that valued the male, God chose to work this miracle through a female.

In a society that valued old age and seniority, God chose to work it through a girl.

In a society that expected girls to be submissive and obedient to males, God chose a girl feisty enough to argue with an archangel when what it was saying didn't seem to her to make any sense, and then adventurous enough on the basis of the archangel's word to undertake a 160 kilometer journey over rough country, apparently unaccompanied by her male kin.

In a society that valued rank and priesthood, God chose to work this greatest of miracles through someone who, simply in virtue of being a young and female, didn't have much of either.

It is true—I almost omitted to mention it!—that Mary did possess one fragment of earthly status. Through her affianced husband Joseph she had a connection to the house of David; and Joseph was a righteous man and a craftsman and thereby, we may reasonably suppose, also a person of some standing in his own small community.

But then, in that same righteousness, dear Joseph very nearly blew the whole thing and had to be stopped in his tracks by an angel.

I find all that both amusing and delightful.

And I rather think that God does too.

APPENDIX A

ACCORDING TO LUKE, WHO SAYS THE MAGNIFICAT? AND DID THE EVANGELIST TAKE THE TEXT FROM A SOURCE?

According to all Greek witnesses and almost all versional and patristic witnesses, Luke attributes the *Magnificat* to Mary. Why, then, is there any question about the matter? Because a very few other witnesses—mostly, but not quite all, Latin—attribute it or possibly attribute it to Elizabeth.[1] Which group represents Luke's intention? There has been debate about this since 1897, which saw the publication of a sermon by Nicetas, fifth-century Bishop of Remesiana, in which he attributed the *Magnificat* to Elizabeth.[2] In the same year, a paper appeared in reaction by Alfred Loisy (writing under the pseudonym François Jacobé).[3] Loisy thought that the content of the Magnificat was actually more appropriate to Elizabeth than to Mary: "The content ... of the canticle has nothing that is personal to Mary.... The Magnificat is only a copy of the song of Hannah, Samuel's mother. Does not Elisabeth's situation have more analogy with that of Hannah than Mary's? [Le contenu... du cantique n'a rien qui soit personnel a Marie.... le Magnificat n'est qu'un décalque du cantique d'Anne, mère de Samuel. La situation d'Elisabeth n'a-t-elle pas plus d'analogie avec celle d'Anne que celle de Marie?]"[4] He also suggested that both the

Magnificat and *Benedictus* were in fact rather loosely attached to their present context: they "look a little like pieces inserted into the story, where they are only partly framed [ont un peu l'air des pièces rapportées dans le récit, où ils ne sont qu'à moitié encadrés]."[5] He came, however, to no conclusions as a result of these reflections beyond saying that ascertaining Luke's intention was a problem that needed to be addressed.[6]

Later discussions have picked up on Loisy's uncertainties without, perhaps, sharing his caution. John Martin Creed considered apropos Luke 1.46 that "despite the support of all Greek MSS. and almost all versions, the conclusion should probably be drawn that Μαριάμ is not original," and suggested that Elizabeth's position was closer to Hannah's than was Mary's, so making the *Magnificat* more appropriate in her mouth than Mary's (*Luke* 22). Paul Winter went further and found the *Magnificat* to be unconnected, "even in the mouth of Elishebha (sic)," but was, nevertheless, overall of the opinion "that the Third Evangelist intended his readers to understand that the Magnificat was spoken by the mother of John."[7] Benko, following a lengthy survey of the debate, suggested a "popular desire which sought to give Jesus higher honors than John, and Mary than Elizabeth," in which frame of mind "one would naturally think of Mary when reading the words: '. . . henceforth all generations will call me blessed; for he who is mighty has done great things for me. . . .'" Thus, in Benko's view, "it came to pass that a Jewish hymn of praise, first adopted as a song of Elizabeth, the mother of John, was quickly attributed to Mary, the mother of the Christ."[8]

What, then, do these commentators imagine was the *origin* of the *Magnificat*? Winter suggested that it and the *Benedictus* had their origin among the Maccabees:

> It is most likely that both the Magnificat and the first part of the Benedictus which speak of past manifestations

> of God's power and God's mercy toward Israel, which speak of salvation as an event known to have happened in the past… not as one awaiting the speaker in future, were written by some Jewish poet who wished to express gratitude for the help God had given in the struggle against the Syro-Macedonian armies.[9]

Even scholars such as Raymond Brown, who continue to follow the main text tradition and attribute the *Magnificat* to Mary in Luke's intention, nonetheless see it as stemming from a source. Brown considered its past tense significant and suggested a Jewish-Christian community of Anawim or Poor Ones, since they would have been in a position to celebrate the whole event of Christ.[10] Fitzmyer largely follows Brown.[11] Similarly, Evans, who notes, however, that this hypothesis does not "get rid of the artificiality" of the connections between the hymn and Mary's situation.[12] Bovon, by contrast, refers the aorists to God's action in creation and history, and places the hymn's origin in the Pharisaic movement.[13]

Clearly, many share Loisy's questions, if not his caution. But there is no consensus at all as to how those questions should be answered.

For my own view, as regards Luke's *intention* with regard to the speaker of the *Magnificat*, suffice it to say that, with the UBS Committee, I consider the weight of the external evidence overwhelming. To set that witness aside, as did Winter and others, for the sake of "half a dozen witnesses, chiefly Latin" is preposterous. Luke's intended subject of εἶπεν was Μαριάμ, and he intended the *Magnificat* to be regarded as hers.[14]

As for *origins* of the *Magnificat*, Luke Timothy Johnson has, I think, shown us the path we ought to follow: the *Magnificat* is Luke's composition and shows us "an important aspect of Luke's own compositional technique."[15] As I noted in my main text, it is, as are *Benedictus* and *Nunc Dimittis*, an example of what ancient rhetoricians and grammarians would have called *prosōpopoiía*: forms of composition not intended to be regarded as verbatim reports of what was said on particular occasions but rather what the individuals concerned will have intended and would have said had they had leisure for composition and the narrator's skills in that art.[16] There is nothing un-Lukan about the style of this particular example of *prosōpopoiía* and, granted that Luke obviously enjoyed imitating the Septuagint and was rather good at it, the alleged "disconnect" of both hymns from their present contexts has been, to say the least, vastly overstated (as, at least with regard to the *Magnificat*, I believe I have demonstrated in my main text). Quite evidently, Luke was influenced by the Song of Hannah in his composition of the *Magnificat*. Beyond that, arguments put forward as to why we should seek further sources for either the *Magnificat* or *Benedictus* are far from compelling.

APPENDIX B

IS MARY TO BE REGARDED AS A VIRGIN MOTHER, OR WAS SHE A VICTIM OF RAPE? THE QUESTION AS IT HAS BEEN POSED IN THE TWENTIETH AND TWENTY-FIRST CENTURIES.

The situation is markedly changed from that of the early church wherein, as we have seen, rejection of the virginal conception seems largely to come from those who are opposed to Christianity. In the twentieth and twenty-first centuries, there are certainly those who are by no means opposed to Christianity—who would, indeed, regard themselves as profoundly committed Christians—by whom the notion of a virginal conception is either outright denied on theological or even moral grounds, or else regarded as, at most, an optional extra.

Jane Schaberg, a Roman Catholic, is clear that, while she retains her Christian faith, she rejects the virgin birth either as history or even as theologoumenon. In conversation with the Jesus Seminar, she declared that in her view it was a deeply anti-sexual notion that made neither human nor theological sense. Even if it is "in the text" of the infancy narratives, she could not believe that it was historical, and she did not even want it to be, which meant that she felt "no need to defend or fear a church that thinks of it as such."[1] One has the impression that, for Schaberg, far from manifesting a desire to undermine Christian faith, witnessing to Mary's experience as Schaberg believes it to have been is at once to honor Mary and her Son and also to stand in solidarity with those many women throughout history who have been victimized and brutalized.

Protestant theologians such as Emil Brunner and Wolfhart Pannenberg rejected virginal conception precisely because, in their view, it *contradicts* the notion of incarnation.[2] More recently another Protestant, Kyle Roberts, contrasts the first-century understanding of conception, in which there was nothing inherently contradictory in the notion that the *mechanism* of the incarnation was a virginal conception, with the modern understanding of how conception works, whereby sperm meets egg, fertilization leads to life, and both male and female are required to make a true human. This means, in Robert's view, that the virginal conception isn't just a miracle, but something that undermines the meaning of the incarnation itself. It works *against* the idea.[3]

But does it? There are assumptions inherent in these views that are evidently open to question.

Obviously no single human being can share every possible human experience or characteristic—race, sex, sexual orientation and so on. On what basis, then, do we assume that the *sine qua non* for true humanity must involve being conceived according to what we know as the normal generative process? For those at all sensitive to the biblical salvation history (*Heilsgeschichte*), an immediate and obvious objection to such an assumption must be that if we accept it, then we can regard neither Adam nor Eve as truly human, since evidently neither was conceived by such a process. But then, the premise once granted, neither can their children be regarded as human—any of them. So, pursuing the logic of this claim, we are left—*reductio ad absurdum*—with the inevitable conclusion that there have *never* been any human beings.

Even leaving aside such logical absurdities, and simply accepting that human beings *do* exist and do normally come into existence in the same way, i.e., as a result of sexual intercourse, should we then accept that sexual intercourse must therefore be the "one thing necessary" for true humanity? Personally, I doubt it. Sara Maitland in *A Big-Enough God* makes the point nicely (in both senses of the word "nicely"): debating with a group of male clergy on the virginity of Mary, something which for some reason "they felt it important to deny," the debate devolved into this:

> [T]hey wanted Mary not to be a virgin so that Jesus could come into the world 'just like them', could be born in 'the usual way'. This seemed to me to open a whole new can of worms. I feel there is something deeply sexist about all this, since from the point of view of women Jesus did indeed get born in exactly the usual way—down a woman's vagina and out between a woman's legs just like everyone else. The only difference being that maleness was made redundant in this myth. Was it this that they found intolerable?[4]

Perhaps it was! And in any case, Archbishop Rowan Williams surely makes the essential point:

> If Jesus is *perceived* as human, enters into the lives of other human beings as human, shares fully what a human psychology and physiology are open to, including pain, subjective doubt or uncertainty and ignorance about contingent matters of fact, and exists as an embodied person whose corporeal reality is exactly the same in

> character as our own, what does the natural generative process add to a claim that Jesus shares our nature in every respect of significance? It is obviously impossible for Jesus to share every *possible* human condition. … the difficult question is whether sharing the characteristic of having been born as the result of sexual intercourse, or at least (with modern biotechnology suggesting a refinement of this) of the fertilization of an ovum by a sperm provided by a male, is essential to any claim about sharing human nature.[5]

Precisely. Traditional theology has associated the incarnation with God's will for the deification of humankind and, indeed, of the whole creation. It has also very clearly distinguished its *acknowledgment* of that divine will from any presumption to claim that it *understood the nature of that union* or *how God might bring it about*.[6] There is absolutely no reason to suppose—and, indeed, there seem to be rather a lot of good reasons *not* to suppose—that in respect of the conception of Jesus, this distinction between what we believe we may glimpse of God's *purposes* and what we can know as to *how God may bring them about* has been shown to be mistaken or untenable. Moreover, we must surely beware of assuming that *any* particular feature of our being that we can identify is also a criterion by which we may establish who is or is not human. The dangers of such an assumption are evident throughout human history. Racism, xenophobia, antisemitism, slavery, sexism, islamophobia, and homophobia are all examples of precisely this kind of assumption, and their fruits are evidence of the poison that they bring.

Indeed, our own science already points us to another way in which the question may well face us. Dolly the sheep was cloned: she had neither male nor female parent. Yet no one, so far as I know, ever suggested that Dolly, in all evident respects a perfectly normal sheep who became the mother of numerous perfectly normal lambs, was not a sheep. That a human being could be cloned even as Dolly was cloned is—regardless of the morality of such a proceeding, which I do not presume here to discuss—virtually a certainty, and I have little doubt that at some point someone will do it. Will we deny that person's humanity, even though they speak, think, feel, and even fall in love just as the rest of us do? The suggestion that Jesus cannot really have been human if he did not have a human father because he was "not like" the rest of us who were "born in the usual way" seems to suggest that we will. And I fear we may.[7]

Some, while regarding Jesus' virginal conception as unhistorical, retain acceptance of it as theologoumenon. That's the view of Marianne Sawicki, also a Roman Catholic, who builds on archaeological field work in Israel in the 1990s and a wide knowledge of anthropology, as well as on sensitive study of Christian tradition. Sawicki suggests that Mary may have been raped *prior* to her engagement to Joseph—an engagement which would not have been the original intention of her family, who would have intended her to be the bride of a priest. A girl who was raped, however, would lose her high caste marriageability. Supposing that Mary found herself a victim in, say, Sepphoris, when it was seized by Roman soldiers in 4 BCE, then the direction of her life will have been irretrievably changed. Sawicki's reflection on this is powerful:

> Christian belief in Mary's free assent to a divine invitation would not be overturned, but it would have to be directed toward an even more courageous decision on her part. Not an archangel but an enemy soldier would then be the one to deliver the news to Mary that her future was to be quite different from that which she had planned. The assent that the Almighty asked of Mary was her decision to go on living, to survive rather than taking her own life after realizing that she had lost eligibility to become a mother in a legitimate Israelite lineage. She chose not

> to prevent the birth of an out-caste child in her father's house.... Joseph was the solution to the problem of Mary's pregnancy, from her family's point of view. Joseph was the family's second choice but God's first choice, we may surmise, and Joseph made his own courageous assent to this proposal. (*Crossing Galilee* 192-93: cf. the whole passage, 192-93).

A number of prominent Roman Catholic theologians—among them Hans Kung, Richard McBrien and Edward Schillebeeckx—while not necessarily subscribing to the view that Mary was raped—appear likewise to subscribe to the view that the virgin birth is theologoumenon rather than history.[8] The ecumenical group responsible for the papers that made up *Mary in the New Testament: A Collaborative Assessment by Protestant and Roman Catholic Scholars*, which included Raymond Brown as a joint editor, while in agreement that the NT narratives told of virginal conception, were also agreed that it was impossible to categorize it as "historical" by the usual methods and criteria of historical research, and that individuals' decisions to consider the virginal conception historical fact or theologoumenon must finally depend on their attitude toward the church's tradition.[9] Historical-critical method can only take us so far.

Indeed that is true. Historical-critical method *can* only take us so far. But that, of course, is a double-edged sword. It is evident that notions such as Schaberg's or Sawicki's of a natural pregnancy that was uniquely used or imbued or inspired by the Holy Spirit make it possible for some to believe in the incarnation who otherwise could not or would not believe—and, as a Christian, surely I rejoice in that. Indeed, I think I can understand why a miracle that seems to remain within the confines of normal experience—in this case, that conception normally follows sexual intercourse between a woman and a man—is easier to accept than one that bursts such boundaries. All that granted, however, from a strictly theological or philosophical viewpoint, I cannot see that anything of any great significance has been achieved. Even if the virginal conception *is* theologoumenon, still, that leaves us, in the conception and birth of Jesus of Nazareth, with the notion of a unique inspiration by the Holy Spirit, such inspiration being an act of God. In this we either believe or do not believe, but with regard to it, so far as I can see, historical-critical method can have nothing to say.

ENDNOTES

Prologue

1. "Gherardo delle Notti," that is, "Gerard of the nights," the name by which the Dutch painter Gerard van Honthorst (Dutch: *Gerrit van Honthorst*) (4 November 1592–27 April 1656) became known in Italy as a result of his skill in painting scenes that were lit from within.
2. Gaventa, *Mary: Glimpses of the Mother of Jesus* 100.
3. Fiorenza, *In Memory of Her* 45.
4. Gal. 4.4; Mark 3.20-35, 6.3; Matt. 1.18-25; 2.11, 13-14, 19-21; 12.46-50; Luke 1.26-56; 2.1-52; 8.19-21, Acts 1.14; John 2.1-12, 19.25-27.
5. Rev. 12.5 citing Ps. 2.9.
6. M. Eugene Boring, *Revelation* 152; cf. Ian Boxall, "Who is the Woman clothed with the Sun?" 144-45.
7. Simon Gathercole, *The Gospel and the Gospels* (Grand Rapids, Michigan: Eerdmans, 2022). In my opinion, *Gospel and the Gospels* is the most important single work of New Testament scholarship to be published since Burridge's *What are the Gospels* was published in 1992.
8. Gathercole, *Gospel and Gospels* 502. The essential point regarding the unviersality of the Pauline kerygma was made as early as C. H. Dodd's *The Apostolic Preaching and Its Developments: three lectures with an appendix on eschatology and history* (London: Hodder and Stoughton, 1936)—still valuable reading after nearly a century!
9. An example of the kind of thing to which I am referring is Robert J. Miller, ed., *The Complete Gospels* (HarperSanFrancisco, 1992).
10. John P. Meier, *A Marginal Jew: Re-Thinking the Historical Jesus* (New York: Doubleday, 1991) 113; Meier's discussion of the *agrapha* and apocryphal gospels (112-141) is still worth reading.
11. Common Latin renderings of Θεοτόκος are *Mater Dei* and/or *Dei Genitrix*; common in English are "God-bearer" or "Mother of God"—none of them perfect or without problems. but none, it seems, without sticking power.
12. Jenson, *Systematic Theology* 2.204.

1. Paul

1. Proverbs 8.27-31; cf. J. B. Lightfoot, *Galatians* 168; de Witt Burton, *Galatians* 216-17; Frank J. Matera, *Galatians* 150. Matera's caution in this respect—"the pre-existence of Christ… is *probably* implied" (my emphasis)—is in my view unnecessary, as is his insistence that Paul's expressions at 4.4, though "entirely harmonious with the idea of personal pre-existence… can also be read apart from that idea" (407, n.62).
2. Judges 13.3-24.
3. I am aware of commentators' objections to such a description of the passage. Thus Boring declares that Jesus "is not bested in an argument, does not 'capitulate,' but, like God does reverse a previous decision." Yet Boring also concedes that in her dialogue with Jesus, the woman,

> does not merely acquiesce… but like Abraham, Moses, Job, and the biblical psalmists, argues with the Lord. She does not dispute the priority of Israel, but relativizes the diachronic scheme of "first to the Jews, then to the Greeks" by positing a synchronic alternative or supplement to it: the "dogs" do not *only* have to wait to be fed later ("not yet") but *also* receive the overflow ("crumbs") of the messianic extravagance even now ("already"). (*Mark: A Commentary* 214)

Following this,

> Jesus reverses his original response and acts *on the basis of what the woman has said.* (Ibid, my emphasis).

I find Boring's careful analysis here both apt and insightful. But that does not alter the fact that he appears to me to have described, with admirable precision and care, something that in any other connection I would have referred to as being "bested in an argument"!
4. Mark 7.24-30, 14.1-9.
5. "Of the 1,426 people given names in the Hebrew scriptures, only 111 of them are female. The proportion is twice as great in the New Testament, but there, in contrast to Andrew, James, John, and Judas, we meet the Samaritan woman, the Canaanite woman, the widow of Nain." (Coffey, *Hidden Women of the Gospels* 13).
6. Paul even, at Romans 16.7, speaks of a woman, Junia, as "apostle" in service of the gospel; see C. E. B. Cranfield, *Romans* 2.788-790; James D. G. Dunn,

Romans 2.894; Joseph A. Fitzmyer, S.J., *Romans* 737-38; Arland J. Hultgren, *Romans* 574-75; Eldon J. Epp, *Junia: The First Woman Apostle* passim. Allegations that there is confusion or uncertainty about Paul's meaning (such as the suggestion that by "of note among [ἐπίσημοι ἐν]" he meant "known to") are in my view ill-founded: "Junia" is a common woman's name, whereas there is no evidence at all of a male name "Junia," or of a male apostle with that name. Some ancient texts do, indeed, offer a variant reading at 16.7, "Julia": but that, of course, is also a woman's name. Modern translations increasingly represent this awareness: e.g., NRSV, NAB, REB, TILC.

7. See Dunn, *Romans 9-16* 900; Cranfield, *Romans* 2.789; Bryan, *Preface to Romans* 229.

8. Philippians 4.2 is especially striking in this respect: Euodia and Syntache are among "the rest of my fellow-workers (τῶν ʿλοιπῶν συνεργῶν μου)" who "shared my struggles (συνήθλησάν μοι)" on behalf of the gospel. Apropos "ἐδηλώθη γάρ μοι... ὑπὸ τῶν Χλόης" (1 Cor. 1.11), some commentators suggest that Chloe herself was not a Christian and compare "ἀσπάσασθε τοὺς ἐκ τῶν Ἀριστοβούλου... ἀσπάσασθε τοὺς ἐκ τῶν Ναρκίσσου τοὺς ὄντας ἐν κυρίῳ" (Rom. 16.10b-11). But the contrast is more marked than the parallel: Paul's omission in Chloe's case of the partitive "ἐκ" suggests that in this case the entire household was Christian, given which, it is scarcely credible that Chloe herself was not among them.

9. Lightfoot, *Galatians* 168; Matera, *Galatians* 150; Martyn, *Galatians* 390.

10. Apropos Job 14.1, Dhorme points to the phrase "יְלוּד אִשָּׁה" parallel to "אֱנוֹשׁ" at Job 15.14, 25.4, and Sir. 10.18, and compares ἐν γεννητοῖς γυναικῶν at Matt. 11.11//Luke 7.28 (*Job* 194).

11. J. R. R. Tolkein uses a form of the same theme in *Lord of the Rings*. The evil Lord of the Nazgûl, also called the Witch-king of Angmar, is defeated and killed by the hobbit Merry Brandybuck and a noblewoman of Rhohann, Éowyn, niece of King Theoden: thus fulfilling the elf-lord Glorfindel's prophecy that that the Lord of the Nazgûl would not die by the hand of man.

12. Gal. 3.16. As Martyn points out, one might be tempted to offer the paraphrase "born a Jew," since Paul knows that Jesus was a Jew and takes that fact seriously: thus, writing to the Roman church, he quotes a formula identifying Christ as "of the seed of David, according to the flesh" (Rom. 1.3; cf. 9.5) (Martyn, *Galatians* 390).

13. ἐξαγοράζω is used in matters of commerce meaning simply "buy," "purchase" or "buy up." It occurs only once in the LXX, at Dan. 2.8 where Nebuchadnezzor accuses the magicians of using delaying tactics in an effort

to "buy" time ("Επ' ἀληθείας οἶδα ὅτι καιρὸν ὑμεῖς ἐξαγοράζετε"), and in the Pauline literature it is used in a similar sense of "buying" time at Col. 4.5, Eph. 5.16. Diodorus Siculus (first-century BCE historian) uses the word, however, in the sense of "purchase" in order to "redeem" (*Bibliotheca historica* 3.3), and that is the sense in which Paul uses it at Galatians 3.13 and 4.4-5. As Martyn points out, these are the only two places in the NT "at which the verb is connected to God's action in Christ" (*Galatians* 390). Cf. Caird, *New Testament Theology* 148; Wright, *Climax of the Covenant* 151-52.

14. It is indeed possible that the matrilinear principle of identifying Jewishness was known in some circles as early as the late second temple period. I hint at such a possibility myself in a note I wrote some years ago (see Christopher Bryan, "A Further Look at Acts 16.1-3" *JBL* 107 [1988] 292-94). The fact, however, remains: *we have no clear and unambiguous witness to such a principle earlier than the Mishnah*, wherein it appears, as Yehuda Leib Maimon puts it, "like a bolt from the blue" ("The Matrilinear Principle" in Shaye Cohen, *The Beginnings of Jewishness*).

15. Mary's Jewishness is assumed in the rest of the NT and later Christian tradition, e.g., *Protevangelium of James* 1.1-5.2.

16. Ernest de Witt Burton cites Friedrich Sieffert, *Der Brief an die Galater* (Göttingen, 1880) *in loc.* (*Galatians* 217).

17. Burton, *Galatians* 217; so, more recently, J. Louis Martyn: "In the tradition 'born of a woman,' there is no hint that Paul knew and drew upon the tradition that Jesus was born of a virgin" (*Galatians,* 407 n.63). Martyn does add, however, a striking qualification: "The theological intention behind the tradition of Jesus' virgin birth is, however, harmonious with the intention of Gal. 4.4-5" (ibid).

18. 1 Corinthians 11.23-26. See Christopher Bryan, *Resurrection of the Messiah* 51. I also argue there that 1 Corinthians 15.1-11 indicates Paul's awareness of the empty tomb tradition. I believe that to be correct, but I am aware that it is more controversial. Apropos Paul's silence on the virginal conception, John McHugh surely had a point: "it is difficult to believe that he, Luke's friend and fellow-traveller, had never even heard the story of the virginal conception" (*Mother of Jesus* 276).

19. Still basic here is C. H. Dodd, *The Apostolic Preaching and Its Development*; see also Caird, *New Testament Theology* 27-73, Bryan, *Listening to the Bible* 66-87.

20. Ambrose of Milan (attributed): Hymn: *Veni, Redemptor gentium.*

21. Crean, "Mary as a New Eve in the Thought of St Paul" *NB* 103 (2022) 662-677.

22. That is, in this particular case, effectively the past participle. "The employment of the aorist presents the birth and subjection to law as in each case a simple fact and leaves the temporal relation to be inferred solely from the nature of the facts referred to" (Burton, *Galatians* 218).
23. So Burton rendered Paul's γενόμενον ἐκ γυναικός by "born of woman," since he regarded γυναικός as "not indefinite, but qualitative," but rendered γενόμενον ὑπὸ νόμον by "made subject to law" since he also regarded νόμον as qualitative. He pointed out that "though γενόμενον ἐκ γυναικός evidently refers to the birth, that reference is neither conveyed by, nor imparted to, the participle, but lies wholly in the limiting phrase" (Galatians 216-18). Cf. LSJ γίνομαι, II; and GELS γίνομαι. (The normally impeccable BDAG is perhaps, in this matter, misleading, since BDAG γίνομαι 1 appears to suggest that birth is implied by γίνομαι standing alone).
24. Galatians 4.23, 24, 29.
25. Romans 9.11.
26. Crean, "Mary as the New Eve" 667. Cf. McHugh: "Thus Paul, on every occasion where he refers even distantly to Christ's entry into this world of time, never once uses the verb 'to be begotten'. Is this purely accident?" (*Mother of Jesus* 276).
27. Crean, "Mary as the New Eve" 669.
28. In rendering the four definite articles in 1 Cor. 11.12, I again change from the NRSV (which omits them in all four cases) to the KJV and DR, which translate the verse exactly.
29. 1 Corinthians 11.8-9.
30. Genesis 2.18: for the connection cf. e.g., Conzelmann, *1 Corinthians* 188; Raymond Collins, *First Corinthians* 410; Fitzmyer, *First Corinthians* 415-16.
31. 1 Corinthians 11.11.
32. 1 Corinthians 11.12.
33. Crean, "Mary as the New Eve" 665: cf. e.g., Robertson and Plummer, *First Epistle of St Paul to the Corinthians* 234; Hèring, *Première Épître aux Corinthiens* 96; Conzelmann, *1 Corinthians* 190; C. K. Barrett, *First Epistle to the Corinthians* 255; Collins, *First Corinthians* 403.
34. Crean, "Mary as the New Eve" 666.
35. Crean, "Mary as the New Eve" 667.
36. Matera correctly points out apropos Galatians 4.4 that Paul's expression "neither affirms nor denies the virgin birth" (*Galatians* 150).

2. Mark

1. NRSV "his family" renders Greek "οἱ παρ᾽αὐτοῦ." Although earlier translations rendered the phrase by "his friends" (KJV, RV), occurrences in papyri indicate that the koine "uses this expression to denote others who are intimately connected with someone, e.g., family, relatives" (BDAG παρά 3.a.β.ב).

2. Mark says that "they came out to get him (ἐξῆλθον κρατῆσαι αὐτόν)": κρατῆσαι is a strong word and certainly does not preclude the use of force. See BDAG κρατέω 3.

3. Collins, *Mark* 227 not inaptly compares Philo *Ebr.* 145-46.

4. For discussion of the three views, still of immense value is J. B. Lightfoot, "The Brethren of the Lord," in *Galatians* 252-91 (supports the Epiphanian view); see also McHugh, *Mother of Jesus* 200-254 (rejects all three, and finally offers his own view that the *adelphoi* are "foster-brothers"); John P. Meier, *A Marginal Jew* 1.327-32 (claims that in the NT "*adelphos*" never means half-brother or stepbrother; most likely the brothers and sisters of Jesus were true siblings); Richard Bauckham, "The Brothers and Sisters of Jesus: An Epiphanian Response" 686-700 (Bauckham notes, against Meier, that the claim that ἀδελφός cannot mean "half-brother" or "stepbrother" is linguistically unsound, and points to the tradition, widespread by the mid-second century, that Jesus' brothers were Joseph's children by an earlier marriage: so, e.g., *Gospel of Peter* and *Protoevangelium of James*). That Jesus' brothers and sisters were older than he, possibly regarding him and even his mother as in some sense intruders, would fit with the somewhat painful dynamics of their relationship as hinted at in the NT.

5. My use of italics here is deliberate: Mark's use as a particle of the imperative ἴδε (*Look! See!*) is clearly emphatic: see BDAG ἴδε 1, 3.

6. Bultmann viewed the pericope as an ideal scene constructed from a proverbial saying preserved in the Oxyrhinchus Papyri (cf. Huck-Leitzmann, *Synopsis* 18, fn. on Luke 4.24). What might have led to such a view of Jesus by his fellow townsfolk we do not know (cf. Vincent Taylor, *St. Mark* 298), but the pericope surely contains too much detail embarrassing to the church (notably Jesus' inability to perform many mighty works in Nazareth) for Bultmann's view of it to be plausible.

7. Greek τέκτων: "one who constructs, builder, carpenter" (BAGD τέκτων; cf. LSJ τέκτων). The word can cover workers in stone or metal, but the most common usage points to one who works with wood: cf. Brown, *Birth* 539 n.21.

8. With the NRSV, I follow the reading ὁ τέκτων, ὁ υἱὸς τῆς Μαρίας attested by all uncials and many minuscules and early versions. Some texts, however, including 𝔓45, read "του τεκτονος υιος και" for "ὁ τέκτων," possibly an assimilation to Matt. 13.55 (so *TCNT* 88-89). Some commentators think this represents what Mark originally wrote, and that Matthew followed such an early text (so, e.g., Taylor, *Mark* 300; cf. discussion in Brown, *Birth* 537-39; Meir, *Marginal Jew* 225-26).<

9. *Against Celsus* 6.36.

10. So Sirach:

> The wisdom of the scribe depends on the opportunity of leisure;
> only the one who has little business can become wise. (38.24)

Thus, despite his awareness of their necessity for society, Sirach goes on to specify among those incapable of wisdom, "every artisan (τέκτων) and master artisan (ἀρχιτέκτων)" (38.27).

11. Taylor, *Mark* 299-300; Ettiene Trocmé, *La Formation de l'évangile selon Marc* (Paris: Universitaires de France, 1963) 104 n.107; Brown, *Birth* 537-41; Morna Hooker, *A Commentary on the Gospel according to St Mark* (London: A & C Black) 153; Jane Schaberg, *The Illegitimacy of Jesus: A Feminist Interpretation of the Infancy Narratives*, Expanded Twentieth-Century Edition (Sheffield: Sheffield Phoenix, 2006) 141-45; Meier, *Marginal Jew* 1.226-27.

12. C. E. B. Cranfield points to belief that Jesus was illegitimate as *therefore* "evidence in support of the historicity of the Virgin Birth" (*The Gospel according to Saint Mark*. 3rd ed. Cambridge: Cambridge University Press, 1977 195). As my long-time barrister friend Leslie Stemp used to point out to me in conversation, it is in matters of law generally regarded as a sound assumption that where two parties are in dispute, anything they actually agree on is quite likely to be the case.

13. Harvey K. McArthur, "Son of Mary," *NovT* 15 (1973) 38-58; also Bauckham, "The Brothers and Sisters of Jesus." Bauckham suggests "that in Nazareth Jesus would have been known as 'the son of Mary' because this distinguished him from the children of Joseph by his first wife." This practice is implicit in several Old Testament and rabbinic texts, and it would have been a way of making a distinction between Jesus and the rest of his family in Nazareth.

14. This is, incidentally, also the only occurrence of the phrase "the son of Mary (ὁ υἱὸς τῆς Μαρίας)" in the New Testament, although Jesus is referred to elsewhere as "her firstborn son (τὸν υἱὸν αὐτῆς τὸν πρωτότοκον)" (Luke 2.7) where the possessive evidently refers to Mary.

15. Tal Ilan, *Lexicon of Jewish Names in Late Antiquity: 330 BCE - 650 CE*, 4 vols. TSAJ 148 (Tübingen: Mohr Siebeck, 2002-2012).
16. Marianne Sawicki, *Crossing Galilee: Architectures of Contact in the Occupied Land of Jesus.* (Harrisburg, Pennsylvania: Trinity International, 2000) 137-38.
17. Whatever their attitude to Jesus at this stage of his ministry, such evidence as there is implies that Jesus' brothers did become prominent in the later Christian movement (1 Cor. 19.5, Gal. 1.19, Eusebius, *Ecclesiastical History* 1.2-5): which noted, that the tradition also preserved the less palatable memory of their original hostility to Jesus suggests a rather remarkable honesty in the handing on of the tradition.
18. M. Eugene Boring, *Mark: A Commentary.* (Louisville and London: Westminster John Knox, 2006) 164.
19. Alan Richardson, *An Introduction to the Theology of the New Testament* (London: SCM, 1958) 60-61; cf. Cranfield: "their very familiarity with him is a hindrance to knowing him truly, for it makes it all the more hard for them to see through the veil of his ordinariness" (*Mark* 193).

3. Matthew

1. For convenience I refer to the author of the gospel as Matthew. We are invariably reminded—not, in my view, entirely convincingly—how unlikely it is that an actual eyewitness of Jesus' ministry would have relied on Mark as the foundation for his work. That aside, however, if the group for whom Matthew wrote had at some time some degree of significant, formative contact with a disciple called Matthew, that might explain their gospel being described as "according to" him. That it *was* so called is a fact of their history that must be accounted for somehow (cf. Luz, *Matthew* 1.59). For my views on the gospel's authorship and purpose, see Bryan, *Resurrection of the Messiah* 83-87.
2. NRSV renders Matthew's "βίβλος γενέσεως" as "an account of the genealogy." This translation is certainly possible, since in the Greek Scriptures γένεσις is at times linked to genealogies, e.g., at Genesis 5.1 where LXX βίβλος γενέσεως renders Hebrew סֵפֶר תּוֹלְדֹת. Later rabbinic exegesis declared of Genesis 5.1 (and also 2.4, where the same expression occurs) that "[This] teaches that the Holy Blessed One showed [Adam] all the generations that would come from him, as if they rose up (and played) before him" (*Avot D'Rabbi Natan* 31, William Davidson Talmud transl.). Since, however, these conversations date from c650 to 950 of the Christian era, and in any case I believe that Matthew 1.1 is intended as a title for the entire gospel, *not* just for

the genealogy, I prefer to render "βίβλος γενέσεως" by "Book of Genesis," i.e., book of "the origin or mode of formation of something" (see *OED* "genesis": which offers as synonyms such expressons as "coming into being, inception, origination, birth, creation." These would certainly cover the main senses in which γένεσις is commonly used in our texts (cf. BDAG γένεσις 1; *GELS* γένεσις 1).

3. Examples from the Scriptures are Proverbs, Ecclesiastes, Canticles, Hosea, Amos, Joel, Nahum, Tobit, Baruch; from Qumran, the *Community Rule* and the *War Rule.* On Matthew 1.1 as a general title for the entire work, see further the definitive note in W. D. Davies and Dale C. Allison, *A Critical and Exegetical Commentary on the Gospel according to Saint Matthew.* 3 vols. (Edinburgh: T. & T. Clark, 1988–97) 1.149-54.

4. Is the expression "of Jesus Christ" subjective or objective? In other words, are we to hear how Jesus Christ began, or of the new beginning Jesus Christ has brought about for us? As so often in both Greek and English usage, there is no need to attempt such a distinction. We may look to hear both. I am struck by the fact that grammarians seem in general far more willing than commentators to admit such ambiguity as a part of normal discourse. So,

> The division of the genitive into objective, subjective, etc., is really only an attempt to set off several special types among the manifold possibilities of the general function of the adnominal genitive, which is to denote a relationship (BDF §163).
>
> The genitive with substantives denotes in general a connection or dependence between two words.... The same construction may often be placed under more than one of the different classes... and the connection between the two substantives is often so loose that it is difficult to include with precision all cases under specific grammatical classes" (Smyth, *Grammar*, § 1295).

For the same point, see also Moule, *Idiom*, 40, 203.

5. See Daniel Harrington, S.J., *Matthew* 30-32. Not, of course, that this is a purely ancient phenomenon. Genealogy remains, in Thomas Laqueuer's view,

> one of the great feats of the human imagination; a vast collection of stories, both intimate and cosmic, that bind the living to the dead and to one another, the past to the present and the present to what is to come. It is a primal work of culture, a narrative cornucopia encompassing stories

> about the origins of heroes and kings; stories about nations, whose gnarly, almost metaphysical genealogical connections are bound up in the Latin root *natus* and its cognates; stories about ancestors told around campfires, in books and now in hyperspace. (Laqueur, "The Pocahontas Exception," 3, 5-8).

Laqueur goes on to review Francesca Morgan's *A Nation of Descendants: Politics and the Practice of Genealogy in U.S. History* (Chapel Hill: University of North Carolina Press, 2021). The book's title alone speaks (as, of course, does its content and Laqueur's review) of the value Americans throughout U.S. history have placed on the genealogical witness.

6. Schaberg, *Illegitmacy* 46-47.

7. Are Greek-speaking readers of Matthew's gospel likely to have known this? Luz asks the question, implying, as it seems to me, that the obvious answer is "No." (Luz, *Matthew* 1.85). I am not so sure. Responsible scholarship sees in the gospel's author someone who wrote and spoke in Greek but also knew Hebrew (e.g., Brown, *Birth of the Messiah* 47). It seems not unreasonable to imagine that the evangelist might look for similar abilities among at least some of those for whom he wrote.

8. Rabbi Eliyahu Safran says of the number seven,

> It is the perfect number. More than that, it is Judaism's most sacred number. Seven is completeness and wholesomeness. My uncle, Rabbi Alexandre Safran Z'L, concludes his prolific discussion of "Jewish time /Sabbath time" in his *Israel in Time & Space* by noting that the number seven thus joins for all eternity the Creator and His Creation, God and His people; and the hyphen uniting them, is the holy Shabbat. For, as we know, the Sabbath is the seventh day. *Shemittah*, the seventh year. *Yovel*, the culmination of seven cycles of seven years ("Seven: The Power of Numbers" [May 15, 2022] Online at https://ourtorah.org/p/24545/).

9. An aspect of Matthew's genealogy that has puzzled commentators is the origin of some of his names. Other examples, however, of expanded biblical genealogies from approximately the same period—such as those in the *Biblical Antiquities* of Pseudo-Philo (which expands on the genealogies in Genesis 4 to 5 and 10 to 11) or in *Jubilees* (which supplies the names of wives of the patriarchs missing from the biblical narrative)—suggest that a degree of creative freedom was acceptable in such compositions, and that appears to be the case here.

10. "Jesus is the Son of David (and of Abraham) and was born at an opportune time in Israel's history. For the Matthean community, it served to root Jesus firmly within the history of God's people—something that was important both for Jewish and Gentile Christians" (Harrington, *Matthew* 32.2).
11. *Joseph and Asenath* 21.4.
12. Genesis 38.
13. Joshua 2.1-22, 6.22-25.
14. It is sometimes suggested that Bathsheba was also a gentile, but there is no evidence of that, rather the contrary. As well as being called "the wife of Uriah the Hittite," she is also described by her patronymic, "daughter of Eliam" (2 Samuel 11.3). That is unusual, so perhaps it is significant. A possible connection is that one Eliam, "son of Ahitophel the Gilonite," was, like Uriah her husband, among David's elite warriors (2 Samuel 23.34, 39; cf. *b Sanhedrin* 69b).
15. Cf. Brown, *Birth* 73-74; Harrington, *Matthew* 32. Marianne Sawicki takes essentially this view, with the irregularity in Mary's case involving her being raped prior to her engagement to Joseph—an engagement which will not actually have been the original intention of her family, who would have intended her as the bride of a priest. "Joseph was the family's second choice but God's first choice, we may surmise, and Joseph made his own courageous assent to this proposal" (*Crossing Galilee* 93: cf. the whole passage, 192-93). See further Additional Note B.
16. I follow Raymond Brown and others in using the expression "virginal conception" (*virginitas ante partum*) to refer to that miraculous element in the birth of Jesus which in the view of most ancient and modern commentators is affirmed by Matthew and Luke. "Virgin birth" (*virginitas in partu*) and, by implication though less clearly, "perpetual virginity" (*virginitas post partum*) are affirmed by the *Protoevangelium of James* 19.2-20.3 (second half of the second century).
17. Elizabeth Schüssler Fiorenza, *In Memory of Her* 45.
18. Beverly Roberts Gaventa, *Mary: Glimpses of the Mother of Jesus* 33-39.
19. Likewise *Re-Va 1995*, which has "genealogía" at Matt. 1.1 and "nacimiento" at 1.18; and TILC, which gives up on the parallel completely, rendering 1.1 "Gesù Cristo è discendente di Davide" and 1.18 "Ecco come è nato Gesù Cristo." An honorable exception to all this is *TOB*, which has "origines" at both 1.1 and 1.18.
20. Jerome preserved the verbal link between the genealogy at Matthew 1.1 and the following narrative at 1.18 by in both cases rendering γένεσις by Latin *generatio*. Strikingly, Wiclif and Douay-Rheims, the two English translations

based directly on Jerome rather than the Greek text, follow Jerome here, in each place rendering his *generatio* by "generacioun" / "generation."

21. See Safrai and Stern, *The Jewish People in the First Century* 1.752-92; also Brown, *Birth of the Messiah* 123-28; Schaberg, *Illegitimacy* 49-69. Historically, the rabbinic customs here described have not been by any means so remote from our own customs as we perhaps imagine. There was, in fact, a considerable degree of similarity between rabbinic marriage customs and the custom of the "marriage contract" as it still existed in Tudor England and later. As Richard Greenham, a Tudor jurist, put it, such a marriage contract, "although it be a degree under marriage, yet it is more than a determined purpose, yea more than a simple promise" (*A Treatise of Contract* in *Works* [1599]; cited in Bawcutt, *Measure for Measure* 6). Strikingly, the majority of medieval marriage litigation involved attempts by one party to repudiate a marriage contract that the other party wished to enforce—a recurring problem that was not resolved until the Marriage Bill of 1752 laid it down that only a church wedding properly witnessed was legally binding and valid. Thus seventeenth century understandings—and disputes—about the marriage contract are pivotal to the plot of Shakespeare's *Measure for Measure*. They lie behind the notion—to modern audiences, ridiculous, but to Jacobeans, whatever their personal views on the matter, entirely familiar—that a young man should be sentenced to death for getting his fiancée pregnant (1.2.142-169), and also behind Marianna's saying that she has never been married but claiming nonetheless that she and Angelo are wife and husband (5.1.169-234). See further discussion in N. W. Bawcutt, *Shakespeare: Measure for Measure* 6-12.

22. Harrington, *Matthew* 34.

23. See Additional Note B.

24. If it stood alone, Matthew's expression at 1.18 could certainly be taken to imply that Joseph realized at once that the Holy Spirit was involved in Mary's pregnancy, and even that he was told of this. This is the view of 1.18 taken by Xavier Léon-Dufour, S.J. ("L'annonce à Joseph," 65-81). *Pace* Léon-Dufour, however, what follows in Matthew 1.19-20 makes it very hard to suppose that this is *actually* what the evangelist intended. It is not merely, as Ceslas Spicq points out, that "cette foi en la divinité de Jésus est bien précoce! [this faith in the divinity of Jesus is very precocious!]" ("'Joseph, son mari, étant juste…' [Mt., I.19]" *RB* 71 [1964] 206-207)—although it certainly would be!—but also because it seems absolutely ruled out by (a) Joseph's considering the possibility of exposing Mary "to public disgrace"—a consideration that surely requires his supposing her to be an adulteress? and (b) the fact that when the angel instructs Joseph to take Mary into his home, the statement that the

child is "through the Holy Spirit" is most naturally understood as intended to provide Joseph with important information *that he does not yet have* (cf. Brown, *Birth of the Messiah* 124; Schaberg, *Illegitimacy* 51). Léon-Dufour's view that Joseph already knows that the child is from God obliges him to a strained and, as it seems to most exegetes, unlikely interpretation of this announcement.

25. For discussion of the Torah issues that would have faced Joseph on discovering that Mary was pregnant, see Schaberg, *Illegitimacy* 49-64. The obvious question raised by our text is, What is the connection between Joseph's decision to divorce Mary quietly and his being "righteous (δίκαιος)"? Are we to understand that he is righteous *and therefore* unwilling to disgrace Mary (understanding καὶ in its usual connective sense [BDAG καὶ 1, 2])? Or that he is righteous *but nevertheless* unwilling to disgrace Mary (understanding καὶ as adversative, equivalent to καίτοι [BDAG καὶ 2iδ])? The former, put forward by Clement of Alexandria and Jerome, is certainly the easier and more obvious sense (so Luz, *Matthew* 1.95); and *pace* Allison and Davies, it does not mean that δίκαιος loses its normal Matthean sense of being obedient to Torah, merely that mercy is seen as a key element in such obedience (cf. Ps. 112.4, Mal. 6.8, Wisd. 12.19). Brown's objection here that it is not clear whether justice consists in mercy or is tempered by mercy (*Birth* 126) is beside the point: if "mercy" is a required element of justice, then "justice" that lacks mercy not truly justice. So Spicq says about Joseph's decision,

> C'est une décision de clémence, qui ne révèle pas seulement sa sagesse et sa maîtrise de lui-même, mais une bienveillance insigne, de la miséricorde généreuse et de la magnanimité. Toutes ces nuances de la justice sont parfaitement bibliques, puisque Dieu avait enseigné à son peuple que le juste doit être humain (δει τον δίκαιον είναι φιλάνθρωπον, Sag., χιι, 19) et miséricordieux, puisque la *tsedaqah* était associée à la *hésèd* et que la δικαιοσύνη dans les écrits tardifs était équivalente à l'ἐλεημοσύνη. [It is a kindly decision that reveals not only his wisdom and self-control but also a remarkable benevolence, born of generous mercy and magnanimity. All these nuances of justice are perfectly biblical, since God taught his people that the just should be humane (δει τον δίκαιον είναι φιλάνθρωπον, Wisd. 12.19) and merciful, since *tsedaqah* was associated with *hesed* and in the Scriptures δικαιοσύνη was eqivalent to ἐλεημοσύνη.] ("Joseph, son mari..." 213-14).

26. On this point see particularly Gaventa, *Mary* 33-46.

27. The divorce procedure was public and was intended to be, not least in that it left the woman free to marry someone else. To that extent "λάθρᾳ (secretly)" is a strange choice of word for Joseph's planned course of action. The obvious response to that, I suppose, is that in this particular case divorce would nonetheless be a good deal *less* public and humiliating than the procedure (involving the death penalty) specified in Deuteronomy 19.22-27 (cf. Harrington, *Matthew* 34-35). It is perhaps significant that Matthew will go on to use the same word to describe Herod taking counsel "secretly" with the Magi: this too will be a threat to the child and to his mother.
28. Matthew will again introduce an angel as God's messenger in the context of a dream at 2.13 and 19. For this, there is precedent in Scripture (e.g., Gen. 28.10-17, 37.5-11) and elsewhere in Jewish tradition (Pseudo-Philo, *Biblical Antiquities* 9.10; Josephus, *Antiquities* 2.210-17); see Davies and Allison, *Matthew* 1.206-7; Harrington, *Matthew* 37-38. The angel's message regarding Jesus' birth and future likewise follow a well-established pattern: e.g., Gen. 16.11-12 (about Ishmael); Gen. 17.19, 21 (Isaac); 1 Kings 13.2 (Josiah); 1 Chron. 22.9-10 (Solomon). Belief in divination by dreams remained widespread in antiquity, despite the caution and even scepticism of influential thinkers such as Aristotle (*Parva Naturalia* 462b 12-464b 18a; cf. David Ross, *Aristotle Parva Naturalia* 47-49).
29. Isaiah 64.6.
30. Karl A. Plank, "The Human Face of Otherness" 73; cited in Gaventa, *Mary* 48n.18.
31. It has been asserted that adoption such as Matthew here implies had no place in Jewish tradition: notably by Y. Levin, "Jesus, 'Son of God' and 'Son of David': The 'Adoption' of Jesus into the Davidic Line," 415-42. This, however, is not correct: see the devastating critique of Levin by Caleb T. Friedeman, "Jesus' Davidic Lineage and the Case for Jewish Adoption," 249-67.
32. We are, of course, to think here and at 1.18 of God's creative intervention by the Spirit, and not of the Spirit as Mary's sexual partner (cf. Luz, *Matthew 1-7*, 95). See further Additional Note B.
33. On the formula quotations, see Davies and Allison, *Matthew* 3.573-77.
34. The feminine form (ἡ) of παρθένος "generally refers to a young woman of marriagable age, with or without focus on viriginity" (BDAG παρθένος; cf. LSJ παρθένος A.2, *TDNT* 5.835; see e.g. LXX Gen. 34.3, *Iliad* 2.514). At LXX 7.14, παρθένος is used to render Hebrew הָמְלַעָה, "an adolescent woman, one of marriagable age. The contention that the word must necessarily connote 'virgin' is unwarranted. The Hebrew for 'virgin' is *bethulah*, though

almah too sometimes bears this meaning" (Slotki, *Isaiah 35;* cf. Kaiser, *Isaiah 1-12* 101).

35. See, e.g., I. W. Slotki, *Isaiah* (London and Bournemouth: Soncino, 1949) 35; cf. Otto Kaiser, *Isaiah 1-12.* (Philadelphia: Westminster, 1972) 102. I am not nearly so convinced of the improbability of the Rabbis' suggestion as Kaiser appears to be.

36. The promise of YHWH's presence ran (and runs) deep in Israel. It was, according to Exodus, the presence of YHWH that had enabled Moses to face Pharaoh (Exod. 3.11-12). In the situation of exile, the promise of presence becomes especially marked: "I will be their God, and they shall be my people" (Jer. 31.33) cf. Walter Brueggemann, *Theology of the Old Testament: Testimony, Dispute, Advocacy.* (Minneapolis: Fortress, 1997) 171-72. The question will also be addressed by the author of Revelation, who in the verses leading up to his picture of the woman crowned with the sun, begins with a view of the heavenly temple, and the ark visible within it—the ark being, of course, the sign of God's presence (Rev. 11.19).

37. NRSV renders simply, "And remember, I am with you always, to the end of the age" (Matt. 28.30): but Matthew's grammatically unnecessary ἐγὼ is emphatic.

38. Matthew 28.20. I largely owe this, as it appears to me, entirely satisfactory explanation of Matthew's appeal to Isaiah 7.14 to Jane Schaberg, (*Illegitimacy* 70-73). It has the advantage of indicating an evident parallel between Ahaz's and Joseph's situations that justifies Matthew's choice of text, whilst, *pace* numerous biblical commentators ancient and modern, not requiring us to assume that Matthew completely misunderstood the passage he had chosen to quote. Isaiah 7.14 had, of course, and has, no bearing on the tradition of virginal conception, whether considered in its Hebrew dress, where הָעַלְמָה, in Biblical as in modern Hebrew, simply means "the young woman" (*HED* עַלְמָה; cf. Slotki, *Isaiah* 35; Kaiser, *Isaiah 1-12* 100-101) or in Greek, where other Greek versions—Aquila, Symmachus and Theodotion—render עלמה by νεᾶνις, and the LXX's παρθένος, though not its usual practice (it too usually renders עַלְמָה by νεᾶνις: e.g., LXX Exod. 2.8) was a perfectly reasonable translation, since in ordinary usage παρθένος does *not* necessarily imply virginity, merely youth (LSJ παρθένος A2; *GELS* παρθένος; BDAG παρθένος). Schaberg herself associates this with her understanding of Matthew as conveying, in however veiled a form, a tradition of Mary having been raped, as opposed to Jesus' virginal conception. In this I do not follow her. It is the case, however, that Isaiah 7.14 and Matthew's use of it are no more witnesses for his belief in the virginal conception of Jesus than they are witnesses against.

39. That Joseph could not have been Jesus' biological father is also, of course, *all* that Matthew 1.25 affirms. What then of traditions of Mary's perpetual virginity (*virginitas post partum*)? It is doubtless true, as Davies and Allison point out, that "had Matthew held to Mary's perpetual virginity… he would almost certainly have chosen a less ambiguous expression" (*Matthew* 1.219). But that, of course, would be equally true had he wished to deny it. The point is, we have no way of knowing whether the evangelist was even aware of the question.
40. *m. Bava Batra* 8.6.
41. That the Messiah should be of the house of David and come in fulfilment of God's promise to David in 1 Samual 7 is not a *sine qua non* of Messianism and certainly not universal in expressions of Messianic hope. Both ideas are, however, quite widely present and often seem simply to be assumed. As Matthew V. Novenson puts it, "one could claim the Judaean kingship intelligibly either on the grounds of ancestry, as a rightful son of David, or on the grounds of merit, as one divinely appointed as was David. Those who could claim Davidic ancestry often did or, alternatively, their followers or biographers claimed it for them" (*The Grammar of Messianism* 96; cf. 104-113 and passim). In other words, you don't have to be a son of David to be the Messiah, but it helps.
42. See the discussion of Matthew 13.53-58, and nn 131, 132.
43. I transliterate "Magi" (Greek μάγοι) rather than using one of the common construals such as "wise men" (too vague), "astrologers" (inappropriate associations, at least in modern parlance) or "kings" (traditional, but wrong—although as I recall in *The Man Born to be King* Dorothy Sayers made a spirited and enjoyable case for it). The term "Magi" combined with "from the east" suggests that Matthew thought of them as coming from Persia ("Magi" originally referred to a caste of Persian priests who claimed special skills to interpret dreams) and their reading the stars suggests Babylon. But in view of their role in this particular narrative perhaps the most important thing about them is that they are exotic figures; which is to say, foreign; which is to say, gentiles.
44. Genesis 12.3.
45. Cf. Exod. 1.16, 22; 2.15; 2.23, 4.19; Pseudo-Philo, *Biblical Antiquities* 9.12; Josephus, *Antiquities* 2.205-237. For a summary and discussion of parallels between Matthew's account of Jesus' birth and Moses' traditions, see Harrington, *Matthew* 47-49.
46. Dorothy Sayers, *The Man Born to be King* (London: Victor Gallancz, 1946) 58; for "ὁ μέγας" in antiquity, see Josephus, *Antiquities* 18.5.4. See further on Herod *HJPAJC* 1.287-329; Martin Goodman, *Rome and Jerusalem: The Clash of Ancient Civilizations.* (London: Allen Lane, 2007) 59-63,

357-58, 222, 227, 397; Stewart Perowne, *The Life and Times of Herod the Great* (London: The History Press, 2003). (Strikingly, Herod is by far the most rounded and interesting of the characters in *Kings in Judaea*—the first of Sayers's *The Man Born to be King* series. From an actor's point of view, it is quite the best part in the play.)

47. "King Herod was disturbed (ὁ βασιλεὺς Ἡρῴδης ἐταράχθη)" (2.3): KJV has "he was troubled" and REB "greatly perturbed."

48. Epiphanius, *Panarion* 1.20.1.1; see Jerome, *Altercatio Luciferiani* 23.

49. See above n. 112.

50. Zech. 6.12; 1 Enoch 53.6. Cf. Joan E. Taylor, *The Essenes, the Scrolls, and the Dead Sea* 124-26; Novenson, *Grammar of Messianism* 77-82.

51. See J. Priest, "Testament of Moses" in *OTP* 1.920-21.

52. *Testament of Moses* 6.4; cf. R. T. France, "Herod and the Children of Bethlehem" *NovT.* 21 (1979) 98-120.

53. Brown, *Birth of the Messiah* 142; Gaventa, *Mary* 42.

54. So Christina Rossetti's

> Angels and Archangels
> May have gathered there,
> Cherubim and seraphim
> Thronged the air;
> But only His Mother
> In her maiden bliss
> Worshipped the Beloved
> With a kiss.
> ("In the bleak midwinter," published as "A Christmas Carol" in *Scribner's Monthly* January 1872)

55. E.g., Exod. 7.8-12, Dan. 2.1-49.

56. Lancelot Andrewes made the point:

> [1] Their faith first: faith in that they never ask "Whether He be?" but "Where He is born?" for that born He is, that they steadfastly believe.
> [2] Then their confessing of it; they were no sooner come, but they tell it out; confess Him and His birth to be the cause of their coming.
> [3] [Then] the steps of their faith, their coming on such a journey, at such a time, with such speed.
> [4] Fourthly, their diligent enquiring Him out.

> [5] Last, when they had found Him, the end of their seeing, coming, seeking; to worship Him. Worship with Him with their bodies, worship Him with their goods; their worship and ours; the true worship of Christ.
>
> (Sermon preached on Christmas Day, 1622)

57. Matthew 28.19.
58. Archelaus' mismanagement would eventually lead Augustus in AD 6 to strip him of his role as Ethnarch and banish him to Vienne in Gaul. At the same time, Augustus also reduced Judaea to a province under direct Roman rule by a Procurator (Josephus, *War* 2.114-117; *Ant.* 17.339-355).
59. NRSV's "was ruling" correctly renders Matthew's "βασιλεύει" (Matt. 2.22). The evanglist's choice of word is not, however, entirely accurate, since "βασιλεύει" strictly means "was ruling as king." Rome never granted Archelaus the title "king," allowing him to rule only as "Ethnarch" ("ruler of a people").
60. This verse is a notorious problem for interpreters. Matthew makes three changes from his usual formula for introducing quotations from Scripture. (1) He replaces "the prophet" with "the prophets." (2) Instead of the participle "saying" he has the conjunction "that (ὅτι)." (3) The text itself, "He shall be called a Nazarene (Ναζωραῖος κληθήσεται)" corresponds to no known biblical text. These changes have led some commentators to suppose that Matthew intends not to quote directly from a single passage in his customary fashion, but to summarize what he regards as the import of prophecy in general, having in mind more than one text. Three main sources may be seen for his summary: the title נזיר, of holy persons dedicated to God (cf. Judges 3.2-7); Isaiah's messianic promise of "a shoot out of the stock of Jesse and a branch (נֵצֶר) out of his roots" (11.1); and, of course, the place name "Nazareth" itself, which has suggested the linking of these ideas and the person of Jesus. That there is no *actual* etymological connection between נזיר, נֵצֶר and Ναζαρέτ is, of course, beside the point: the only point that matters is what Christians may have made of the evident homeophonies between the three words (cf. Davies and Allison, *Matthew* 1.275-81; Harrington, *Matthew* 45-46). To declare that the return of Jesus to Nazareth was "in order that" all this might be fulfilled may be Matthew's intention.
61. Sara Maitland, *Daughter of Jerusalem* (London: Frederick Muller, 1978) 239-40.
62. See, e.g., Schaberg, *Illegitimacy* 138-56.

63. Sawicki, *Crossing Galilee* 186. There is, incidentally, a rather striking parallel here with traditions about the prophet Mohammed, an orphan from the powerful Quraish tribe in Mecca, who was adopted by his uncle. "In a culture where the lineage of horses, even, were carefully recorded and the most prized animals prevented from mating with others of inferior pedigree, Muhammed's orphan status—his disrupted lineage—was frowned on." (Tariq Ali, "Winged Words" 11-12).
64. Cf. Sawicki: "[I]n Judean religious law the lines of imputed entitlement to the productivity of land and people followed the lines of perceived kinship, which were congruent with the trajectories of the real displacement of brides from the households of their fathers to those of their husbands. Any anomaly in a bride's trajectory could deprive her *and her children* of property and the fruits of labor that otherwise would have been theirs" (*Crossing Galilee* 191, my emphasis).
65. For discussion of the question, see Meier, *Marginal Jew* 1.322-45. Cf. Sawicki, *Crossing Galilee* 193.
66. See Sawicki, *Crossing Galilee* 193.
67. Sawicki, *Crossing Galilee* 186-87. I would connect this with the interesting suggestion of Halvor Moxnes in his study, *Putting Jesus in His Place*—namely, that in origin "eunuch" was an insult thrown at Jesus that he then appropriated to describe his and his followers' "place"—somewhat as British 7th Armoured Division and other allied troops defending Tobruk in World War II accepted the name "desert rats" or "rats of Tobruk," originally applied to them and intended as an insult by the Nazi propogandist William Joyce ("Lord Haw-Haw"). For further reflection on these issues see Helen King, "The 'Trans' Body of Jesus and Transgressive Theologies" in *Via Media News*, December 6, 2022.
68. See E. Meyers and J. Strange, *Archaeology, the Rabbis, and Early Christianity* (Nashville: Abingdon, 1981); also "Nazareth" in *ABD*.
69. Mark 4.6.

4. Luke

1. Again, for convenience I refer to the author of the third gospel and Acts as Luke, and indeed I see no good reason for assuming that name to be wrong. For my views on the author of Luke-Acts and his purpose, see Bryan, *Resurrection of the Messiah* 101-105.
2. See Loveday Alexander, *Preface to Luke's Gospel:* passim. On "the scientific tradition," see especially 21-22, where Alexander points out that she uses the word "science" in a sense perhaps closer to its usage in French than in English.

Luke has a narrative style which is both distinctive and powerful, telling us what we need to know *but no more*. God is always in the background, with depths unrevealed (so Auerbach of Israel's Scriptures in general: see *Mimesis* 3-23). Like much of the NT, moreover, Luke tells stories about people low on the social ladder, yet the stories are neither scurrilous nor farcical. We take seriously the spiritual lives of ordinary people (again see Auerbach, *Mimesis* 42-46, also my discussion in *Listening to the Bible* 60-64).

3. I owe this entirely apt description to Soares Prabhu, "'Rejoice, Favored One!' Mary in the Annunciation Story of Luke" in *Biblebhashyam* 3 (1977) 259.

4. *Pesikta de Rav Kahana* (S. Buber, ed. [Lyck, 1868]) 20 (141b); *Pesikta Rabbati* 32 (M. Friedmann, ed. [Vienna, 1880]) 148a.

5. On the theme of the barren woman in Scripture in general, there is useful material in Mary Callaway, *Sing, O Barren One: A Study in Comparative Midrash*. SBL Dissertation Series 91 (Atlanta, Georgia: Scholars Press, 1986).

6. Luke "shows amongst his various literary styles a marked fondness for that of the LXX i.e., for the hallowed idiom of sacred scripture" (C. F. Evans, *Saint Luke* [London: SCM, 1990] 57). This stylistic adaptation is, as other commentators have pointed out, "classicism" of a kind, though not a kind that would have been approved by those who looked to the evolving and more generally recognized classicism of the first century or the Atticism of the second: cf. Loveday C. A. Alexander, *Acts in Its Ancient Literary Context: A Classicist Looks at the Acts of the Apostles* (London: T & T Clark, 2005) 242-52. Luke could also, on occasion, mimic other styles, such as the rhetoric of a somewhat self-serving "officialese" (Acts 23.26-30, 24.2b-8), and he probably enjoyed doing it.

7. Cf. Gen. 17.15-19; Judges 13.2.

8. Cf. Gen. 17.1-15; Judges 13.3-22; Dan. 10.5-7.

9. Cf. Exod. 15.16, Judges 13.22-23; Dan. 10.7.

10. Cf. Gen. 17.19, Dan. 10.11-12.

11. Cf. Gen. 15.8, 17.18, 18.9b-15, Judg, 6.37-40; 2 Kings 20.8-11.

12. Cf. Judg. 6.37-40; Dan. 10.15.

13. See *m. Tamid* 5.4-6, 6.1-3, 7.2 cf. Num. 6.24-26; Brown, *Birth of the Messiah* 263, Fitzmyer, *Luke* 328-29, Bovon *Luke* 1.39. Whether Luke actually knew the temple rituals as they would later be described in the Mishnah, but abbreviated description of them so as to focus on his main storyline, or whether he was unaware of the details, is not clear. The most we can say is that his narrative, as it stands, coheres reasonably well with such details.

14. Cf. Dan. 10.15.

15. Fitzmyer, *Luke I-IX* 315.

16. By naming Gabriel, Luke establishes a second link between his narrative about Zachariah and Elizabeth and his narrative about Mary. But why Gabriel? According to Tobit, Gabriel is one of the "seven holy angels which present the prayers of the saints and go in before the glory of the Holy One" [Tobit 12:16]. The comments of Gregory the Great are still apposite: "You should be aware that the word 'angel' denotes a function rather than a nature. Those holy spirits of heaven have indeed always been spirits. They can only be called angels when they deliver some message. Moreover, those who deliver messages of lesser importance are called angels; and those who proclaim messages of supreme importance are called archangels. And so it was that not merely an angel but the archangel Gabriel was sent to the Virgin Mary. It was only fitting that the highest angel should come to announce the greatest of all messages.... So too Gabriel, who is called God's strength, was sent to Mary. He came to announce the One who appeared as a humble man to quell the cosmic powers. Thus God's strength announced the coming of the Lord of the heavenly powers, mighty in battle" (Gregory the Great, *Hom.* 32, 8-9 [*PL* 76, 1250-1251]).

17. Before the alleged discovery at Caesarea Maritima in 1962 of a fragmentary Hebrew inscription, it seemed that there was extant *no* early reference to Nazareth outside the New Testament. This fragment, cited as authentic e.g., by Fitzmyer (*Luke* 1.343) and C. F. Evans (*Luke* 159), was held to date from the late third or early fourth century CE. It apparently listed the twenty-four priestly "courses" (cf. Luke 1.5) and the towns where they resided, locating the eighteenth course, (cf. 1 Chron. 24.15) at נצרת. The authenticity of the fragment itself has, however, been questioned (see Enrico Tuccinardi, "Nazareth, the Caesarea Inscription, and the Hand of God"), and forgery of such a nature and quality as this would seem to be would by no means be unique: cf. James Lasdun, "Bats on the Ceiling,": a fascinating review of Ariel Sabar, *Veritas*. Even if the Nazareth fragment is a fraud—and it may be—I see little reason to doubt the historicity of Nazareth itself in the life of Jesus, since there is no reason for it to have been invented. Rather, one senses that Jesus' origin in Nazareth is if anything an *embarrassment* to the tradition (again: John 1.46!). If any origin for Jesus had been invented, it would surely have been Bethlehem. On the possibility of historical links between a town in Galilee and Bethlehem, see below p. 182, n. 62.

18. See above, p. 168, n. 34.

19. See above, n. 103.

20. On Schaberg's view of Luke 1.26-28, see Additional Note B.
21. On the names of Jesus' family see also discussion of Mark 6.3 on pp. 15-16 above.
22. Bovon correctly poses the question for those who interpret this passage, "Is χαῖρε… a simple 'good morning' or a genuine invitation to rejoice?" (*Luke 1* 50): whether he correctly answers it is another matter. Given the nature of the entire passage and Luke's evident imitation of Septuagintal style, together with the explanatory description of Mary that follows—κεχαριτωμένη: "favored one" or "graced one" and the message that Gabriel brings—"εὗρες γὰρ χάριν παρὰ τῷ θεῷ"—the answer is surely not in doubt. Gabriel invites Mary to rejoice. I believe TOB has it perfectly—"Sois joyeuse, toi qui as la faveur de Dieu!"
23. Cf. LXX Soph. 3.14, Joel 2.12; cf. also, ironic usage at LXX Lam. 2.21.
24. L. T. Johnson, *Luke* 37.
25. E.g., NRSV Ephesians 1.6.
26. E.g., Luke 1.30.
27. Luke could have expected his koine-speaking audience naturally to have associated the word with any or all of three notions: with qualities of winsomeness or charm *in Mary herself*; with feelings of goodwill or benevolence *towards Mary*; and with notions of benefits *conferred on Mary*—the two latter tending to overlap, it being, as Ceslas Spicq points out, often "impossible to distinguish between benevolent feelings and a favor granted" (Spicq, *Lexicon* 3.503; for the three senses I have distinguished, cf. BDAG χάρις 1, 2 and 3; LSJ χάρις I, II and III). In the two latter senses, and as having its source in God and /or Christ, χάρις and its cognates (not used by either Matthew or Mark) is quite an important Lucan word, especially in Acts, and particularly when he is speaking of Paul (1.28, 1.30, 2.40, 2.52, Acts 4.33, 6.8, 7.10, 7.46, 11.23, 13.43, 14.3, 14.26, 15.11, 15.40, 18.27, 20.24, 20.32). It is, of course, also an important Pauline word which, given the tradition that the evangelist was a companion of Paul, may not be merely coincidental. See further n.28, below.
28. LXX Ps. 83.12 // MT Ps . 84.11. In the LXX, χάρις commonly translates Hebrew חֵן. Hebrew חֵן derives from the verb חנן, which speaks primarily of someone's graciousness to another in terms of generous action: as in the formula describing YHWH:

> YHWH, YHWH, God, merciful and gracious (יְהוָה יְהוָה, אֵל רַחוּם וְחַנּוּן) (Exod. 34.6; cf. 2 Chron. 30.9, Neh. 9.17, 31; Ps. 86.15, 103.8, 111.4, 112.4, 145.8, Joel 2.13, Jonah 4.2).

חֵן appears, however, to undergo a development of meaning whereby it speaks not only of the giver and the giver's gracious act, but also—and perhaps mainly—of the gift thereby established for the recipient, which is visible to others. Thus in Ps. 84.11 (cited in my main text) the writer says that, "YHWH gives grace and glory (חֵן וְכָבוֹד יִתֵּן יְהוָה) to those who walk uprightly"—the expression being rendered in Greek by "χάριν καὶ δόξαν δώσει" (LXX Ps. 83.12). Such is the חֵן / χάρις spoken of by YHWH in Exod. 3.21: "וְנָתַתִּי אֶת-חֵן הָעָם-הַזֶּה (And I will give this people grace in the sight of the Egyptians)" rendered in the LXX, "καὶ δώσω χάριν τῷ λαῷ τούτῳ ἐναντίον τῶν Αἰγυπτίων" cf. other examples at Gen. 39.21, Exod. 11.3, 12.36. For fuller discussion, see *TDNT* IX, 376-81.

29. Ernest Best, *A Critical and Exegetical Commentary on Ephesians.* ICC. (Edinburgh: T. & T. Clark, 1998) 104. At Ephesians 1.6, Best says, "We take ἐχαρίτωσεν then with the same sense as χάρις and as indicating God's graciousness towards those whom he has foreordained… it is difficult to find a precise one-word English equivalent to the verb which conveys the same sense as the noun. The double use of the root reinforces the idea of the free abundance of God's grace. It is grace which controls his ordaining power and it is this grace which is displayed to us 'in the loved one'" (*Ephesians* 128).

30. The expression occurs twice in Israel's Scriptures as here in the greeting to Mary, without a verb: in Boaz's greeting to the reapers at Ruth 2.4 and in the angel's greeting to Gideon at Judges 6.12. The two greetings, identical in wording, are not therefore identical in meaning. Boaz is evidently a pious man (cf. Ruth 2.12, 3.10) and his address to the reapers should be heard as an invocation of divine blessing (cf. Katherine Doob Sakenfeld, *Ruth* 40; André LaCocque, *Ruth* 65; against Tod Linafelt, *Ruth* 29); moreover, "the audience is led to feel that Boaz's arrival is another facet of Ruth's good fortune in hitting upon the particular portion of the field where she is working" (Edward E. Cambell, *Ruth* 93). The greeting to Gideon is rather a declaration (cf. the REB, "the LORD is with you") (and is met, as will be Gabriel's to Mary, with a challenge--Judges 6.12!). Gabriel's greeting to Mary seems closer to the greeting to Gideon, although it has elements of both.

31. 2 Chronicles 13.12; 1 Esdras 1.27 (Pharoah against Israel!)

32. NRSV renders "terrified" both at 1.12 and at 1.29, making nothing of Luke's use of ταράσσω in the case of Zachariah and the more emphatic διαταράσσω of Mary, the latter clearly implying that Mary's reaction was the stronger. The foundational sense of the verb is, moreover, as BDAG indicates, "to cause movement by shaking or stirring," and thus, in its metaphorical use, "to stir up, disturb, unsettle, throw into confusion" (ταράσσω 1, 2). Hence

Jerome in both cases translates by Latin *turbo*, which has more or less exactly the range of senses as possessed by the Greek verb (see *OLD turbo*, 1 to 8, especially 7 and 8). Douey-Rheims, following Jerome, gets this nicely in English with "troubled," and KJV, following the Greek *textus receptus* but possibly influenced by Douey-Rheims, does the same. The English RV of 1880 follows its predecessors, only improving them by using "greatly troubled" in Mary's case, reflecting the more emphatic form of the verb used by the evangelist. I follow all three in the use of "troubled," and reflect the emphatic form of the verb (following the NEB of 1961) by the adverb "deeply."

33. Thus the angel of YHWH to Hagar (Gen. 16.11) and to the wife of Manoah (Judg. 13.2-5 [6-24]).

34. Evans, *Luke* 160. Luke's two verbs at 1.29, διεταράχθη and διελογίζετο, are marked by a change of tense and voice which is hard to bring out in English: διεταράχθη is in the aorist passive, implying a single, immediate action—or, in this case, perhaps we should say reaction: Mary's being troubled and perplexed. But διελογίζετο is an imperfect active, implying her going on *to consider the implications* of what has happened (see LSJ διαλογίζομαι 2; BDAG διαλογίζομαι 1). The combination of tenses is perhaps a "means of pointing to (but not emphasizing) the onset of an event that is portrayed as a process" (*LHGT* 50).

35. Bovon, *Luke 1* 50; see LXX Gen. 6.8, 18.3, 1 Kingd. 1.18.

36. NRSV's "And now" seems an extraordinarily weak rendering of "καὶ ἰδοὺ"—an expression used as "a prompter of attention" and "marker of strong emphasis" (BDAG ἰδοὺ 1 and 2).

37. Brown, *Birth* 280.

38. E.g., LXX Gen. 4.1, 19.8, 24.16

39. See LSJ γινώσκω III, BDAG γινώσκω 5, *GELS* γινώσκω 13.

40. So Fitzmyer, *Luke* 1.350.

41. See above on Matthew 1.18-19, cf. Deut. 22.24.

42. That is the storyline: a promise, and a question that arises directly from that promise. So generations of readers and listeners have naturally understood the narrative. There is no need—and, in my view, no room—for complicated additional hypotheses, such as that Mary had already made a vow of perpetual virginity: a notion that, however understandable it may be in the light of later Christian reflection on Mary, Brown rightly describes as "totally implausible" in the context supposed by Luke (*Birth of the Messiah* 306).

43. Bovon, *Luke 1* 51.

44. "The story itself unfolds according to the Hebrew Bible genre of the birth prophecy. Such legends are concerned with a certain individual who is

sought out by a messenger of God." This messenger "determines the entire interaction and the course of the conversation" (Bovon, *Luke* 1.47). What are striking and significant therefore are those elements in the conversation that deviate from or add to the Biblical traditions, of which the most obvious in the annunciation to Mary is the stress on her virginity.

45. Perhaps it was the avoidance of a possible element of contradiction here—in other words, doctrinal rather than linguistic reasons—that led the Greek fathers, (followed by the NRSV and REB) to favor "declared" or "proclaimed" as the meaning of "ὁρισθέντος," at Romans 1.4, rather than "appointed" (so TILC "costuito," TOB "établi") which does indeed appear to have been its normal sense at this period (cf. Cranfield, *Romans* 161-62). That granted, in interpreting nuances of rhetoric, I am always cautious in preferring our understanding to that of the Greek fathers, who were, after all, reading their own language.

46. At Genesis 18.14 the LXX renders Masoretic "הֲיִפָּלֵא מֵיְהוָה דָּבָר (Is anything too hard for YHWH?)" by "μὴ ἀδυνατεῖ παρὰ τῷ θεῷ ῥῆμα (Can it be that anything is impossible with God?)"; cf. Luke 1.37: "οὐκ ἀδυνατήσει παρὰ τοῦ θεοῦ πᾶν ῥῆμα." Commentators generally suggest that ῥῆμα at LXX Genesis 18.14 renders Hebrew דָּבָר and therefore, in addition to its usual senses in classical and koine Greek ("that which is said, word, saying, expression or statement") has also, following דָּבָר, the further force of an "event that can be spoken about, thing, object, matter event" (BDAG ῥῆμα 1 and 2; LSJ ῥῆμα A3; cf. *TDNT* 4.92-93). We need not doubt that this is broadly true of ῥῆμα in the LXX. I am indebted, however, to my friend Christopher Palmer for pointing out to me in conversation that in Mary's response to Gabriel, "Be it to me according to your word (ῥῆμα)," she actually appears to be using ῥῆμα simply in what would be its usual Greek sense. This leads me to wonder whether Luke cared about the enriched sense of ῥῆμα, which is not actually necessary in order to make sense of Gabriel's words, or whether the evangelist was even aware of it (*pace* Fitzmyer, *Luke* 1.352). In my view, far more significant than possible Hebraic implications of ῥῆμα at Luke 1.37 is the change in its relationship to God that I refer to in my main text and discuss in n.47, below.

47. The reading "παρὰ τοῦ θεοῦ (from God)" (παρὰ followed by the genitive) appears to be what Luke wrote at 1.37 and probably represents his deliberate rephrasing of LXX Gen. 18.14 "παρὰ τῷ θεῷ (with God)" (παρὰ followed by the dative) (cf. NA28; *TCGNT* 130; *TDNT* 5.729-30; Bovon, *Luke 1* 53). Παρὰ followed by the dative speaks of *closeness*: hence, used figuratively, it means "in the sight or judgment of someone" (BDAG παρὰ B.2). Παρὰ

followed by the genitive speaks of that *from which* something proceeds, and hence is the "marker of one who originates or directs" (BDAG παρὰ A.2; cf. *GAGNT* 172; *GGNT* §237). It is unfortunate that the relatively poorly attested variant reading for Luke 1.37, "παρὰ τῷ θεῷ [with God]" was in the *Textus Receptus* used by King James's translators—a variant that is very likely the creation of early copyists "correcting" Luke in the light of LXX Gen. 18.14. But at Luke 1.37, as Luke wrote it, Gabriel is *not* saying, "With (or, In the sight of) God no word shall be powerless" but, "No word *from God* shall be powerless." The only English translations of which I am aware that spell out clearly the implications of this are the RV of 1880, which has "For no word from God shall be void of power" (which I have followed in my own translation in my main text), and NEB and REB, whose "God's promises can never fail" is a paraphrase that makes the essential point: Gabriel is talking about a word that comes *from* God. The revisers of 1880 were, no doubt, acutely aware of what were then recent improvements in the text of the NT resulting from the work of Westcott and Hort, and the creators of NEB (1970) and REB (1990) did not forget them. Alas, by contrast, the revisers of 1952 (RSV), 1970 (NAB) and 1989 (NRSV) ignored the significance of this, essentially returning to the KJV translators' rendering of *Textus Receptus*: all, in other words, taking a massive step backwards.

48. Despite the practice of the NRSV, REB and EVV generally (and other modern versions: cf. TOB, *la servante* and TILC, *la serva*), it is a mistake to render δοῦλος / δούλη as "servant," thus disguising the significance of the word in the koine of the first Christian century. (The same should be said, incidentally, of NAB's "handmaid," certainly if that word is understood in the sense offered by *OED*: "a female servant.") As Spicq points out, to begin with, "before it came to be used for slaves, *doulos* was an adjective meaning 'unfree,' as opposed to *eleutheros*, and this dichotomy remained basic in the first century: *eite douloi, eite eleutheroi* ['slaves or free,' 1 Cor. 12.13 NRSV]. As the Roman jurist Gaius (*fl.* 130-180) would later define the matter, 'The principal legal distinction between persons is that of free and slave. Further, among free men, some are *ingenuus,* other are manumitted. The *ingenii* are those who are born free: the manumitted are those who are freed from servitude by a legal proceeding" (*TLNT* 3.380-81 citing Gaius, *Institutes* 1.9-11). See further nn. 50 and 51 below.

49. LXX Gen. 22.1; Isa. 6.8.

50. Dale B. Martin, *Slavery as Salvation* xiii, 1–49, 61–62; also Bartchy, *First Century Slavery and the Interpretation of 1 Corinthians 7:21* especially 114-120.

On Greco-Roman slavery in general, see Yvon Thébert, "The Slave," 138-174, and literature there cited.

51. The notion of being "slave of the god" (though not common) is occasionally found in pagan contexts. Apuleius, after his deliverance by the grace of Isis, rejoices that he has begun to be "slave to the goddess" and is in his turn exhorted to accept willingly "the yoke of service" (*Metamorphoses* 11.15).

52. Gaventa, "Nothing Will Be Impossible with God" 25.

53. Soares Prabhu, "'Rejoice, Favored One!'" 276 n.24. Schaberg's *Illegitimacy of Jesus* is a striking example of such negative interpretation: see further Additional Note B.

54. Bovon, *Luke 3* 201.

55. Ibid.

56. *BHGNT Luke,* 36; cf. BDF §384. "Luke uses the optative *genoito,* expressing a wish that is obtainable" (Fitzmyer, *Luke I-IX* 352). Cf. Prabhu, "'Rejoice, Favored One!'" 276 n.24; J. McHugh, *The Mother of Jesus in the New Testament* (New York: Doubleday, 1979) 65; Brown, *Birth* 319.

57. "In none of the Hebrew Bible parallels does one find such an explicitly formulated assent as in this passage" (Bovon, *Luke 1* 53 n.96).

58. For the two senses (by no means incompatible with each other) here attributed to μετὰ σπουδῆς, see BDAG, σπουδή 1 and 2; LSJ σπουδή (I) and II. Blaise Hospodar ("*Meta spoudēs* in Luke 1,39," 14-18), eager to emphasize the latter sense (he renders μετὰ σπουδῆς at Luke 1.48 by "in a serious mood of mind" and/or with "grave pensiveness") produces striking examples from Jewish and pagan literature, but perhaps overstresses the latter sense at the expense of the former.

59. So, e.g., classically, Karl Barth:

> "Born of the Virgin Mary." Once again, and now from the human standpoint, the male is excluded here. The male has nothing to do with this birth. What is involved here is, if you like, a divine act of judgement. To what is to begin here, humankind is to contribute nothing by his action and initiative. Humanity is not simply excluded, for the Virgin is there. But the male, as the specific agent of human action and history, with his responsibility for directing the human species, must now retire into the background, as the powerless figure of Joseph. That is the Christian reply to the problem of woman: here the woman stands absolutely in the foreground, moreover the *virgo*, the Virgin Mary. God did not choose humanity in its pride and its defiance, but humanity in its weakness and humility, not humanity in its historical role, but

> humanity in the weakness of its nature as represented by the woman, the human creature who can confront God only with the words, 'Behold, the handmaid of the Lord; be it unto me according as Thou hast said.' Such is the human co-operation in this matter, that and only that! (*Dogmatics in Outline,* G. T. Thomson, transl. altered. 99-100).

David Brown seems determined to read the Biblical Marian texts so as to strip Mary of any personality whatever. Thus,

> Mary's fiat is really incidental to the main focus of the text, God's involvement in acting upon her. Her role is not properly as an individual but rather as a foil, so that through her various objections and difficulties the marvelous character of what God is doing may be more effectively highlighted. Even the allusion to the sword piecing her heart could be a reference merely to the incident in the Temple which follows since Luke makes… no indicator of any active or deep involvement in the mission of her son. (*Discipleship and Imagination* 234-35).

I find these comments quite extraordinary, and the more so in light of a footnote that Brown attaches conceding that, "Luke's text leaves open the possibility of an alternative trajectory that could legitimate a different way of approaching the story" (op. cit. 235 n.27). Indeed it does!—and in a storyteller as good as Luke, that is probably not an accident.

60. Ann Loades, *Grace is not Faceless* (London: Darton, Longman and Todd) 40.

61. Laurentin, *Mary* 14.

62. While my purpose is, as I have said, to speak of Mary and the traditions surrounding her *as she was remembered*, I have also pointed out that memory is not necessarily utterly divorced from what may actually have been the case. In the present instance, it is interesting to note that recent archeological research increasingly points to strong links between Lower Galilee and Judaea at this period (James H. Charlesworth, "The Historical Jesus in the Fourth Gospel: A Paradigm Shift?" *Journal for the Study of the Historical Jesus* 8(1) 24-26). Archaeological study in a number of sites in Lower Galilee indicate that Jewish settlements there began in the Hasmonean period between 135–76 BCE, and were culturally linked to Judaea (Mordechai Aviam, "The Hasmonaean Dynasty's Activities in the Galilee" in *Jews, Pagans and Christians in the Galilee* 41-50). By the time of Jannaeus (103–76 BCE), Galilee, especially in the middle and east, was dominated by Jews and Gamla in the Golan

had become a Jewish town (S. Gutman, "Gamla" in *The New Encyclopedia of Archaeological Excavations in the Holy Land*, E. Stern ed. 4 vols. [New York: Simon & Schuster, 1993] 2.459-63). If the archeologists are right, then they lend credence to Luke's assertion that Jesus' family had relatives in Judea and in the hill country west of Jerusalem (Lk. 1.36, 39-40). They also lay open the possibility that a claim made in both Matthew and Luke—namely, that while Jesus was "of Nazareth" (as Mark and John imply), his ancestry originated in Bethlehem—might just possibly be correct (cf. Charlesworth, "Historical Jesus in the Fourth Gospel" 26).

63. Hospodar, "Meta spoudes" 14.

64. Cf. Gathercole, *Gospel and the Gospels* 464: the trope is, of course, from Arthur Conan Doyle's *The Adventure of Silver Blaze.*

65. *Pace* Bovon, who has Mary "hike" for the journey! This seems extraordinarily unlikely to be how Luke will have envisaged a respectable young Jewish woman travelling alone at this period (Bovon, *Luke* 1.58).

66. The expression "καὶ ἐγένετο" should "be recognized as a Septuagintism, since this asyndetic form is used in that translation of the Old Testament for Hebrew *wayyĕhî... wĕ-*, "and it happened... that" (Fitzmyer, *Luke I-IX* 119).

67. This slowness and solemnity are even more evident in Luke's Greek than in English, for in the sentence that immediately follows ἐγένετο, each time a proper noun appears it is accompanied by the definite article, "...τῆς Μαρίας ἡ Ἐλισάβετ... ἡ Ἐλισάβετ" (see *LHGT* 38-39).

68. Bovon (*Luke* 1.58-59) compares Jacob and Esau in the womb (Gen. 25.22-28), although the contrasts here are surely as marked as the similarities.

69. On "εὐλογημένη" cf. BDAG εὐλογέω 3; *GAGNT* 172-3, n. 125.

70. The NT uses two Greek words to describe those who are in a right relationship with God, namely, εὐλογημένος, perfect passive participle of εὐλογέω (BDAG: "speak well of, praise, extol... call down God's gracious power, bless...bestow a favor, provide with benefits"), and μακάριος and its cognates (BDAG: "fortunate or happy because of circumstances... fortunate, happy, privileged, blessed... *privileged recipient of divine favor*"). In the LXX, εὐλογημένος and its cognates frequently render Hebrew ברכה/ברך (e.g., Gen. 2.3), and μακάριος and its cognates renders several Hebrew words, notably among them אַשְׁרֵי (e.g., Ps. 1.1). Evidently, the two expressions, in both Hebrew and Greek, overlap in meaning but also extend that meaning in different directions: the former tending to indicate what *causes* our right relationship with God (i.e., God's gracious word), the latter what *follows* from it. English translations of the NT from Wycliffe onward (including KJV, D-R and NRSV) do not, however, generally reflect this distinction, rendering both

words by "blessed." In my own renderings, I try to indicate the distinction by rendering εὐλογημένη/εὐλογημένος by "blessed," μακαρία by "happy," and μακαριοῦσίν by "will call happy."

71. In Koine Greek of the first century of the Christian Era, πιστεύω and its cognates, while at various times appropriately rendered by a number of English words including "belief" and "faith," is at its heart a word expressing relationship and, in particular, relationship of *trust*, understood as a virtue, but also as something fragile and easily betrayed: cf. Teresa Morgan, *Roman Faith and Christian Faith* passim.

72. Cf. "Elizabeth perceives that Mary's true joy and her true value lie in her faith" (Laurentin, *Mary* 14). As Morgan points out, "The language of faith is central to Christianity as to no other religious tradition" (*Roman Faith and Christian Faith* 1).

73. "Because you did not trust (ἀνθ' ὧν οὐκ ἐπίστευσας)" (1.20) and "happy is she that trusted (μακαρία ἡ πιστεύσασα)" (1.45): I have translated so as to make clear what our English translations often do not make clear, that the verb is in each case the same.

74. Bovon, *Luke* 2, 132; he cites Rachel C. Wahlberg, "Jesus and the Uterus Image," *ThTo* 31 (1974-75) 228-30. I found Bovon's entire discussion of Luke 11.27ff helpful: see Bovon, *Luke* 2, 128-34. Similarly Fitzmyer, who points out that, "The particle *menoun* does not mean "nay, rather..." but "yes, rather..." for v.28 admits that Jesus' mother is worthy of praise, not just because she has given birth to him, but because she too—in the Lucan story—is among those who have listened to the word of God, believed it (1.45), and acted on it (8.21; cf. Acts 1.14)" (*Luke X-XXIV* 927).

75. Caird, *New Testament Theology* 28; cf. McHugh: "When she speaks of what God has done for her, she speaks of what God has done for Israel: that is, she speaks of herself as the Daughter of Zion" (*Mother of Jesus in the New Testament* 76).

76. On *prosōpopoiía* and the origin of the *Magnificat*, see further Appendix B.

77. On *prosōpopoiía* in Romans see further Christopher Bryan, *Preface to Romans* 142-45.

78. BDAG μακάριος 1 and 2.

79. On the significance of the Name of God in biblical tradition, see Pedersen, *Israel* I-II, 245-47.

80. Evans, *Luke* 171; but Evans is by no means alone. See additional Note A.

81. Shakespeare, *Midsummer Night's Dream* 1.1.229.

82. The Catonsville Nine were Father Daniel Berrigan and eight other Roman Catholic activists who on May 17, 1968, took 378 draft files from the draft board office in Catonsville, Maryland, and burned them in the parking lot to protest the Vietnam War. They then recited the Lord's Prayer and made impassioned speeches denouncing the war.

83. Greenham Common Women's Peace Camp was a succession of protest camps protesting the siting of nuclear weapons at the then Royal Air Force station in the civil parishes of Greenham and Thatcham in Berkshire, England. The camp began on 5 September 1981 when a Welsh group, Women for Life on Earth, came to Greenham to protest the British government's decision to allow cruise missiles to be stored there. After realizing that the march alone was not going to get them the attention that they needed if their protest was to be effective, the women began to stay at Greenham. A Commemorative and Historic Site at Yellow Gate, Greenham Common, now marks the site of the original Peace Camp between 1981 and 2000.

84. Bovon, *Luke 1* 65, citing Gustavo Guttiérez, *A Theology of Liberation: History, Politics, and Salvation* 116-20.

85. C. S. Lewis, *Reflections on the Psalms* (London: Geoffrey Bles, 1958) 6.

86. Dorothy Sayers, *The Man Born to Be King* [London: Victor Gallancz, 1946] 46).

87. "The antithetical terms *kiddush ha-Shem* ("sanctification of the [Divine] Name") and *ḥillul ha-Shem* ("defamation of the [Divine] Name") are complementary antonyms and denote the two aspects of one of the most significant concepts in Judaism. They imply, respectively, the glorification of the God of Israel and the diminution of His honor. The specific terms are rabbinic; the concepts themselves, however, are biblical in origin and are included among the 613 commandments: "Ye shall keep My commandments and do them: I am the Lord. Ye shall not profane My holy Name; but I will be hallowed among the children of Israel; I am the Lord who hallow you" (Lev. 22:31, 32). The entire people was subject to these principles, although the priests were especially cautioned to avoid *ḥillul ha-Shem* (Lev. 21:6; 22:2)" (*Encyclopedia Judaica*: "KIDDUSH HA-SHEM AND ḤILLUL HA-SHEM"; cited online at jewishvirtuallibrary.org).

88. Herbert McCabe, O.P., *God Matters* 211.

89. See, e.g., Raymond Brown, "The Qumran Scrolls and the Johannine Gospel and Epistles" *CBQ* 17 (1955): 403-19, 559-74.

90. Cf. Josephus, *Antiquities* 17.13.5; 18.1.1; 18.2.1. Attempts to reconcile the two narratives have not in general been found convincing: see Brown,

Birth 394-96; Fitzmyer, *Luke* 1.392-93; Evans, *Luke* 191-93; Johnson, *Luke* 49.

91. Bovon, *Luke* 1.83.

92. See BDF §5 (3).

93. Cf. Brown, *Birth of the Messiah* 415.

94. Cf. Micah 5.2; Matt. 2.5.

95. Fragments of the altar were discovered as early as 1568 and more came to light in 1859; their incorporation into a reconstruction of the altar during the first half of the twentieth century has been and remains controversial. See, online at time of writing, a useful Wikipedia article, "Ara Pacis" (https://en.wikipedia.org/wiki/Ara_Pacis).

96. If Luke is correct in his initial dating of the events recorded in his birth narrative as being "in the days of Herod the king of Judaea" (1.5), then a Roman census could not have applied in Judaea either: see Sherwin-White, *Roman Society and Roman Law* 163 n.4. Sherwin-White has useful information generally on the subject of Roman census, although his apparent assumption that Luke is concerned to revise Matthew appears to most of us unlikely to be correct.

97. One may grant Luke's particular concern to show a positive relationship between Christianity and Roman *imperium*. Nevertheless, the attitude to Rome manifested here accords generally with biblical views of pagan empire. There was in the '90s and '00s a fad in NT scholarship (now mercifully passing) which was anxious to make the NT anti-Roman. It is neither anti- nor pro-. On Jesus and Rome, see my *Render to Caesar* (2005). On relations generally between Rome and Israel at this period, see Martin Goodman's magnificent *Rome and Jerusalem* (2007).

98. Pierre Benoit, "Quirinius (Recensement de)" *DBSup* 9 (1977) 693-720 esp. 700.

99. NRSV "expecting a child" renders οὔσῃ ἐγκύῳ: οὔσῃ being attributive qualifying Μαριὰμ, and ἐγκύῳ predicate dative.

100. Luke 1.39-40.

101. Kelley Nikondeha, *The First Advent in Palestine* 84. Such family ties alone would be adequate reason for Mary undertaking the journey. As I have indicated in my main text, Nikondeha is mistaken, however, in supposing that the imperial decree *obliged* Mary to be present at the registration (*First Advent* 82-83). I am obliged to my friend and colleague Sheila Swarbrick for drawing my attention to Nikondeha's book.

102. Luke Timothy Johnson, *The Gospel of Luke* 51.

103. That, of course, is *all* that it makes clear. The word πρωτότοκος neither excludes nor requires the birth of later children. Occasionally in our literature the word μονογενής ("the only member of a kin") is added to πρωτότοκος, so as to make it clear that an only child is the referent: thus in the *Psalms of Solomon*: "Your discipline is upon us as on a firstborn, an only son (ὡς υἱὸν πρωτότοκον μονογενῆ)" (Ps. Sol. 18.4).

It may be worth noting, however, that πρωτότοκος is also used to speak of pre-eminence or special status (BDAG πρωτότοκος 2). Given that Luke has already told us through an angel that Mary's child is to be called "son of the Most high," it has been suggested that what the evangelist may have had in mind as he wrote or dictated "**her firstborn son**" are other occasions and other contexts in which Jesus is spoken of as "the firstborn" (such as Rom. 8.29; Col. 1.15; Heb. 1.6 citing LXX Ps.88.28/MT Ps. 89.27). We might even translate Luke's expression here as, "**her son, the firstborn,**" rendering τὸν πρωτότοκον as a noun substantive in apposition to τὸν υἱὸν αὐτῆς (*BHGNT Luke* 68). In other words, the issue hinted at by speaking of Jesus as "**firstborn**" may not be to do with Mary at all, but with Jesus' relationship to God and to humankind. "Has it become a Christological title that designates the Lord, in his incarnation and resurrection, as the firstborn of a new human race?" (Bovon, *Luke 1* 85). The suggestion is attractive, although, as Bovon himself seems to imply, rendered somewhat less plausible by the fact that Luke for his part "does not use this attribute in the context of the resurrection account or the kerygma" (ibid).

104. Gaventa, *Mary* 61.

105. Cf. Wisdom 7.4. Brown observes that the fact that Mary (rather than Joseph or someone helping with the birth) wraps the child in cloths is hardly evidence that Mary's bringing Jesus to birth was miraculous or painless (Brown, *Birth of the Messiah* 399). This is surely correct. Brown's reference, however, to the *Protoevangelium of James*, which certainly understands the birth as miraculous but does not connect that claim to Jesus' being wrapped in bands of cloth, appears to be somewhat beside the point.

106. So Tyndale (1534), Cranmer (1539), D-R, KJV, RV, NEB, RSV, REB, NRSV, NAB. The only exceptions I can find are Wiclif (1380) "cracche" and similarly Geneva (1557) "cretche."

107. See Martin Hengel, φάτνη in *TDNT* IX, 49-55.

108. Rossetti, *Christmas Carol.*

109. BDAG τόπος a, b, c and e; cf. LSJ τόπος A 1, 2.

110. See BDAG κατάλυμα. Noun κατάλυμα is cognate with verb καταλύω, used to mean "unloose," "unharness" or "unyoke," and hence "to take up one's

quarters," "to lodge" (LSJ καταλύω II, 1 and 2). Elsewhere, Luke uses another word, πανδοχεῖον, to speak of what appears to be an inn in more or less our sense (see Luke 10.34).

111. So also Tyndale (1534); the only exception of which I am aware is Wicliffe who, translating from the Vulgate in 1380, rendered the passage by "ther was no place to hym in no chaumbre" (following Vlg. vl "ei" rather than "eis").

112. Brown, *Birth* 400; Johnson, *Luke* 49.

113. Johnson, *Luke* 52. One seems regularly to hear preachers around Christmas making this point, and in view of the materialism and excess that have come to surround our commemoration of the Saviour's birth, perhaps they cannot make it too loudly or too often. But there is no clear basis for it in Luke's narrative.

114. Fitzmyer, *Luke* 1.408.

115. Commentators have found themselves puzzled that Luke tells us so briefly about Jesus' birth and then cuts at once to the shepherds: "It remains a riddle why Luke does not narrate Jesus' birth in greater detail" (Bovon, *Luke* 1.86; cf. Brown *Birth* 410-11)—a puzzlement that perhaps says more about the commentators than about Luke's narrative. In my view, Luke here gives us a perfect example of an effective narrative style in which "less is more." His description of Jesus' birth has done exactly what is needed to get our imaginations working. The two thousand or so years of imaginative and artistic reflection to which his work has led are the unarguable testimony to that.

116. While rabbinic tradition was at times somewhat dismissive of shepherds (e.g., *b. Sanh.* 25b), in the Scriptures shepherds generally get a good press: suffice it to recall that Moses was a shepherd, David was a shepherd, and God is pictured as the shepherd of Israel (Exod. 3.1; 1 Sam. 16.11; Ps. 23.1). Those who heard Luke from a pagan background would perhaps recall traditions of the shepherd Faustulus and his wife Acca Larentia who raised Romulus and Remus as their own (e.g., Livy, *History of Rome* 1.4.6-8).

117. Luke's description of the shepherds as ἀγραυλοῦντες (KJV "abiding in the fields") (Luke 2.8)—that is, as having the fields as their dwelling—already had ancient precedent. Homer spoke of ποιμένες ἄγραυλοι (*Iliad* 18.162).

118. With Luke's expression "φυλάσσοντες φυλακὰς τῆς νυκτὸς" we might compare Xenophon speaking of a soldier's duty "to watch the watches (φυλακὰς φυλάξειν)," i.e., to take his turn on guard duty (*Anabasis* 2.6.10).

119. In my translation at Luke 14b, I follow the paraphrase offered by the NEB, although I confess I am much drawn by REB's "and on earth peace to all in whom he delights." The ending of the angelic hymn at Luke 2.14 presents a notorious textual problem. Two readings have good support: "ἐπὶ γῆς εἰρήνη ἐν ἀνθρώποις εὐδοκία," with εὐδοκία in the nominative (this is the reading followed by the KJV: "on earth peace, good will towards men"); and "ἐπὶ γῆς εἰρήνη ἐν ἀνθρώποις εὐδοκίας," with εὐδοκία in the genitive (this is the reading followed by Jerome ["in terra pax in hominibus bonae voluntatis"] and therefore by Douay-Rheims: "on earth peace towards men of good will"). NA28 (followed by the NRSV) favours εὐδοκία in the genitive as being "the more difficult reading" (*TCGNT* 133). There is, in fact, not so much difference in meaning between the two readings as might at first appear. If εὐδοκία is understood in its frequent LXX sense of *divine* goodwill or good pleasure (as, e.g., at LXX 1 Chron. 16.10 or rendering Hebrew ןוֹצָר at LXX Ps. 5.13), then whichever reading of Luke 2.14 we follow, Luke is to be understood as speaking of *God's benevolence towards humankind*, not of human benevolence: "εὐδοκία in the angel's song refers to God's gracious counsel addressed in free and incomprehensible favour to the people of His elect" (Gottlob Schrenk, *TDNT* 2.750; cf. 2.742-51; also Fitzmyer, *Luke* 1.410-12; *GAGNT* 177; BDAG εὐδοκία 1 and especially 2; *LHGT* 73). Hence NRSV's "peace among those whom [God] favours," though clumsy, is acceptable.

120. Luke 10.21 // Matt.11.25. Of course, Jesus is not perceived as thanking God because the wise have been left out, any more than as imagining that only the very young will follow him. "The wise" is clearly ironic. See Bryan, *Son of God* 99.

121. The verb itself, συντηρέω, which the NRSV and REB render by "treasure up," does indeed carry the sense of "to preserve," and hence "to store information in one's mind for careful consideration, hold or treasure up in one's memory," cf. LXX Sir. 39.2; Dan. 7.28 [Theod]; *T. Levi* 6.2; also LSJ συντηρέω; BDAG συντηρέω 3.

122. The verb συμβάλλω, which with REB I render "ponder," means literally "to throw together or bring together" (cf BDAG συμβάλλω 1, 2 and 3). It occurs in the LXX and elsewhere in a number of senses. Luke is the only New Testament writer to use it and seems to understand it as implying "give careful thought to, consider, ponder," but not without an element of perplexity: cf. Luke [11.53 vl], 14.31, Acts 4.15, 17.18.

123. See Burridge, *What are the Gospels* 199.

124. Schaberg, *Illegitimacy* 136. I do not, of course, by any means share Schaberg's view that these traditions were to do with Mary's being raped.

Schaberg herself, always scrupulous, admits that it is "impossible to be certain that this was the case" (137). Rather, I would connect these traditions with the mystery of a virginal conception. Nevertheless, Schaberg's entire reflection on the likely role of women in the creation and transmission of Jesus' story is well worth study and reflection (*Illegitimacy* 136-38).

125. Schaberg, *Illegitimacy of Jesus* 136-38.

126. Bovon, *Luke* 1.92, citing the research of W. C. Van Unnik, "Die rechte Bedeutung des Wortes treffen: Lukas 2,29" (*Sparsa Collecta* 1.72-91).

127. Gaventa, *Mary* 62. We might bear in mind (and will discuss in their place) Mary's reaction to Jesus' enigmatic words to her in John 2.4-5.

128. *Daughter of Jerusalem* 29

129. Luke 24.52-53.

130. Leviticus 12.4-6.

131. Granted it is obviously the more difficult reading, "their (αὐτῶν)" is surely correct. Variant "his (αυτου)" is perhaps best seen as a "transcriptional error for αὐτῶν (in cursive Greek script the pronoun was abbreviated αὐτ with the termination expressed by a 'shorthand' stroke), or as a deliberate modification because afterwards (ver. 27), Jesus is the object of the presentation in the Temple" (*TCGNT* 134). Be that as it may, Jerome followed the variant reading αυτου, rendering it by "eius." Latin "eius" can, however, be either masculine or feminine, which was convenient for the DRB translators who, following Jerome, were able to render "eius" by "her," thereby satisfying at once both the requirements of Lev. 12.4-6 and the text they were translating. KJV, though based on Greek texts rather than Jerome, also has "her," presumably following the reading αὐτῆς, a "late correction" (ibid.) found in the edition of the NT published by Beza (1565). That said, the KJV translators will certainly have been aware of Vg, and presumably of D-R (of which the NT had been published in 1589).

132. 1 Sam. 1.21-28.

133. Johnson, *Luke* 35.

134. Mal. 3.1; see René Laurentin, *Structure et Théologie de Luc I-II* (Paris: Gabalda, 1957); so Brown, *Birth* 445, but contrast Evans, *Luke* 213. Luke surely had Malachi in mind earlier at 1.17 where he had the angel speak to Zachariah of John going before the Lord "in the spirit and power of Elijah" (cf. Mal. 4.5).

135. See, e.g., *RCL*, proper for the Presentation. Many artists have likewise registered the connection: cf. e.g., Ambrosio Lorenzetti's *Presentation in the Temple* (1342: now in the Uffizi).

136. There is no reason to suppose on the basis of the expression τοὺς γονεῖς (also at 2.48) and references to Joseph as Jesus' "father" (e.g., 2.33, 48) that

Luke is drawing upon an earlier source that did not know of the virginal conception tradition and in which this is the first intimation the parents have that their child has a special destiny (as suggested by Creed, *Luke* 41-42). Luke, who obviously *did* know of the virginal conception tradition, apparently did not find the expressions objectionable, and neither have generations of Christians listening to them over centuries, so there is no reason to suppose that a hypothetical source would have done so. Indeed, in view of his acceptance of Jesus, Joseph *was* Jesus' father for legal and genealogical purposes, as we have already noted in our discussion of Matthew.

137. See BDAG δέχομαι 1, "to receive something offered or transmitted by another," specifically citing Luke 2.28.

138. As Creed pointed out, Simeon's confidence and joy are a striking contrast to the attitude of the aged sage Asita to the birth of the Buddha, with which this narrative of Simeon is sometimes compared (Creed, *Luke* 37-38: cf. Bovon, *Luke* 1.97).

139. As at Luke 1.69, 3.6, 19.9, Acts 4.12, 13.26, 16.17, 28.28.

140. Shake off this downy sleep, death's counterfeit,
And look on death itself! (*Macbeth* 2.3.76-77)

141. So Adriaen Isenbrandt's "Our Lady of the Seven Sorrows" (grisaille), painted at some time between 1510 and 1551 and at present in the collection of the Royal Museums of Fine Art in Belgium.

142. Examples are the nineteenth-century Russian icon of "Our Lady Who Softens Evil Hearts" and the "Seven Swords Piercing the Sorrowful Heart of Mary" statue in the Church of the Holy Cross in Salamanca.

143. In addition to the present instance, examples of such pairing are Mary and Zechariah in the birth narratives; the widow of Zarephath and Naaman the Syrian (4:26-27); the "woman who was a sinner" and Simon the Pharisee (7:36-50); the twelve male disciples and the women who "provided for them out of their own resources" (8.1-3); and the parables of the lost sheep and the ten coins (15:4-10).

144. BDAG ἀνθομολογέομαι; cf. LSJ "confess freely and openly" (ἀνθομολογέομαι A.II). This is the only time this verb is used in the NT.

145. Bovon, *Luke 1* 106. Some versions, notably some readings of the Vulgate, read "Israel" here. At the time of the disastrous second revolt against Rome (A.D. 132-35), documents were actually dated to years from "the redemption of Israel" and "the redemption of Jerusalem"—in other words,

Luke's expression clearly reflects real Jewish aspirations of the period (see Fitzmyer, *Luke* 1.432).

146. This is one of those cases where derivation is some use as an indicator of sense: λύτρωσις and its cognates are all related directly or indirectly to λύω ("to loose, to set free, to untie") and they are invariably used in connection with some kind of liberation. In the LXX, the verb generally has God as its subject and renders Hebrew *ga'al* "set free," *padah* "deliver, redeem, save" or *paraq* "pull away (i.e., from danger)." "I am the Lord… and I will deliver you from slavery and I will redeem (λυτρώσομαι) you by a raised arm and great judgment" (LXX Exod. 6:6); "because the Lord loved you… the Lord brought you out with a strong and a high arm and redeemed (ἐλυτρώσατο) you from a house of slavery, from the hand of Pharaoh king of Egypt" (LXX Deut. 7:8); "because with the Lord there is mercy, and much redemption (λύτρωσις) is with him, and it he who will redeem (λυτρώσεται) Israel from all its acts of lawlessness" (LXX Ps. 129.7-8). This is precisely the way in which Luke uses λύτρωσις and its cognates, e.g., at 1:68, 21:28, 24:21 and here at 2:38. The point at issue is not the *means*—although in secular usage the word normally implies payment of a ransom—but the *fact* of deliverance (cf. Isa. 52:3). Hence, as Fitzmyer points out, "the redemption of Jerusalem" at 2:38 is more or less synonymous with the earlier expression, "the consolation of Israel" (2:25) (Fitzmyer, *Luke* 1.432).

147. "Saint Simeon the receiver of God holds the infant Christ in his arms, who gives him his blessing. The Virgin on the other side of the altar stretches out her arms to the child, and behind her Joseph carries two doves in his robe; near him the prophetess Anna points out Christ and holds a scroll with these words: 'This child has created heaven and earth'" (Dionysius of Fourna, *Painter's Manual*, trans. Paul Hetherington [Torrance, California: Oakwood, 1996] [London: Sagittarius, 1974] 32). Dionysius lived from c1670 to sometime after 1744.

148. Cf. Luke 11.49, 21.15.

149. Cf. Luke 1.28, 30; 4.22.

150. E.g., Plutarch, *Alexander* 4.4-10.4 and *Cicero* 2.2-4. Cf. Burridge, *What are the Gospels* 142, 174.

151. Luke's word is "ἐξεπλάγησαν," aorist passive of "ἐκπλήσσω," meaning "drive out of one's senses by a sudden shock, amaze, astound" (LSJ ἐκπλήσσω II); "to cause to be filled with amazement to the point of being overwhelmed" (BDAG ἐκπλήσσω). In rendering "ἐξεπλάγησαν" at Luke 2.48 by "were dumbfounded," I follow the suggestion of BDAG (ibid).

152. "Look, your father and I have been searching for you in great anxiety (ὀδυνώμενοι)" (Luke 2.48b. The word expressing their anxiety—ὀδυνώμενοι—is strong (cf. TOB "tout angoissés"): the same word that Luke uses for the torture of the rich man in the flames of Hades (16.24) and for the grief of the Ephesian elders on knowing that they will not see Paul's face again (Acts 20.38) (cf. BDAG ὀδυνάω 1 and 2).

153. Between Jesus and Mary "a first episode of separation occurs when Jesus is lost and eventually found in the temple. Luke says this separation lasted three days, which, of course, prefigures the death of Christ. According to him, Mary, in contemplating these events, and her three days of anxiety in search of Jesus, receives the first taste of the sword that Simeon mentioned" (Laurentin, *Mary* 34).

154. We may note, incidentally, that Luke here uses τὸ ῥῆμα in what appears to be its normal Greek sense (cf. n. 183).

155. FitzMyer, *Luke* 1.444-45 ; Bovon, *Luke* 1.114.

156. Bovon, *Luke* 1.115, citing Laurentin, *Jésus au temple* 84.

157. While Acts is evidently not an example of Greco-Roman βίος/*vita* in the way in which the four canonical gospels are broadly examples of that genre, it and Luke's gospel are evidently and intentionally closely related works. Apropos Act's own genre, suffice it here to say that I find persuasive Richard Burridge's cautious conclusion. Following discussion of various possibilities that have been mooted in recent scholarship, he finds Acts' generic features to be,

> very close to historical monograph, but without the wider focus, scale and variety of verbal subject found in historiography. Its concentration upon early church leaders, especially Peter and Paul, suggests that it is best described as a "biographical monograph."

Burridge continues with a distinction that is particularly helpful:

> If Luke's first volume (Τὸν μὲν πρῶτον λόγον) is all about "what Jesus *began* to do and teach" in his life and ministry (ὧν ἤρξατο ὁ Ἰησοῦς ποιεῖν τε καὶ διδάσκειν), then the second part is what Jesus *continues* "to do and teach" through the deeds and words of Peter, Paul and the early church. (*Reading Acts Today* 26; cf. 1-26; *What are the Gospels* [25th Anniversary edition] 366: cf. 341-66).

Precisely.

158. Calvin understood σὺν γυναιξὶν to mean "with their wives," which would be the most natural way to take the expression: that some early readers understood the text in that way is indicated by the amplification in Codex Bezae (D) which reads "σὺν γυναιξὶν και τέκνοις," and probably by the Dura fragment of Tatian's Diatesseron (see *TCGNT* 284). This is, of course, disputed by those who believe that those being named are intended as witnesses, which would naturally point to the women witnesses of the resurrection as being the intended referents (see C. K. Barrett, *A Critical and Exegetical Commentary on the Acts of the Apostles.* ICC. 2 vols. [Edinburgh: T. & T. Clark, 1994–98] 89; Richard I. Pervo, *Acts: A Commentary.* Hermeneia. [Minneapolis: Fortress, 2009] 46-47).

159. Luke reduces the pericope on "Christ's Real Brethren" (Mark 3.31-35/ Matthew 12.46-50) so that it exists entirely for Jesus' *logion* (Luke 8.19-21) and says, in effect, nothing at all of Mary, nor indeed of his family. He omits all the negative implications regarding Jesus' family that we have noted in the other versions of this pericope, as well as entirely omitting the "Rejection at Nazareth" pericope (Mark 6.1-6 // Matt. 13.53-58). Hence in Pervo's view, "Luke does not portray the family of Jesus as hostile to his mission; he idealizes them" (Pervo, *Acts* 47). Or ignores them? Does that come to the same thing?

160. We have already noted Elisabeth Schüssler Fiorenza's observation that in narratives written in patriarchal societies, the presence of women will as a rule be mentioned only when their behavior can no longer be taken for granted, as when it "presents a problem or when women are exceptional individuals." What I have drawn attention to above as implicit in Luke's narrative is then an example (as I suppose) of what Sandra M. Schneiders calls "Revealing the Text's Secrets": that is, attempting "to extract from the biblical text the 'secrets' about women that are buried beneath its androcentric surface, especially the hidden history of women, which has been largely obscured or distorted, if not erased altogether, by male control of the tradition." Often—as, I believe, in this case—what is needed is no more than to point to "what is plainly in the text but has remained 'unnoticed' or even been denied by exegetes" (Schneiders, *The Revelatory Text: Interpreting the New Testament as Sacred Scripture*, 2nd edition [Collegeville, Minnesota: The Liturgical Press, 1999] 185).

5. John

1. That is to say, Hebrew "בְּרֵאשִׁית בָּרָא אֱלֹהִים" should be understood syntactically not (as in all ancient versions and many modern translations) as an independent sentence, but as a dependent clause: see, e.g., John Skinner, *A Critical and Exegetical Commentary on Genesis.* ICC. (Edinburgh : T. & T. Clark, 1910) 12 n.1; E. A. Speiser, *Genesis.* AB 1. (New York: Doubleday, 1964) 12-13; cf. Robert Alter, *Genesis.* (New York: W. W. Norton, 1996) 3.

2. Thus, we may contrast, e.g., Brooke Foss Westcott, who interprets 1.10-12 in terms of God's activity in the world throughout Israel's history (*The Gospel according to St. John.* [London: John Murray, 1898] 8-10) with Raymond E. Brown, who regards the verses as referring to the ministry of Jesus (Brown, *The Gospel according to John I-XII.* AB 29. [New York: Doubleday, 1966] 28-29).

3. "In other words, the reception of the Word of God under the Old Covenant was repeated at the coming of the Word made flesh" (John F. McHugh, *A Critical and Exegetical Commentary on John 1-4.* ICC. [London and New York: T & T Clark, 2009] 43). We might add that this imperfect reception manifestly continues into the life of the church and the world subsequent to the Incarnation.

4. Several ancient witnesses, mostly Latin, have the singular verb "was born"; the Curetonian Syriac and six manuscripts of the Peshitta Syriac have the plural "those who" but then the singular verb "was born." By contrast with this very patchy witness, *all* Greek manuscripts, together with all other patristic witnesses and versions, witness to the plural verb (see *TCGNT* 196-97).

5. E.g., the Editorial Committee of the United Bible Society's Greek New Testament: see *TCGNT* 197.

6. In his commentary Brown lists "Boismard, Blass, Braun, Burney, Dupont, Mollat (SB), Zahn, and others" as opting for the singular reading (*John I-IXX* 11-12). In the year in which Brown's commentary was published (1966), the first edition of the Jerusalem Bible also opted for it, and had Brown been writing a decade later, he would no doubt have included John McHugh's *The Mother of Jesus in the New Testament* 255-77, which offered a defense of the singular reading that John Wenham (while clearly disagreeing) memorably described as "lusty and attractive." Opting for the plural, however, Brown listed "J. Schmid... Barrett, Bultmann, Lightfoot, Wikenhauser, and others"—including, of course, Brown himself. Major commentators since Brown who have supported the plural reading include, e.g., J. N. Sanders and B. A. Mastin (1968), Rudolf Schnackenburg (1982), Mark W. G. Stibbe (1993), Francis

J. Moloney (1998), and arguably, though somewhat ambiguously, John McHugh himself in his commentary on John, destined not to be completed, of which the first four chapters were published posthumously in 2009.
7. McHugh, *John 1-4* 47.
8. Thus:

> "Bloods" is not Latin; but since it is plural in the Greek, the one who was translating preferred to speak poor Latin, according to the grammarians, that he might make plain the truth to the understanding of the weak among his hearers (Sanguina non est latinum, sed quia graece positum est pluraliter, maluit ille qui interpretabatur minus latine loqui secundim grammaticos et tamen explicare veritatem secundum auditum infirmorum). (Augustine, *Tractates on John*, cited in McHugh, *John* 47 cf. nn. 61 and 62).

9. McHugh, *John 1-4* 47.
10. Barrett, *The Gospel according to St. John. 2nd ed.* (London: SPCK, 1978) 164; similarly, J. N. Sanders and B. A. Mastin, *A Commentary on the Gospel according to St John.* (London: Adam & Charles Black, 1968) 79. Granted the change of metaphor, for the essential sentiment we might compare, on the one hand, the Matthean Jesus' response to Peter's confession, "Blessed are you, Simon son of Jonah! For flesh and blood has not revealed this to you, but my Father in heaven" (Matt. 16.17), and on the other hand, the *logion* as to Jesus' true family attributed to him by all three Synoptics (Mark 3.34b-35/ Matt.12.49-50/Luke 8.21).
11. Westcott *John* 10; cf. McHugh, *John 1-4* 49-50.
12. "Item legi ibi, quia verbum, deus, non ex carne, non ex sanguine, neque ex voluntate viri, neque ex voluntate carnis, sed ex deo natus est; sed quia verbum caro factus est et habitavit in nobis, non ibi legi" (Augustine, *Confessions* 7.9.14).
13. "To write ὁ λόγος σὰρξ ἐγένετο is to exclude any possibility that the human flesh of Jesus was something similar to clothing which he had put on, something quite external to him, which he could discard at will.... The sense is that the Logos became a human being without ceasing to be God" (McHugh, *John* 53).
14. Exod. 29.45. "People expect the Revealer to appear as a shining, mysterious, fascinating figure, as a hero or *theios anthrōpos*, as a miracle worker or mystagogue. His humanity must be no more than a disguise; it must be transparent. People want to look away from the humanity and see or sense

the divinity, they want to penetrate the disguise—or they will expect the humanity to be no more than the visualisation or the 'form' of the divine. All such desires are cut short by the statement: the Word became flesh. It is in his sheer humanity that he is the Revealer." (Bultmann, *The Gospel of John.* [Oxford: Basil Blackwell, 1971] 63). (I have slightly altered Beasley-Murray's translation).

15. The verb "dwelt (ἐσκήνωσεν)" (1.14b)—"live or dwell in a tent" (LSJ σκηνόω)—is not especially common in Greek, and its use here is perhaps best explained by reference to the Scriptures—and, as seems rather often to be the case with John, to the MT rather than the LXX. YHWH's command from the beginning is that Israel shall "make me a sanctuary so that I may dwell among them" (Exod. 25.8). Here and at other key moments when YHWH promises to be present with God's people (Exod. 29.45; 1 Kings 6.13, Ezek.43.7, Zech. 2.10-11), the Hebrew verb שָׁכַן (to dwell, reside) is used. Hebrew שָׁכַן we may transliterate as *sakan*; the Greek σκηνόω as *skēnoō*. The identity of consonants and similarity in meaning were surely noted by the evangelist (as apparently by Aquila: cf. McHugh, *John* 1-4 56). What John seems to be telling his hearers is then that the incarnate Word is the presence of God among God's people, God's full and complete "tabernacle" or "dwelling" (מִשְׁכָּן) (cf. Exod. 25.9): cf. Brown, *John* 1.32-35; McHugh, *John* 1-4 55-57; for a note of caution, however, see Barrett, *John* 165-66.

16. "ὁ ἄνθρωπος φύσει πολιτικὸν ζῷον (human beings are a social animals)" (Aristotle, *Politics* 1.1253a:). The word "πολιτικὸν" ("of or pertaining to the *polis*") is often translated "political," but in this context surely refers more to our natural characteristic of "living in community" than to what we normally understand as "politics" (cf. LSJ πολιτικός A.4: which specifically refers to this passage). Hence "social" is probably the more appropriate rendering.

17. Sara Maitland, *A Big Enough God: Artful Theology* (London: Mowbray, 1995) 99.

18. John 18.15, 20.2.

19. John 13.23; 19.26, 21.7, 20.

20. John 19.26-27.

21. John 4.21, 8.10, 20.13 cf. Matt.15.28, Luke 13.12.

22. "Certainly it contains none of the disrespect the English vocative has come to possess" (*GAGNT* 290); see LS γυνή I, II; BDAG γυνή 1; Brown, *John* 1.99.

23. Hebrew: "מַה-לִּי וָלָךְ" (e.g., Judges 11.12) or "2) "מַה-לִּי וְלָכֶם Sam. 16.10). The former clearly implies a sense of injury, virtually, "Why are you treating me like this?" The latter, by contrast, appears to be a simple refusal.

24. I quote from the Venerable Calhoun Walpole in personal correspondence, responding to my asking her to comment on the significance of "Qué tiene que ver esto con nosotros?"—which is how Jesus replies to his mother at John 2.4 according to Riene-Valera 1995.
25. Barrett, *John* 191.
26. Aquinas, *Commentary on John*, James A. Weisheipl, O.P. transl.
27. Westcott, *John* 37.
28. ἀρχιτρίκλινος: perhaps the slave who was responsible for managing the banquet; or possibly a guest appointed as *arbiter bibendi*. The commentators are generally uncertain: cf. Barrett, *John* 192-93; Brown, *John I-XII* 100.
29. Barret, *John* 193.
30. "It is difficult to treat this verse as a real connective between Cana and the next scene at Jerusalem, for a journey to Capernaum is a long detour from the road to Jerusalem" (Brown, *John I-XII* 113).
31. On the basis of his surmise that the gospel as we have it is a result of an editing of the author's disordered "literary remains" by a "redactor," Bultmann claimed that "the *Evangelist's Redaction* in 2.1-12 may perhaps be responsible for the date in v.1, but not for v.12, which must have been in the source, since it does not link up with the following section." In the source, "v.12 probably led on to 4.46-54" (Bultmann, *John* 114 and 114 n.4).
32. "If the verse was an attempt to harmonize the Johannine and Synoptic chronologies, it has not been successful" (Brown, *John I-XII* 113).
33. Luke 2.41-52.
34. Barrett, *John* 347-48; cf. Brown, who is slightly more cautious: "the Jews may be turning to an *ad hominem* argument against Jesus. He has been talking about his heavenly father and their father, but were there not rumours about his own birth? Was there not some question of whether he was really the son of Joseph?" (*John I-XII* 357).
35. I do not share the conviction of some (e.g., Barrett, *John* 551) that the presence of women followers of Jesus at the cross cannot be historical. No doubt it is hard to imagine that "a potentially dangerous" group of Jesus' male disciples would have been allowed to approach; by contrast, it is entirely plausible that soldiers guarding the cross would have been untroubled by the approach of a tiny group of grieving women who could hardly constitute a threat to anyone (which is, as Richard Bauckham points out, the "gist" of what happens according to all four gospels (Bauckham, *Jesus and the Eyewitnesses: The Gospels as Eyewitness Testimony*. 2nd edition [Grand Rapids, Michigan: W. B. Eerdmans 2017] 344), and with them a youth, possibly a young man, *not one of the twelve*, as Bauckham, again, has argued strongly and in my view

convincingly (*Jesus and the Eyewitnesses* 384-411, 550-89), whom the synoptic (apostolic) tradition did not even notice or bother to mention. What the boy himself would remember is, of course, entirely another matter.

Nothing whatever should to be made of the contrast between the women "at a distance (ἀπὸ μακρόθεν)" (Mark 15.40) and "near the cross (παρὰ τῷ σταυρῷ)" (John 19.25). The terms are imprecise, and their sense entirely dictated by context and point of view: one person's "at a distance" may well be another's "near." More to the point, and what many critics seem to forget in these connections, is that crucifixion was *intended* to be public. Crucified persons might find their sufferings watched many people—friends and enemies alike (Emil Stauffer, *Jesus and His Story* [London: SCM, 1960] 111, 179)—which is, again, just what the evangelists describe. For discussion of the vexed (and, on the basis of what John tells us, ultimately insoluble) question as to how many and who are the women whom the evangelist places at the cross with the mother of Jesus, see Brown, *John XIII-XXI* 904-6.

36. Bultmann, *John* 673.

37. Brown, *John XIII-XXI* 925.

38. C. H. Dodd, *The Interpretation of the Fourth Gospel* (Cambridge: Cambridge University Press, 1953) 428 n2.

39. C. H. Dodd, *Historical Tradition* 127.

40. Ernst Heanchen, *John 2* 193.

41. See my *Son of God* 48-50.

6. Revelation, or the Apocalypse

1. The seer of Revelation is deeply conscious of his "prophecy" as *text*, and therefore as something that could be altered but that, since it is the testimony of Jesus himself, *must not* be altered (Rev. 22.18-20); cf. Caird, *Revelation* 287-88.

2. Guffey, *Revelation and the Visual Culture of Asia Minor* 197.

3. In a series of books and papers, Margaret Barker sees a connection between developing early Christian theology and the faith and ritual of the first Temple, eclipsed but not forgotten since the temple reform—or "purge"—under Josiah (*Temple Theology* 76-78), but returned to by early Christians who found in it concepts of "incarnation and atonement, the sons of God and the life of the age to come, the day of judgment, justification, salvation, the renewed covenant and the kingdom of God" (*Temple Theology* vii). No doubt at significant points in the New Testament—notably in Hebrews—early Christians did draw biblical traditions of the first temple. I am not convinced, however, that an eclipsed faith of the first Temple is necessary to account

for—or, indeed, *can* account for—the evolution of Christian belief in its early decades, any more than that it is to be accounted for on the basis of Greek culture or Roman imperial religion. At times, all and any of these doubtless played a part. Nevertheless, the only sufficient explanation for Christian belief lies with his followers' experience of Jesus himself (see my *Son of God,* passim). To be fair, I do not think Barker would deny that. She argues that Jesus himself was his own first and best interpreter (*Temple Theology* viii). But she would probably consider I underestimate the significance of the eclipsed but not forgotten temple theology.

4. See Guffey, *Revelation* 183-86.

5. For a summary of patristic material identifying the woman as a figure of the people of God and identifying her with Mary, Jesus' mother, see McHugh, *Mother of Jesus* 470-71.

6. Cf. e.g., G. B. Caird, *Revelation* 147-48; Boring, *Revelation* 151; Wilfred J. Harrington, S. J., *Revelation* 129.

7. The seer follows the LXX's gentler version of the implied narrative wherein God's promise to the Messiah is that "you shall shepherd (ποιμανεῖς)" the nations, rather than the MT's declaration that "you shall break (תְּרֹעֵם)" them (LXX/MT Ps.2.9a). It is perhaps not without significance that the seer does *not* go on to allude also to Ps.2.9b, where the LXX pretty well follows the MT. For the messianic associations of this psalm, see Avrohom Chaim Feuer, *Tehillim 1* 65, 67.

8. Revelation 2.26-27, 11.15b.

9. We need not here enter into disputes as to whether the seer means by the birth of the Messiah to speak of the nativity of Jesus or of his cross (so, e.g., Caird, *Revelation* 149)—or, as I would incline to add, of his resurrection and exaltation. Indeed, I would argue that we *ought* not to enter into such disputes. In the proclamation of the church, these elements—nativity, cross, resurrection and exaltation—are all in the divine ordering, just as the δεῖ of Jesus' passion predictions indicates, and they stand together.

10. The Hebrew "uses what appear to be homonyms, the first verb meaning 'to trample,' the second, identical in form, probably referring to the hissing sound of the snake just before it bites" (Alter, *Genesis* 13).

11. Caird, *Revelation* 149.

12. Not, *pace* one of the cathdral's own guide books, "Eve tempting Adam"!

13. Beatrice is "realtà storica e simbolo… Pur rappresentando, come apparirà in modo indubbio alla fine del *Purgatorio*, una realtà che la trascende, Beatrice non cessa mai di essere se stessa, movendo l'animo di Dante allo stesso tremore e commozione dei giorni fiorentini" (Leonardi, *Dante Alighieri Commedia* 59).

14. Walpole, *Lessons from the Angel Oak* vii.
15. Cf. Mark 8.33 // Matthew 16.23.
16. Cf. Revelation 6.4. Since I now live in Exeter, little over an hour away from the border with Wales, I ought as a matter of courtesy to point out that the evil seven-headed red dragon of Revelation must not be confused with the (single-headed) Red Dragon of Wales. The Red (or Golden) Dragon is from a quite different mythology. It stands originally for Romano-British defiance of Saxon invaders, and perhaps derives from Dragon standards of Sarmatian Cavalry who served the Emperor. It has come to stand for liberty, justice and freedom from usurpers and oppressors—the usurpers and oppressors in this case having been, alas, mostly the English.
17. Psalm 74.13-14; cf. Dahood, *Psalms* 2.206; Brueggemann, *The Message of the Psalms* 70.
18. Cf. Caird, *Revelation* 159.
19. Boring, *Revelation* 160.
20. Boring, *Revelation* 160; cf. Rom. 8.19-22.
21. John 19.26-27.
22. Pursuing the metaphor elsewhere in the NT tradition, we might say that all whom Jesus called members of his family (Mark 3.34) and who call on God "Abba" as he did (Mark 14.36, Rom. 8.15) are children of Mary his mother.
23. John 1.13.

7. Mary as the Early Christians Remembered Her

1. David Brown, *Discipleship and Imagination* 228.
2. Ann Loades, *Grace is Not Faceless* 59-60.
3. E. L. Mascall, "The Dogmatic Theology of the Mother of God" 28.
4. Cf. Rowan Williams, "The Seal of Orthodoxy: Mary and the Heart of Christian Doctrine," 18ff. As Williams points out, while we must beware of attempting to analyze Jesus' psychology, we must beware equally of presenting him as a sort of automaton with no psychology or personality at all. Evidently, he had an extraordinarily powerful personality that led some to adoration and others to violent hostility.
5. "Der zwölfjährige Jesus": Luke 2.41-52.
6. John 2.1-8.
7. John 2.11.
8. John 19.25-27.
9. Acts 1.12-14, 2.1-4.

10. Still basic for consideration here is Dodd, *Apostolic Preaching* (1936); see further Caird, *New Testament Theology* 27-73.
11. So McHugh: "if Jesus was in fact virginally conceived, is it not likely that Mary, during her earthly life, would have entrusted such a secret only to those who were closest to her, and to Jesus?" (*Mother of Jesus* 324).
12. See Origen, *Against Celsus* 1.28; also (probably) "Rabbi Shimon ben Azzai said: I found a scroll recording people's lineages in Jerusalem, and it was written in it that so-and-so is a *mamzer* from an adulterous union with a married woman" (*m. Yevamot* 4.13).
13. See above, chapter 1.
14. That in Matthew and Luke we have two witnesses from the seventies or eighties of the first Christian century who testify to the virginal conception of Jesus has been and remains the view of most exegetes throughout Christian history, and is my view. It was, however, notably challenged by Jane Schaberg in her book, *The Illegitimacy of Jesus*, originally published in 1987 and several times republished. In Schaberg's opinion (I quote from the 2006 edition), "It was the intention—or better, *an* intention—of Matthew and Luke to pass down the tradition they inherited: that Jesus the Messiah had been illegitimately conceived during the period when his mother Mary was betrothed to Joseph" (*Illegitimacy* 17). Schaberg's understanding of Matthew and Luke has not been found generally persuasive even among scholars who hold Jesus was indeed conceived illegitimately. For thoughtful critique of her work (which, though often criticized, has not always been *fairly* criticized), see the review article by David T. Landry, "Illegitimacy Reconsidered," in the 2006 ("Twentieth Anniversary") edition of *Illegitimacy*, 283-299.
15. See above, n. 261.

Postscript: The Significance of Mary for Christians in the Twenty-First Century

1. Mark 6.3, Gal. 4.4.
2. FitzGerald, "Mary the *Theotokos*" 84.
3. The Chalcedonian definition declares of Jesus that he

> was begotten before the ages from the Father according to his deity, but in the last days for us and our salvation, the same one was born of the Virgin Mary, the bearer of God (ἐκ Μαρίας τῆς παρθένου τῆς θεοτόκου), according to his humanity. He is one and the same Christ, Son, Lord, and Only Begotten, who is made known in two natures united without

> confusion [ἀσυγχύτως], without change [ἀτρέπτως], without division [ἀδιαιρέτως], without separation [ἀχωρίστως]).

Evidently, these statements are not directly about Mary: they are about Jesus.
4. "Dogmatic Theology" 39. As Robert Hughes has pointed out, in Christian understanding, the Holy Spirit is the Mediator of God's grace to humankind. "But it is through Mary's womb, pelvis, and vagina that this grace, this ultimate superfluous graciousness that is the Holy Spirit, is poured out in the Christian dispensation, and with her free (although informed by prevenient grace) consent and assent. In that sense, and in that sense alone, it is appropriate to call her Mediatrix of All Graces precisely as *Theotokos*, God bearer" (*Beloved Dust* 120).
5. "For as the Incarnation of the Word is unrepeatable, so is the vocation to be his mother. And it is surely natural to expect that one who has a unique vocation, a vocation moreover which surpasses in sublimity that of all other creatures, should be prepared for it by unique graces and rewarded by unique privileges" (Mascall, "Dogmatic Theology" 45).
6. Debated by medieval theologians, it was not defined as a dogma until 1854, by Pope Pius IX in the papal bull *Ineffabilis Deus*, which states that Mary, through God's grace, was conceived free from the stain of original sin through her role as the Mother of God:

> We declare, pronounce, and define that the doctrine which holds that the most Blessed Virgin Mary, in the first instance of her conception, by a singular grace and privilege granted by Almighty God, in view of the merits of Jesus Christ, the Saviour of the human race, was preserved free from all stain of original sin, is a doctrine revealed by God and therefore to be believed firmly and constantly by all the faithful.

According to Karl Rahner and Herbert Vorgrimler, this dogma

> means that through the prevenient redemptive grace of Christ Mary was preserved from original sin from the first moment of her existence and thus began her life possessed of the grace of justification (as the grace of Christ).... The maternity which God predestined for her, which she was freely to accept, is for her from the beginning what infant baptism is for others: the efficacious pledge of Christ's grace which excludes original sin and always precedes man's own free salutary acts" (*CTD* 223).

7. Pope Pius XII defined the dogma of the Assumption of Mary in 1950 in his apostolic constitution *Munificentissimus Deus* as follows:

> We proclaim and define it to be a dogma revealed by God that the immaculate Mother of God, Mary ever virgin, when the course of her earthly life was finished, was taken up body and soul into the glory of heaven.

A result of this teaching that "even now a perfect and glorified corporeality is part of the total fulfilment of Mary since the close of her earthly life" is, in the view of Rahner and Herbert Vorgrimler "that our present position vis-à-vis salvation is clarified: she, who by faith has received salvation in her body for herself and for us all, has received it *totally*, for it is the salvation of the *whole* human being" (*CDT* 39).

According to the Anglican-Roman Catholic International Commission's "Seattle Statement," released in 2004, "the teaching about Mary in the two definitions of the Assumption and the Immaculate Conception, understood within the biblical pattern of the economy of hope and grace, can be said to be consonant with the teaching of the Scriptures and the ancient common traditions." The difference between Roman Catholics and Anglicans would appear to be not over the doctrine itself but over the propriety of its being regarded as dogma: so E. L. Mascall: "I do not myself think these beliefs form part of the central core of the dogmatic system of Christianity… I should myself regret it very much if, for example, the authorities of the Church of England resolved to exclude from communion anyone who would not make an explicit *ex animo* profession of them." Even here, however, perhaps the differences are not insurmountable. In Karl Rahner's view, "theological reflection is possible about *whether and why* it was opportune for Pius XII to define this dogma, and on this point a Catholic is certainly not obliged by the dogma to hold one particular opinion" (*Foundations of Christian Faith* 388).

8. There is evidence that Mary's Conception was celebrated in the East since the seventh century, and in the West (in England at Canterbury and Exeter) since the tenth; celebration of her Nativity certainly took place in Rome in 701 under Pope Sergius I; celebration of her Falling Asleep (Dormitian) or Assumption is placed by some authorities as early as the fourth century. Its early place in the devotions of Welsh Christianity was demonstrated to me only a few weeks ago when I had the privilege of being taken to the ancient and beautiful church of St. Bridget's, Skenrith, which was consecrated in 1207. Among the church's treasures, Fr. Julian Gray, the parish priest, pointed us with justifiable pride to the "Skenrith Cope." The Cope, which is dated to the late 1400s, is made of red velvet, embroidered

with a central image of the Assumption of the Blessed Virgin Mary, supported by angels (see online at http://Grosmont.wales/st-bridgets-church-skenfrith/).

9. *GAGNT* 171; cf BDAG χαριτόω.

10. See above, n.6. As will be evident, I am not persuaded by David Brown's rejection of the Immaculate Conception (*Discipleship and Imagination* 261-70), usefully critiqued in Tina Beattie, "From Ethics to Eschatology" 64-78. More positively, see Jenson's comments on Mary's exemption from the consequences of original sin and (consequent?) "sinlessness" in Jenson, *Systematic Theology* 2.203-4.

11. See Gen. 5.24, 2 Kings 2.11-12. Scripture is tantalizingly vague about Moses' death and burial although it does say unambiguously, "So Moses the servant of YHWH died there in the land of Moab" (Deut. 34.6). Josephus sees this as specifically denying the possibility "that any should venture to say that by reason of his surpassing virtue Moses had gone back to the Deity" (*Ant.* 4.326; H. St J. Thackeray transl.)—an observation surely reflecting Josephus' awareness of some who made just such a claim.

12. 2 Peter 1.4. In this connection George Florovosky (with whom I have some difficulty in other respects: see below n.14) rightly says, "it is not so much a heavenly reward for her purity and virtue, as an 'implication' of her sublime office, of her being the Mother of God, the *Theotokos*" ("Ever-Virgin Mother" 63).

13. Schaberg quotes a remark that I find very much to the point: "I think that the doctrine of the Virgin Birth as something higher, sweeter, nobler than ordinary motherhood, is a slur on all the natural motherhood of the world." (*Illegitimacy* 25 citing Elizabeth Cady Stanton et al., *The Woman's Bible* 114).

14. Thus, according to George Florovsky, Mary's "perpetual virginity," whatever else it is (and, to be fair to him, it is a good deal more) "excludes first of all any 'erotic' involvement" and implies "bodily integrity or incorruption" ("Ever Virgin Mother" 61). I am not saying that these expressions, in their context, *cannot* be understood in a biblical sense, but they are surely on the brink of sliding into something very different. As Stafford points out,

> The story of our first creation in Genesis still places sexual love at the heart of creation. In Paradise, Adam and Eve were given to each other to know and love. They were clearly different from each other; the glory one glimpses in the beloved is not one's own. Yet they were both human, consubstantial, and in rejoined bodies they became one flesh. (*Disordered Loves* 39)

15. Kyriaki Karidoyanes FitzGerald, "Mary the *Theotokos* and the Call to Holiness" 85-86. Cf. Jenson on the "sinlessness" of Mary: in *Systematic*

Theology 2, 203-204; also Sarah Maitland: "the virginity of Mary is not about biology, but about meaning, about symbol and metaphor" (*A Big Enough God* 188).

16. Stafford, *Disordered Loves* 40.

17. Jenson, *Systematic Theology* 2, 203.

18. Jenson, *Systematic Theology* 2, 204.

19. *qui conceptus est de Spiritu Sancto, natus ex Maria Virgine* (Symbolum Apostolorum, or Symbolum Apostolicum).

20. τὸν δι' ἡμᾶς τοὺς ἀνθρώπους καὶ διὰ τὴν ἡμετέραν σωτηρίαν κατελθόντα ἐκ τῶν οὐρανῶν καὶ σαρκωθέντα ἐκ Πνεύματος Ἁγίου καὶ Μαρίας τῆς παρθένου καὶ ἐνανθρωπήσαντα (Niceno-Constantinopolitan Creed: adopted in more or less its present form at the Second Ecumenical Council in Constantinople in 381).

21. The title Θεοτόκος ("God-bearer") for Mary was affirmed by the third ecumenical council, the Council of Ephesus (431). Certainly the affirmation involved a good deal of politicking and personal rivalry, but the issue involved was real, and the decision arrived at must not be dismissed as a mere matter of politics.

22. There is also, of course, the not-unrelated question, "Why do we need to pray at all, since God already presumably already knows everything about us—including our wants before we are even aware of them ourselves?" A question brilliantly answered by Augustine of Hippo in his *Letter to Probia*, and (brevity being the soul of wit) arguably even more brilliantly by the horse in C. S. Lewis' novel *The Magician's Nephew*:

> "Wouldn't he know without being asked?" said Polly.
>
> "I've no doubt he would," said the Horse (still with his mouth full). "But I've a sort of an idea he likes to be asked."

23. Romans 8.31b, 38-39.

24. Romans 15.30.

25. On early understanding of the "Communion of Saints," see Kelly, *Early Christian Creeds* 392, 397.

26. A battery of NT texts make this point: cf. Acts 1.13-14, Rom. 15.30, 1 Cor. 14.13, 2 Cor. 9.14, 13.9, Col. 4.3, 1 Thess. 5.25, 2 Thess. 1.11, 3.1, Heb. 13.18.

27. Jenson, *Systematic Theology* 2, 202.

28. "Mary has by grace been exalted above all angels and men to a place second only to her Son, as the most holy mother of God who was involved in the mysteries of Christ" (*VCII*, 421).

Additional Note 1. According to Luke, Who Says the Magnificat? And Did the Evangelist Take It from an Outside Source?

1. See *TCGNT* 130-31.
2. G. Morin: " Deux Passages Inédits." 286-88; and "Le *De Psalmodiae Bono* de l'évêque saint Niceta." 385-97; cited in Stephen Benko, "The Magnificat" 264.
3. François Jacobé, "L'origine du Magnificat" 424-32.
4. "L'origine" 431.
5. "L'origine" 429.
6. "L'origine," 432.
7. Paul Winter, "Magnificat and Benedictus—Maccabean Psalms?" 335-36.
8. Benko, "Magnificat," 275.
9. Winter, "Magnificat and Benedictus" 340.
10. Brown, *Birth of the Messiah* 363, cf. Hays, *Echoes of Scripture.* 196-98.
11. Fitzmyer, *Luke I-IX* 361-62.
12. Evans, *Luke* 173.
13. Bovon, *Luke 1* 57.
14. *TCGNT* 130-31. The few variants that attribute the *Magnificat* to Elizabeth may have done so for the reason suggested by Creed: that those who created them thought Elizabeth's situation was closer to Hannah's than was Mary's—as in a sense it was: but not in the more important sense that was evidently central for Luke.
15. See Johnson, *Luke* 43. Paul makes use of *prosōpo-poiía* in a rather different way at Romans 7: see Bryan, *Preface to Romans*, 139-140, and nn. 46 and 47.
16. Lucian described the matter concisely: "If a person has to be introduced to make a speech, above all let his language suit his person and his subject, and next let those be as clear as possible. It is then, however, that you can play the orator and show your eloquence" (*How to Write History* 58, K. Kilburn transl.).

Additional Note 2. Was Mary a Virgin Mother or a Victim of Rape? The Question as Posed in the Twentieth and Twenty-First Centuries.

1. Schaberg, "A Cancelled Father," in *Forum*, n.s., 2. 1 (Spring 1999) 61.
2. Pannenberg, *The Apostles' Creed in the Light of Today's Questions* 76.
3. See further Kyle Roberts, *A Complicated Pregnancy* (2017).
4. Maitland, *Big Enough God* 187-88.
5. Rowan Williams, "Seal of Orthodoxy" 25-26.

6. Cf. e.g., "[St. Maximos] stated plainly that the Incarnation should be regarded as an absolute and primary purpose of God in the act of Creation. *The nature of the Incarnation, of this union of the Divine majesty with human frailty, is indeed an unfathomable mystery*, but we can at least grasp the reason and the purpose of this supreme mystery, its *logos* and *skopos*. And this original reason, or the ultimate purpose, was, in the opinion of St. Maximus, precisely the Incarnation itself and then our own incorporation into the Body of the Incarnate One." ("*Cur Deus Homo?* The Motive of the Incarnation," in *Creation and Redemption*, Vol. III in *The Collected Works of Georges Florovsky* (Belmont, Massachusetts: Nordland, 1976), 168, my emphases.

7. The issue was powerfully presented in Episode 39 of *Star Trek: The Next Generation* entitled *The Measure of a Man* (February 13, 1989), written by novelist Melinda Snodgrass and considered by some to be the first great episode of that series.

8. Küng, *On Being a Christian* 453–57 and n.92; McBrien, *Catholicism* 1:513–18; Schillebeeckx, *Jesus: An Experiment in Christology*, 553–56 and n.5.

9. *Mary in the New Testament: A Collaborative Assessment by Protestant and Roman Catholic Scholars*, 77–97, 107–43, and 289–92.

SELECTED BIBLIOGRAPHY AND SOURCES

Holy Scripture

In quoting the Bible, for the most part I use the NRSV, occasionally referring to the Revised Version of 1880 (a much-undervalued version) or—at the other extreme of things—the Revised English Bible of 1990. Once or twice, if I were to make the point I wanted to make, there seemed to be no alternative to offering my own translation. Certainly it is much easier to be critical of other people's translations than to make one's own, and every translation of every ancient text should be read charitably against the setting of its time as well as against the original. As Stephanie Carter said recently, speaking of her own rendering of Ovid's *Metamorphoses*, "There will never be the translation that we arrive at and say, 'OK, here's the translation of Ovid for all time,' or 'Here's the translation of Homer for all time,' because translation is about merging two moments: the moment of the translator and the moment of the original source text" (In Lily Meyer, "Having Their Say: Stephanie McCarter on her feminist translation of Ovid", *Poetry Foundation* [November 28, 2022; online at www.poetryfoundation.org]). Meyer's point granted, one might perhaps concede that some moments do seem to have been especially appropriate for some texts, or least that such moments have manifested greater sticking-power than others. I say that simply because, after more than four hundred years and counting, one has somehow to explain the continued and continuing success of the "Authorized" or "King James" version of the Bible (1611). But there may be better ways of doing that.

Behind my references to Scripture in the original languages or in the Vulgate lie the following:

Hebrew Scriptures, Masoretic Text (MT): K. Elliger and W. Rudolph, *Biblia Hebraica Stuttgartensia*. Stuttgart: Deutsche Bibelstiftung, 1966–67.

Greek Old Testament (LXX): Alfred Rahlfs, ed. *Septuaginta*: Id est Vetus Testamentum graece iuxta LXX interpretes. 4th ed. 2 vols. Stuttgart: Privilegierte Württembergische Bibelanstalt, 1935–50.

Greek New Testament: *Greek New Testament*: Eberhard Nestle and Erwin Nestle, with Barbara Aland, Kurt Aland, Johannes Karavidopoulos, Carlo M. Martini, and Bruce M. Metzger, Novum Testamentum Graece. 27th edition. Stuttgart: Deutsche Bibelgesellschaft, 1984.

Latin Bible (Vg.): Boniface Fischer, John Gribomont, H. F. D. Sparks, and W. Thiele, *Biblia Sacra: iuxta Vulgatam Versionem*. Stuttgart: Deutsche Bibelgesellschaft, 1969.

Sources (other than Holy Scripture) earlier than the Tenth Century

Ambrose of Milan. *Veni, Redemptor gentium*. Office hymn for the Octave before Christmas. Text in *Hymni Ecclesiae*, John Henry Newman, ed. London: Alexander MacMillan, 1865. 311.

Apuleius. *Metamorphoses*. Text and French translation in Donald Struan Robertson and Paul Vallette, *Apuleius: Les Metamorphoses*. Collection des universités de France. Paris : Les Belles Lettres, 1940–46. English translation in Patrick Gerard Walsh, *Apuleius Lucius: The Golden Ass*. Oxford: Oxford University Press, 1995 [1994].

Aristotle, *Politics*. Text and translation by H. Rackham in *Aristotle Politics*. LCL. London: William Heinmann, 1932.

____, *Parva Naturalia*. Text with introduction and commentary in Sir David Ross, *Aristotle Parva Naturalia*. Oxford: Clarendon, 1955. Text and translation by Walter Stanley Hett in *On the Soul, Parva Naturalia, On Breath*. LCL. Cambridge, Massachusetts: Harvard University, 1989.

Assumption of Moses: see *Testament of Moses*.

Augustine of Hippo, *Confessions*. Text and translation by Caroline J. B. Hammond in *Augustine Confessions*. LCL. Cambridge, Massachusetts:

Harvard University, 2018. Translation in Henry Chadwick, *Saint Augustine: Confessions*. Oxford: Oxford University, 2008.

___. *Tractates on John.* Text in Radbodus Willems, *Sancti Aurelii Augustini: In Iohannis Evangelium tractatus cxxiv.* CC.SL 36. Brepols: Turnholt, 1954. Translation in *Nicene and Post-Nicene Fathers*, first series. Vol. 7. John Gibb, trans., Philip Schaff, ed. Buffalo, New York: Christian Literature Publishing Co., 1888.

Babylonian Talmud. Text and translation in A. Zvi Ehrman, *The Talmud with English Translation and Commentary.* 20 volumes, Jerusalem: El–'Am, 1965. Translation of Babylonian Talmud in *Soncino Hebrew/English Babylonian Talmud.* Isidore Epstein, ed. 30 vols. London: Soncino Press, 1990.

Chalcedonian Definition of the Faith. Text and notes in T. Herbert Bindley and F. W. Green, *The Oecumenical Documents of the Faith.* London: Methuen, 1950. 191-99. Translation in Henry Bettenson, *Documents of the Christian Church.* 2nd edition. Oxford University, 1963. 51-52.

Dead Sea Scrolls. Text and translation in James H. Charlesworth, ed., *The Dead Sea Scrolls: Hebrew, Aramaic and Greek Texts with English Translations.* 10 vols. Tübingen: J. C. B. Mohr (Paul Siebeck); Louisville, Kentucky: Westminster John Knox Press, 1994–. Translation in Geza Vermes, *The Dead Sea Scrolls in English.* Fourth Edition. London and New York: Penguin Books, 1995.

Diodorus Siculus. *Bibliotheca historica.* Text and translation by C. H. Oldfather in *Diodorus Siculus Library of History.* 12 vols. LCL. Cambridge, MA: Harvard University, 1933.

Epiphanius of Salamis, *Panarion.* English translation by Frank Williams in *The Panarion of Epiphanius of Salamis.* 3 volumes. Leiden: Brill, 1987-2009. Available online at the Internet Archive.

Eusebius of Caesarea. *Ecclesiastical History.* Text and French translation in Gustave Bardy, ed., *Eusèbe de Césarée: Histoire ecclésiastique.* Sources chrétiennes 31, 41, 55. Paris: Cerf, 1952-58. Text and translation in Kirsopp Lake and J. E. L. Oulton, *Eusebius. Ecclesiastical History.* 2 vols. LCL. New York: Putnam; London: Heinemann, 1926-32. Translation in *Eusebius: Ecclesiastical History.* Hugh Jackson Lawlor and John Earnest Leonard Oulton, trans. 2 vols. London: S.P.C.K., 1954.

Gospel of Peter. Text and French translation in U. Bouriant, ed. *Mémoires publiés par les membres de la Mission archéologique française au Caire.* Vol. 1. Paris: Leroux, 1892. Text in Henry Barclay Swete, ed., *EUAGGELION KATA PETRON: The Akhmim Fragment of the Apocryphal Gospel of Peter.*

London and New York: Macmillan, 1893. English translation by Chr. Maurer in *NTA* 1.179-87.

Homer, *Iliad.* Text in Thomas W. Allen, *Homer Ilias.* Oxford: Clarendon Press, 1931. Text and translation in A. T. Murray, *Homer: The Iliad.* 2 vols. LCL. Cambridge, Massachusetts: Harvard University Press/ London: Heinemann, 1944.

Jerome, *Altercatio Luciferiani.* Text in Migne, PL, vol. 23, coll. 153-182B. Translation by W. H. Freemantle, "The Dialogue against the Luciferians" in *Nicene and Post-Nicene Fathers*, vol. 6. Edinburgh and New York: T & T Clark, 1893. 319-34.

Joseph and Asenath. Introduction and translation by C. Burchard in *OTP* 2.177-247.

Josephus, *Jewish Antiquities.* Text and translation in H. St. J. Thackeray, Ralph Marcus, Allen Wikgren, and L. H. Feldman, *Josephus.* 10 vols. LCL. Cambridge, Massachusetts: Harvard University Press; London: William Heinemann, 1926-65. Translation of 1-4 in Louis H. Feldman, *Flavius Josephus: Judean Antiquities 1-4.* Boston / Leiden: Brill, 2004.

Justin. *First and Second Apologies.* Text in Miroslav Marcovich, ed., *Iustini Martyris Apologiae pro Christianis.* Patristische Tete und Studien 38. Berlin and New York: Walter de Gruyter, 1994. Translation in Thomas B. Falls, *Saint Justin Martyr.* New York: Christian Heritage, 1949.

Kohelet Rabbah. English translation in *Midrash rabbah.* London: Soncino, 1939.

Livy: see Titus Livius

Lucian, *How to Write History.* Text and translation by K. Kilburn in *Lucian.* Vol. 6. London: William Heinemann / Cambridge, Massachusetts: Harvard University. 1959.

Lucius Apuleius, *Metamorphoses* or *The Golden Ass.* Translation by Robert Graves in *The Transformations of Lucius: otherwise known as the Golden Ass.* London: Penguin, 1950.

Mishnah. Text and translation in Philip Blackman, *Mishnayoth.* Gateshead, N.Y.: Judaica, 1983. Translation in Herbert Danby, *The Mishnah.* Oxford: Clarendon Press, 1933.

Origen of Alexandria. *Against Celsus.* Translation by Frederick Crombie in *Origen of Alexandria against Celsus.* Jackson, Michigan: Ex Fontibus, 2013.

___, *Commentary on St. Paul's Epistle to the Romans.* Available only in fragments: text and French translation of some Greek fragments in Jean Sherer, *Le Commentaire d'Origène sur Rom. III.5—V.7* (Cairo: Institut Français d'Archeologie Orientale, 1957); text of further fragments in

A. Ramsbotham, "The Commentary of Origen on the Epistle to the Romans" in *JTS* 13 (1911-12) 209-224; 13 (1911-12) 357-68; and 14 (1912-13) 10-22. Rufinus' Latin translation (not entirely reliable?) in Migne, *Patrologiae* 14.837-1292).

Pesikta de Rav Kahana. Text in Bernard Mandelbaum, *Pesikta de Rav Kahana.* 2 vols. New York: Jewish Theological Seminary of America, 1962.

Pesikta Rabbati. Text in Meir Friedmann, *Pesiqta Rabbati.* Vienna: Joseph Kaiser, 1880.

Philo, *De Mutatione Nominum.* Text and translation in F. H. Colson and G. H. Whitaker, *Philo.* 10 vols with 2 supp. vols. LCL. Cambridge, Massachusetts: Harvard University; London: William Heinemann, 1968-81.

Plutarch, *Alexander.* Text and translation by Bernadotte Perrin in *Plutarch Lives: Demosthenes and Cicero, Alexander and Caesar.* LCL 99. Harvard University, 1989.

____. *Cicero.* Text and translation by Bernadotte Perrin in *Plutarch Lives: Demosthenes and Cicero, Alexander and Caesar.* LCL 99. Harvard University, 1989.

Protevangelium of James. Text and translation in *The Protevangelium of James: Greek and English Texts.* Vol. 1. George T. Zervos, transl. London: Bloomsbury T&T Clark, 2018. Introduction an English translation by Oscar Cullmann, translated by A. J. B Higgins, in *NTA* 1.370-88.

Pseudo-Philo, *Biblical Antiquities.* Latin text in D. J. Harrington et al., *Pseudo-Philon et Les Antiquités bibliques.* Vol. 1. Translation by D. J. Harrington in *OTP* 2, 297—377.

Quintilian, *Institutio Oratoria.* Text and translation by H. E. Butler in *Quintilian: Institutio Oratoria.* 4 vols. LCL124-27. Cambridge, Massachusetts: Harvard University, 1921.

Qumran: see Dead Sea Scrolls.

Testament of Moses (also known as *Assumption of Moses*). Text in Johannes Tromp, *The Assumption of Moses: A Critical Edition with Commentary.* Studia in Veteris Testamenti Pseudepigrapha 10. Leiden: Brill, 1997. Introduction and English translation by J. Priest in *OTP* 1.919—34.

Titus Livius, *History of Rome* (*Ab urbe condita*). Text in Robert M. Ogilvy and P. G. Walsh, eds. *Ab urbe condita.* 2 vols. Oxford Classical Texts. Oxford: Oxford University Press, 1974-99. Translation in Aubrey de Selincourt, *Livy: The Early History of Rome.* 3rd edition. London: Penguin, 2002.

Xenophon, *Anabasis.* Text and translation by Carleton L. Brownson and John Dillery. LCL. Cambridge, Massachusetts: Harvard University, 1998.

Sources from the Tenth Century to the Present

Lexicons, Dictionaries, Grammars, Documents Collections, and Systematic and Dogmatic Theologies

Barth, Karl. *Dogmatics in Outline.* G. T. Thomson, transl. London: SCM, 1949.

Bauer, Walter, and William F. Arndt, F. Wilbur Gingrich, and Frederick W. Danker, and revised and edited by Frederick William Danker. *A Greek-English Lexicon of the New Testament and Other Early Christian Literature.* 3rd ed. Chicago and London: University of Chicago, 2000.

Bettenson, Henry. *Documents of the Christian Church.* 2nd edition. Oxford University, 1963.

Blass, F., and A. Debrunner. *A Greek Grammar of the New Testament and Other Early Christian Literature.* Translated and revised by Robert W. Funk. Chicago: University of Chicago, 1961.

Flannery, Austin, O.P. *Vatican II: The Conciliar and Post Conciliar Documents.* Revised edition. Collegeville, Minnesota: Liturgical, 1984

Ilan, Tal. *Lexicon of Jewish Names in Late Antiquity*, 4 vols. TSAJ 148 Tübingen: Mohr Siebeck, 2002-2012.

Jenson, Robert W. *Systematic Theology.* 2 vols. Oxford: Oxford University Press, 1997–99.

Kittel, Gerhard (ed. vols. 1–5) and Gerhard Friedrich (ed. vols. 6–9). *Theological Dictionary of the New Testament.* 9 vols. Translated by Geoffrey W. Bromiley. Grand Rapids: Eerdmans, 1964–1974 (1933–1973).

Liddell, Henry George, and Robert Scott. *A Greek-English Lexicon.* Revised by

Sir Henry Stuart Jones, Roderick McKenzie, et al. With Supplement. Edited by E. A. Barber, P. Maas, M. Scheller, and M. L. West. Oxford: Clarendon, 1968.

Lust, Johan and Erik Eynikel and Katrin Hausp. *Greek-English Lexicon of the Septuagint.* Revised edition. Stuttgart: Deutsche Bibelgesellschaft, 2003.

Metzger, Bruce M. A *Textual Commentary on the Greek New Testament: A Companion Volume to the United Bible Societies' Greek New Testament* (third edition). Corrected edition. London and New York: United Bible Societies, 1975.

Moule, C. F. D. *An Idiom Book of New Testament Greek.* Cambridge: Cambridge University, 1953.

Muraoka, T. A *Greek-English Lexicon of the Septuagint*. Louvain, Paris, and Walpole, Mass: Peeters, 2009.

Oxford Dictionary of the Bible. 2nd edition. W. R. F. Browning, ed. Oxford: Oxford University, 2009

Rahner, Karl, and Herbert Vorgrimler. *Concise Theological Dictionary*. Edited by Cornelius Ernst, O.P. Translated by Richard Strachan. Freiburg: Herder/ London: Burns and Oates, 1965.

Smyth, Herbert Weir. *Greek Grammar*. Revised by Gordon M. Messing. Cambridge, Mass.: Harvard University Press, 1956.

Spicq, Ceslas. *Theological Lexicon of the New Testament*. 3 vols. Translated and edited by James D. Ernest. Peabody, Mass.: Hendrickson, 1994.

Zerwick, Maximilian. *A Grammatical Analysis of the New Testament*. Translated by Mary Grosvenor. 4th ed. Rome: Pontificia instituto biblico, 1993.

Commentaries, Monographs, and Essays

Alexander, Loveday C. A. *The Preface to Luke's Gospel: Literary Convention and Social Context Luke 1.1-4 and Acts 1.1*, SNTSMS 78 (Cambridge: Cambridge University Press, 1993.

____. *Acts in Its Ancient Literary Context: A Classicist Looks at the Acts of the Apostles*. London: T. & T. Clark, 2005.

Alter, Robert. *Genesis*. New York: W. W. Norton, 1996.

Aquinas, St Thomas. *Commentary on the Gospel of John 1-5*. Fabian Larcher, O.P. and James A. Weisheipl, O.P. transl. Introduction and notes by Daniel Keating and Matthew Levering. Washington DC: Catholic University of America, 2010.

____. *Commentary on the Gospel of John 6-12*. Fabian Larcher, O.P. and James A. Weisheipl, O.P. transl. Introduction and notes by Daniel Keating and Matthew Levering. Washington DC: Catholic University of America, 2010.

Attridge, Harold W. *The Epistle to the Hebrews*. Philadelphia: Fortress, 1989.

Auerbach, Erich. *Mimesis: The Representation of Reality in Western Literature*. Willard R. Trask, transl. Princeton: Princeton University, 1953.

Aviam, Mordechai. "The Hasmonaean Dynasty's Activities in the Galilee." In *Jews, Pagans and Christians in the Galilee*. Rochester, New York: University of Rochester Press, 2004. 41-50.

Barker, Margaret. *Temple Theology: An Introduction*. London: S.P.C.K., 2004.

Barrett, C. K. *A Commentary on the First Epistle to the Corinthians*. London: A. & C. Black, 1968.

____. *The Gospel according to St. John. 2nd ed.* London: SPCK, 1978.

____. *A Critical and Exegetical Commentary on the Acts of the Apostles.* ICC. 2 vols. Edinburgh: T. & T. Clark, 1994–98.

Bartchy, S. Scott. *First Century Slavery and the Interpretation of 1 Corinthians 7:21.* SBLDS 11. Missoula: Scholars Press, 1973. 114-120.

Bauckham, Richard. "The Brothers and Sisters of Jesus: An Epiphanian Response." In *CBQ* 56 (1994) 686-700.

____. *Jesus and the Eyewitnesses: The Gospels as Eyewitness Testimony.* 2nd edition. Grand Rapids, Michigan: W. B. Eerdmans, 2017.

Beattie, Tina. "From Ethics to Eschatology: The Continuing Validity of the New Eve for Christian Doctrine and Discipleship." In *Theology, Aesthetics, and Culture: Responses to the Work of David Brown*, ed. Robert MacSwain and Taylor Worley. Oxford and New York: Oxford University Press, 2012. 64-78

Benoit, Pierre. "Quirinius (Recensement de)" *DBSup* 9 (1977) 693-720.

Benko, Stephen. "The Magnificat: A History of the Controversy" *JBL* 86 (1967) 263-75.

Best, Ernest. *A Critical and Exegetical Commentary on Ephesians.* ICC. Edinburgh: T & T Clark, 1998.

Boring, M. Eugene. *Revelation.* Louisville: John Knox, 1989.

____. *Mark: A Commentary.* Louisville and London: Westminster John Knox, 2006.

Bovon, François. *A Commentary on the Gospel of Luke 1:1—9:50.* Christina M. Thomas, transl. Hermenaeia. Minneapolis: Fortress, 2002.

____. *A Commentary on the Gospel of Luke 9.51-19.27.* Donald S. Deer, transl. Hermeneia. Minneapolis: Fortress, 2013.

Boxall, Ian. "Who is the Woman clothed with the Sun?" in Martin Warner, ed., *Say Yes to God: Mary and the Revealing of the Word Made Flesh.* London: Tufton, 1999.

Braaten, Carl E. and Robert W. Jenson, *Mary, Mother of God.* Grand Rapids, Michigan: William B. Eerdmans, 2004.

Brown, David. *Discipleship and Imagination.* Oxford and New York: Oxford University, 2000.

Brown S.S., Raymond E. "The Qumran Scrolls and the Johannine Gospel and Epistles" *CBQ* 17 (1955): 403-19, 559-74.

____. *The Gospel according to John I-XII.* AB 29. New York: Doubleday, 1966.

____. *The Gospel according to John XIII-XXI.* AB 29A. New York: Doubleday, 1970.

____. "The Problem of the Virginal Conception of Jesus," *Theological Studies* 33 (1972) 23–33.

____. "Luke's Description of the Virginal Conception," *Theological Studies* 35 (1974) 360–62.

____. *The Birth of the Messiah.* Image. New York: Doubleday,1977.

Brueggemann, Walter. *The Message of the Psalms.* Minneapolis: Augsburg, 1984.

____. *Theology of the Old Testament: Testimony, Dispute, Advocacy.* Minneapolis: Fortress, 1997.

Bryan, Christopher. "A Further Look at Acts 16:1–3." *JBL* 107 (1988): 292–94.

____. *A Preface to Mark: Notes on the Gospel in Its Literary and Cultural Settings.* Oxford: Oxford University Press, 1991.

____. *A Preface to Romans: Notes on the Epistle in Its Literary and Cultural Setting.* Oxford: Oxford University Press, 2000.

____. *Render to Caesar: Jesus, the Early Church, and the Roman Superpower.* Oxford: Oxford University Press, 2005.

____. *Resurrection of the Messiah.* Oxford: Oxford University Press, 2011.

____. *Listening to the Bible: The Art of Faithful Biblical Interpretation* New York and Oxford: Oxford University, 2014.

____. *Son of God: Reflections on a Tradition.* Oxford and New York: Oxford University, 2023.

Bultmann, Rudolf. *The Gospel of John.* Translated by G. R. Beasley-Murray. Oxford: Basil Blackwell, 1971 (1964, with 1966 supplement).

____. *History of the Synoptic Tradition.* Translated by John Marsh. New York: Harper and Row, 1963 (revised edition 1931).

Burridge, Richard A. "The Genre of Acts—Revisited," in *Reading Acts Today: A Festschrift for Loveday Alexander.* S. Walton, L. Pietersen, F. S. Spencer, and T. E. Philips, eds. London: T & T Clark, 2011. 1-26.

____. *What Are the Gospels? A Comparison with Graeco-Roman Biography.* 25th Anniversary Edition. Waco, Texas: Baylor University 2018 (first published 1992 by Cambridge University).

Burton, Ernest de Witt. *A Critical and Exegetical Commentary on the Epistle to the Galatians.* Edinburgh: T. & T. Clark, 1921.

Caird, G. B. *A Commentary on the Revelation of St. John the Divine.* London: Adam and Charles Black, 1966.

____. *New Testament Theology.* Completed and edited by L. D. Hurst. Oxford: Clarendon, 1994.

Campbell, Jr., Edward E. *Ruth.* AB 8. New York: Doubleday, 1975.

Charlesworth, James H. "The Historical Jesus in the Fourth Gospel: A Paradigm Shift?" *Journal for the Study of the Historical Jesus* 8(1):3-46.

Coffey, Kathy Coffey. *Hidden Women of the Gospels.* New York: Crossroad, 1996.

Cohen, Shaye D. *The Beginnings of Jewishness: Boundaries, Varieties, Uncertainties.* Berkeley and Los Angeles: University of California, 1999.

Collins, Raymond F. *First Corinthians.* SP 7. Collegeville, Minnesota: Liturgical, 1999.

Conzelmann, Hans. *1 Corinthians: A Commentary on the First Epistle to the Corinthians.* Translated by James W. Leitch. Bibliography and References by James W. Dunkly. Hermeneia. Philadelphia: Fortress, 1975 (1969).

Cranfield, C. E. B. *The Gospel according to Saint Mark.* 3rd ed. Cambridge: Cambridge University Press, 1977.

____. *A Critical and Exegetical Commentary on the Epistle to the Romans.* 2 vols. ICC. Edinburgh: T. & T. Clark, 1975–79.

Crean OP, Thomas. "Mary as a New Eve in the Thought of St Paul." In *New Blackfriars* 103 (2022) 662-677.

Creed, John Martin. *The Gospel according to St. Luke.* London: Macmillan, 1930.

Dahood, S.J., Mitchell. *Psalms.* 3 Vols. AB 16, 16 B, and 17 A. New York: Doubleday, 1965-70.

Davies, W. D., and Dale C. Allison. *A Critical and Exegetical Commentary on the Gospel according to Saint Matthew.* 3 vols. Edinburgh: T. & T. Clark, 1988–97.

Dhorme, E. *A Commentary on the Book of Job.* Harold Knight, transl. London: Nelson, 1967.

Dodd, C. H. *The Apostolic Preaching and Its Development.* London: Nisbet, 1936.

____. *The Interpretation of the Fourth Gospel.* Cambridge: Cambridge University Press, 1953.

____. *Historical Tradition in the Fourth Gospel.* Cambridge: Cambridge University Press, 1963.

Donahue, John R., and Daniel J. Harrington. *The Gospel of Mark.* SP 2. Collegeville, Minn.: Liturgical Press, 2002.

Dunn, James D. G. *Romans.* 2 vols. WBC38a and 38b. Dallas, Texas: Word Books, 1988.

Epp, Eldon J. *Junia: The First Woman Apostle.* Minneapolis: Fortress, 2005.

Evans, C. F. *Saint Luke.* London: SCM / Philadelphia: Trinity Press International, 1990.

Feuer, Avrohom Chaim. *Tehillim* 1 New York: Mesorah, 1985.

Fiorenza, Elizabeth Schüssler. *In Memory of Her: A Feminist Reconstruction of Christian Origins.* New York: Crossroad, 1984.

FitzGerald, Kyriaki Karidoyanes. "Mary the *Theotokos* and the Call to Holiness." In Carl Braaten and Robert Jenson, *Mary Mother of God.* Grand Rapids, Michigan: William B. Eerdmans, 2004. 85-86.

Fitzmyer, Joseph A. *First Corinthians.* AYB 32. New Haven and London: Yale University Press, 2008.

____. *Romans: A New Translation with Introduction and Commentary.* AB 33. New York: Doubleday, 1993.

____. *The Gospel according to Luke.* 2 vols. AB 28, 28A. New York: Doubleday, 1981–85.

Florovsky, George. "The Ever-Virgin Mother of God." In *The Mother of God: A Symposium by Members of the Fellowship of St Alban and St Sergius.* E. L. Mascall, ed. Westminster: Dacre, 1949. 51-63.

Friedeman, Caleb T. "Jesus' Davidic Lineage and the Case for Jewish Adoption." In *NTS* 66 (2020) 249-67.

Gathercole, Simon J. *The Gospel and the Gospels: Christian Proclamation and Early Jesus Books.* Grand Rapids, Michigan: Eerdmans, 2022.

Gatta, John. *Green Gospel.* New York: Church House, 2024.

Gaventa, Beverly Roberts. *Mary: Glimpses of the Mother of Jesus.* Columbia, South Carolina: University of South Carolina, 1995.

____. "Nothing Will Be Impossible with God." In Carl E. Braaton and Robert Jenson, *Mary, Mother of God.* Grand Rapids, Michigan: William B. Eerdmans, 2004. 19-35.

Goodman, Martin. *Rome and Jerusalem: The Clash of Ancient Civilizations.* London: Allen Lane, 2007.

Guffey, Andrew R. *The Book of Revelation and the Visual Culture of Asia Minor.* Lanham: Lexington/Fortress Academic, 2019.

Gutman, S. "Gamla." In *The New Encyclopedia of Archaeological Excavations in the Holy Land*, E. Stern ed. 4 vols. New York: Simon & Schuster, 1993. 2.459-63.

Guttiérez, Gustavo. *A Theology of Liberation: History, Politics, and Salvation.* (1973). Ed. and transl. C. Inda and J. Eagleson. New York, Maryknoll: Orbis, 1988.

Harrington, S.J., Daniel J. *The Gospel of Matthew.* SP 1. Collegeville, Minnesota: Liturgical Press, 1991.

Harrington, S.J., Wilfrid J. *Revelation.* SP 16. Collegeville, Minn.: Liturgical Press, 1993.

Hawking, Stephen. *Brief Answers to Big Questions.* London: John Murray, 2018.

Hays, Richard B. *Echoes of Scripture in the Gospels.* Waco, Texas: Baylor University, 2016

Heanchen, Ernst. *John 2: A Commentary on the Gospel of John Chapters 7-21.* Robert W. Funk, trans. Hermeneia. Philadelphia: Fortress 1984 [1980].

Hengel, Martin. *Crucifixion in the Ancient World and the Folly of the Message of The Cross.* Translated by John Bowden. Philadelphia: Fortress, 1977 (1976).

Hèring, Jean. *La Première Épître de saint Paul aux Corinthiens.* Neuchatel: Delachaux et Niestle, 1949.

Hooker, Morna D. *A Commentary on the Gospel according to St Mark.* London: A & C Black, 1991.

Hultgren, Arland J. *Paul's Letter to the Romans: A Commentary.* Grand Rapids, Michigan and Cambridge, UK: William B. Eerdmans, 2011.

Hughes, Robert Davis. *Beloved Dust: Tides of the Spirit in the Christian Life.* New York: Continuum, 2008.

Jacobé, François. "L'origine du Magnificat" in *Revue d'histoire et de littérature religieuses*, ii (1897) 424-32.

Jenson, Robert W. *Systematic Theology.* 2 vols. Oxford: Oxford University Press, 1997–99.

____. See Braaton, Carl E.

Johnson, Luke Timothy. *The Gospel of Luke.* SP3. Collegeville, Minnesota: Liturgical Press, 1991.

____. *The Acts of the Apostles.* SP5. Collegeville, Minnesota: Liturgical Press, 1992.

Kaisar, Otto. *Isaiah 1-12.* Philadelphia: Westminster, 1972.

Kelly, J. N. D. *Early Christian Creeds.* London: Longmans, Green, 1950.

Küng, Hans. *On Being a Christian.* Edward Quinn, transl. New York: Doubleday, 1976.

LaCocque, André. *Ruth.* K. C. Hanson, transl. Minneapolis: Fortress, 2004.

Laqueuer, Thomas. "The Pocahontas Exception," *LRB* 25.7 30 March 2023.

Lasdun, James. "Bats on the Ceiling," *LRB* 42.18, 24 September 2020.

Laurentin, René. *Structure et Théologie de Luc I-II.* Paris: Gabalda, 1957.

____. *Mary in Scripture, Liturgy, and the Catholic Tradition.* Sean O'Neill, transl. New York: Paulist, 2014 (2011).

Léon-Dufour, S.J., Xavier. "L'annonce à Joseph" in *Etudes d'Evangile.* Paris: Seuil, 1965.

Levin, Y. "Jesus, 'Son of God' and 'Son of David': The 'Adoption' of Jesus into the Davidic Line." In *JSNT* 28 (2006) 415-42.

Lewis, C. S. *Reflections on the Psalms.* London: Geoffrey Bles, 1958.

___. "Modern Theology and Biblical Criticism." In *Christian Reflections,* Walter Hooper, ed. Grand Rapids, Michigan: Eerdmans, 1995.

Lightfoot, J. B. *Saint Paul's Epistle to the Galatians.* London: MacMillan, 1865.

Linafelt, Tod. *Ruth.* In Tod Linafelt and Timothy K. Beal, *Ruth and Esther.* Berit Olam. Collegeville, Minnesota: Liturgical, 1999.

Loades, Ann. *Grace is Not Faceless.* London: Darton, Longman and Todd, 2021.

Loisy, Alfred. See his nom de plume: Jacobé, François.

Luz, Ulrich. *Matthew.* Translated by James E. Crouch. Hermeneia. 3 vols. Minneapolis: Fortress, 2001–2007.

Maimon, Yehuda Leib. "The Matrilinear Principle." In Shaye D. Cohen, *The Beginnings of Jewishness: Boundaries, Varieties, Uncertainties.* Berkeley and Los Angeles: University of California, 1999.

Maitland, Sara. *A Big Enough God: Artful Theology.* London: Mowbray, 1995.

Marcus, Joel. *Mark 8–16.* AYB 27A. New Haven and London: Yale University Press, 2009.

Martin, Dale B. *Slavery as Salvation: The Metaphor of Slavery in Pauline Christianity.* New Haven and London: Yale University Press, 1990.

Martyn, J. Louis. *Galatians,* AYB 33A. New Haven and London: Yale University, 1997.

Mary in the New Testament: A Collaborative Assessment by Protestant and Roman Catholic Scholars, Raymond E. Brown et al., eds. Philadelphia: Fortress; New York: Paulist, 1978.

Mascall, E. L. "The Dogmatic Theology of the Mother of God," in *The Mother of God: A Symposium by Members of the Fellowship of St Alban and St Sergius.* E. L. Mascall, ed. Westminster: Dacre, 1949. 37-50.

Mastin, B. A. See Sanders, J. N.

Matera, Frank J. *Galatians.* SP9. Collegeville, Minesota: Litugical, 1992.

McArthur, Harvey K. "Son of Mary." *NovT* 15 (1973) 38-58.

McBrien, Richard. *Catholicism.* Minneapolis: Winston, 1980.

McCarter, P. Kyle. *II Samuel.* AB9. New York: Doubleday, 1984.

McHugh, John F. *The Mother of Jesus in the New Testament.* New York: Doubleday, 1975.

___. *A Critical and Exegetical Commentary on John 1-4.* ICC. London and New York: T & T Clark, 2009.

Meier, John P. *A Marginal Jew: Rethinking the Historical Jesus*. 1. *The Roots of the Problem and the Person*. New York: Doubleday, 1991.

___. "The Brothers and Sisters of Jesus in Ecumenical Perspective." *CBQ* 54 (1992) 1-28.

Moloney, Francis J. *The Gospel of Mark: A Commentary*. Peabody, Mass.: Hendrickson, 2002.

___. *The Gospel of John*. Collegeville, Minn.: Liturgical Press, 1998.

Morin, O.S.B., Germain. "Deux Passages Inédits du *De Psalmodiae Bono* de Saint Niceta (IVe-Ve Siècle)," *RB* 6 (1897) 286-88 and "Le *De Psalmodiae Bono* de l'évêque saint Niceta: rédaction primitive, d'après le ms. Vatic. 5729," *Revue Bénédictine* 14 (1897) 385-97.

Morgan, Teresa. *Roman Faith and Christian Faith: Pistis and Fides in the Early Roman Empire and Early Churches*. Oxford: Oxford University, 2015.

Nikondeha, Kelley. *The First Advent in Palestine*. Minneapolis: Broadleaf, 2022.

Novenson, Matthew V. *The Grammar of Messianism: An Ancient Jewish Political Idiom and Its Users*. Oxford: Oxford University, 2017.

Pannenberg, W. *The Apostles' Creed in the Light of Today's Questions*. London: SCM Press, 1972.

Perowne, Stewart. *The Life and Times of Herod the Great*. London: The History Press, 2003.

Pedersen, Johs. *Israel: Its Life and Culture*. I-II. London: Oxford University Press / Copenhagen: Branner og Korch, 1926.

Pervo, Richard I. *Acts: A Commentary*. Hermeneia. Minneapolis: Fortress, 2009.

Plank, Karl A. "The Human Face of Otherness" in *Faith and History: Essays in Honour of Paul W. Meyer*. John T. Carroll, Charles H. Cosgrove, and E. Elizabeth Johnson, eds. Atlanta: Scholars, 1990.

Plummer, Alfred: see Robertson, Archibald.

Prabhu, Soares. "'Rejoice, Favored One!' Mary in the Annunciation Story of Luke." *Biblebhashyam* 3 (1977).

Reilly, Frank. "Jane Schaberg, Raymond E. Brown, and the Problem of the Illegitimacy of Jesus." In *Journal of Feminist Studies in Religion* 21.1 (2005) 64-65.

Richardson, Alan. *An Introduction to the Theology of the New Testament*. London: SCM, 1958.

Roberts, Kyle. *A Complicated Pregnancy: Whether Mary Was a Virgin and Why It Matters*. Fortress Press, 2017.

Robertson, Archibald, and Alfred Plummer. *A Critical and Exegetical Commentary on the First Epistle of St Paul to the Corinthians.* New York: Charles Scribners, 1911.

Sabar, Ariel. *Veritas: A Harvard Professor, a Con Man and the Gospel of Jesus's Wife.* New York: Random House, 2021.

Safrai, Shmuel and M. Stern, eds. *The Jewish People in the First Century*, 2 vols. Van Gorcum, 1974 / Leiden: Brill, 1988.

Sakenfeld, Katherine Doob. *Ruth.* Interpretation. Louisville, Kentucky: John Knox, 1999

Sanders, J. N. and B. A. Mastin, *A Commentary on the Gospel according to St John.* London: Adam & Charles Black, 1968.

Sawicki, Marianne. *Crossing Galilee: Architectures of Contact in the Occupied Land of Jesus.* Harrisburg, Pennsylvania: Trinity International, 2000.

Sayers, Dorothy. *The Man Born to be King.* London: Victor Gollancz, 1946.

Schaberg, Jane. *The Illegitimacy of Jesus: A Feminist Theological Interpretation of the Infancy Narratives.* Expanded Twentieth Anniversary Edition. Sheffield: Sheffield Phoenix Press, 2006 (San Francisco: Harper and Row, 1997).

Schnackenburg, Rudolf. *The Gospel according to St John.* 3 vols. London: Burns & Oates; New York: Crossroad, 1968-1982.

Schillebeeckx, Edward. *Jesus: An Experiment in Christology*, Hubert Hoskins, transl. New York: Seabury, 1979.

Schnackenburg, Rudolf. *The Gospel according to St. John.* Translated by Kevin Smyth, Cecily Hastings, Francis McDonagh, David Smith, Richard Foley, S.J., and G. A. Kon. 3 vols. New York: Crossroad, 1982–87 (1965–75).

Schneiders, Sandra M. *The Revelatory Text: Interpreting the New Testament as Sacred Scripture.* 2nd edition. Collegeville, Minnesota: The Liturgical Press, 1999.

Schürer, Emil, revised by Geza Vermes, Fergus Millar, and Martin Goodman. *The History of the Jewish People in the Age of Jesus Christ.* 3 vols. Edinburgh: T. & T. Clark, 1973-87.

Sieffert, Friedrich. *Der Brief an die Galater.* Göttingen: Vandenhoeck und Ruprecht, 1886.

Skinner, John. *A Critical and Exegetical Commentary on Genesis.* ICC. Edinburgh : T & T Clark, 1910.

Slotki, I. W. *Isaiah.* London and Bournemouth: Soncino, 1949.

Speiser, E. A. *Genesis.* AB 1. New York: Doubleday, 1964.

Spicq, O.P., Ceslas. "'Joseph, son mari, étant juste…' [Mt., I.19]" *RB* 71 (1964) 206-207.

Stafford, William S. *Disordered Loves: Healing the Seven deadly Sins.* Cambridge, Massachusetts: Cowley, 1994.

Stauffer, Emil. *Jesus and His Story.* London: SCM, 1960.

Stern, M. See Saffrai, Shmuel.

Stibbe, Mark W. "'Return to Sender': A Structuralist Approach to John's Gospel." In *Interpretation* 1 (1993) 189-206.1

Taylor, Joan E. *The Essenes, the Scrolls, and the Dead Sea.* Oxford: Oxford University, 2012.

Taylor, Vincent. *The Gospel according to St. Mark.* London: Macmillan, 1957.

Thébert, Yvon. "The Slave." In *The Romans.* Andrea Giardina, ed., Lydia G. Cochrane, transl. Chicago and London: University of Chicago Press, 1993. 138-174.

Trocmé, Ettiene. *La Formation de l'évangile selon Marc.* Paris: Universitaires de France, 1963.

Tuccinardi, Enrico. "Nazareth, the Caesarea Inscription, and the Hand of God." René Salm, transl. Online at www.academia.edu.

Wade, G. W. *The Book of the Prophet Isaiah.* New York: Edwin S. Gorham, 1911.

Wahlberg, Rachel C. "Jesus and the Uterus Image," *ThTo* 31 (1974-75) 228-30.

Westcott, Brooke Foss. *The Gospel according to St. John.* London: John Murray, 1898.

Williams, Rowan. "The Seal of Orthodoxy: Mary and the Heart of Christian Doctrine." In *Saying Yes to God: Mary and the Revealing of the Word Made Flesh*, Martin Warner, ed. London: Tufton, 1999.

Winter, Paul. "Magnificat and Benedictus—Maccabean Psalms?" *BJRL* 37 (1954) 328-47.

Wright, N. T. *The Climax of the Covenant: Christ and the Law in Pauline Theology.* Edinburgh: T & T Clark, 1991.

Other Sources, including Poetry, Novels, Drama, Films, and Music

Ali, Tariq. "Winged Words." *LRB* 43 (June 2021) 12.11-12.

Andrewes, Lancelot. Sermon preached on Christmas Day 1622 before King James, at Whitehall. Text in *Ninety-Six Sermons by Lancelot Andrewes.* Vol.1. *The Nativity, Repentance & Fasting.* Edited by J.P.W. of Magdalen

College in 1841. Kerry, Ireland: CrossReach Publications, 2018. The text is also available online.

Bawcott, N. W. See Shakespeare, William. *Measure for Measure.*

Beauty and the Beast. Animated film, screenplay by Linda Woolverton, based on a 1756 fairy tale *La Belle et la Bête* by Jeanne-Marie Leprince de Beaumont. Directed by Gary Trousdale and Kirk Wise. 1991.

Calon lân ("A Pure Heart"). Written in the 1890s by Daniel James (Gwyrosydd). Normally sung to a tune by John Hughes.

Leonardi, Anna Maria Chiavacci. See Dante Alighieri.

Cunningham, Michael. *Hours.* London: Fourth Estate, 1999.

Chariots of Fire. Film, screenplay by Colin Welland. Directed by Hugh Hudson. 1981.

Dante Alighieri, *Commedia.* Text in Anna Maria Chiavacci Leonardi, *Dante Alighieri Commedia.* 3 vols. Milan: Arnoldo Mondadori, 1991-97.

Dionysius of Fourna. *Painter's Manual.* c.1685—1744? English translation with commentary in Paul Hetherington, *The 'Painter's Manual' of Dionysius of Fourna.* London: Sagittarius /Torrance, California: Oakwood, 1974.

Doyle, Arthur Conan. "The Adventure of Silver Blaze." *The Strand Magazine,* December 1892.

Lewis, C. S. *The Screwtape Letters.* London: Geoffrey Bles, 1942.

Maitland, Sara. *Daughter of Jerusalem.* London: Virago, 1993 (first published: London: Frederick Muller, 1978).

Morgan, Francesca. *A Nation of Descendants: Politics and the Practice of Genealogy in U.S. History.* North Carolina: University of North Carolina, 2021.

Rossetti, Christina. "A Christmas Carol." *Scribner's Monthly,* January 1872

Sayers, Dorothy. *The Man Born to be King.* London: Victor Gallancz, 1946.

Shakespeare, William. *Romeo and Juiet.* Written c.1595. First Quarto 1597.

____. *Cymbelene.* Performed 1610 or 1611; first published in the First Folio (1623).

____. *Macbeth.* Between 1603 and 1606; first published in the First Folio (1623).

____. *Measure for Measure.* Performed on St Stephen's Night 1604. N. W. Bawcutt, ed. *Measure for Measure.* Oxford and New York: Oxford University, 1991.

Snodgrass, Melinda M. *The Measure of a Man.* Season 2, Episode 9 of television series *Star Trek: The Next Generation.* Air date: February 13, 1989.

Tolkien, J. R. R. *The Lord of the Rings.* The trilogy was first published in 1954-55, but best in many ways is the revised fully revised 60th anniversary edition. London: Harper-Collins, 2014.

Walpole, Calhoun. *Lessons from the Angel Oak.* Charleston, South Carolina: Home House, 2022.

Wesley, Charles. "And Can It Be?" In *Psalms and Hymns* (1738). Music: Thomas Cambell, Sagina (Bouquet , 1825).

HOLY SCRIPTURE

AUTHORS

Authors and Sources other than Holy Scripture earlier than 1050

Authors and Sources between 1050 and 1850

Authors and Sources since 1850

SUBJECTS